Introductory
Microsoft® Word 6.0
for Windows™

Introductory
Microsoft® Word 6.0
for Windows™

Cheryl L. Willis
University of Houston, University Park

Course Technology, Inc. One Main Street, Cambridge, MA 02142
An International Thomson Publishing Company

Introductory Microsoft Word 6.0 for Windows is published by Course Technology, Inc.

Managing Editor	Marjorie Schlaikjer
Series Consulting Editor	Susan Solomon
Product Manager	Kathleen Finnegan
Director of Production	Myrna D'Addario
Production Editor	Cynthia H. Anderson
Desktop Publishing Supervisor	Debbie Masi
Desktop Publisher	Andrea Star Greitzer
Production Assistant	Christine Spillett
Copyeditor	Jane Pedicini
Proofreader	Nancy Hannigan
Product Testing and Support Supervisor	Jeff Goding
Technical Reviewers	Mark Vodnik
	James Valente
Manufacturing Manager	Elizabeth Martinez
Prepress Production	Gex, Inc.
Text Designer	Sally Steele
Illustrations	Andrea Star Greitzer
	illustrious, inc.
Cover Designer	John Gamache
Indexer	Alexandra Nickerson

Introductory Microsoft Word 6.0 for Windows © 1994 Course Technology, Inc.

Trademarks

Disclaimer

ISBN 1-56527-153-X (text)

Printed in the United States of America

10 9 8 7 6 5

From the Publisher

At Course Technology, Inc., we believe that technology will transform the way that people teach and learn. We are very excited about bringing you, college professors and students, the most practical and affordable technology-related products available.

The Course Technology Development Process

Our development process is unparalleled in the higher education publishing industry. Every product we create goes through an exacting process of design, development, review, and testing.

Reviewers give us direction and insight that shape our manuscripts and bring them up to the latest standards. Every manuscript is quality tested. Students whose backgrounds match the intended audience work through every keystroke, carefully checking for clarity, and pointing out errors in logic and sequence. Together with our own technical reviewers, these testers help us ensure that everything that carries our name is error-free and easy to use.

Course Technology Products

We show both *how* and *why* technology is critical to solving problems in college and in whatever field you choose to teach or pursue. Our time-tested, step-by-step instructions provide unparalleled clarity. Examples and applications are chosen and crafted to motivate students.

The Course Technology Team

This book will suit your needs because it was delivered quickly, efficiently, and affordably. In every aspect of our business, we rely on a commitment to quality and the use of technology. Every employee contributes to this process. The names of all of our employees are listed below:

Tim Ashe, David Backer, Stephen M. Bayle, Josh Bernoff, Ann Marie Buconjic, Jody Buttafoco, Kerry Cannell, Jim Chrysikos, Barbara Clemens, Susan Collins, John M. Connolly, Kim Crowley, Myrna D'Addario, Lisa D'Alessandro, Howard S. Diamond, Kathryn Dinovo, Katie Donovan, Joseph B. Dougherty, MaryJane Dwyer, Chris Elkhill, Don Fabricant, Kate Gallagher, Laura Ganson, Jeff Goding, Laurie Gomes, Eileen Gorham, Andrea Greitzer, Catherine Griffin, Tim Hale, Roslyn Hooley, Nicole Jones, Matt Kenslea, Susannah Lean, Suzanne Licht, Laurie Lindgren, Kim Mai, Elizabeth Martinez, Debbie Masi, Don Maynard, Dan Mayo, Kathleen McCann, Jay McNamara, Mac Mendelsohn, Laurie Michelangelo, Kim Munsell, Amy Oliver, Michael Ormsby, Kristine Otto, Debbie Parlee, Kristin Patrick, Charlie Patsios, Jodi Paulus, Darren Perl, Kevin Phaneuf, George J. Pilla, Cathy Prindle, Nancy Ray, Marjorie Schlaikjer, Christine Spillett, Susan Stroud, Michelle Tucker, David Upton, Mark Valentine, Karen Wadsworth, Anne Marie Walker, Renee Walkup, Donna Whiting, Janet Wilson, Lisa Yameen.

Preface

Course Technology, Inc. is proud to present this new book in its Windows Series. *Introductory Microsoft Word 6.0 for Windows* is designed for a first course on Word 6.0 for Windows. This book capitalizes on the energy and enthusiasm students have for Windows-based applications and clearly teaches students how to take full advantage of Word's power. It assumes students have learned basic Windows skills and file management from *An Introduction to Microsoft Windows 3.1* by June Jamrich Parsons or from an *equivalent* book.

Organization and Coverage

Introductory Microsoft Word 6.0 for Windows contains six tutorials that provide hands-on instruction. In these tutorials students learn word processing tasks by following a four-step "Productivity Strategy": create, edit, format, then preview and print. This strategy increases both efficiency and proficiency and is thoroughly reinforced throughout the text.

Moreover, the power of Word is unleashed by emphasizing the use of the Standard toolbar and Formatting toolbar. Using this book, students will be able to do more advanced tasks sooner than they would using other introductory texts; a perusal of the table of contents affirms this benefit. By the end of the book, students will have learned such formerly "advanced" tasks as creating bulleted and numbered lists, producing desktop published documents, and using styles to format text.

Approach

Introductory Microsoft Word 6.0 for Windows distinguishes itself from other Windows textbooks because of its unique two-pronged approach. First, it motivates students by demonstrating why they need to learn the concepts and skills. This book teaches Word 6.0 for Windows using a task-driven rather than a feature-driven approach. By working through the tutorials—each motivated by a realistic case—students learn how to use Word 6.0 for Windows in situations they are likely to encounter in the workplace, rather than learn a list of features one-by-one, out of context. Second, the content, organization, and pedagogy of this book make full use of the Windows environment. The content that is presented, when it's presented, and how it's presented capitalize on the power of Word 6.0 for Windows to enable new users to perform complex word processing tasks earlier and more easily than was possible with non-Windows word processing packages.

Features

Introductory Microsoft Word 6.0 for Windows is an exceptional textbook also because it contains the following features:

- **"Read This Before You Begin" Page** This page is consistent with Course Technology's unequaled commitment to helping instructors introduce technology into the classroom. Technical considerations and assumptions about hardware, software, and default settings are listed in one place to help instructors save time and eliminate unnecessary aggravation.

- **Tutorial Case** Each tutorial begins with a word processing problem that students could reasonably encounter in business. Thus, the process of solving the problem will be meaningful to students.

- **Step-by-Step Methodology** The unique Course Technology, Inc. methodology keeps students on track. They click or press keys always within the context of solving the problem posed in the Tutorial Case. The text constantly guides students, letting them know where they are in the process of solving the problem. The numerous screen shots include labels that direct students' attention to what they should look at on the screen.

- **Page Design** Each full-color page is designed to help students easily differentiate between what they are to do and what they are to read. The steps are easily identified by their color background and numbered bullets. Windows default colors are used in the screen shots so instructors can more easily assure that students' screens look like those in the book.

- **TROUBLE?** TROUBLE? paragraphs anticipate the mistakes that students are likely to make and help them recover from these mistakes. This feature facilitates independent learning and frees the instructor to focus on substantive conceptual issues rather than common procedural errors.

- **Reference Windows and Task Reference** Reference Windows provide short, generic summaries of frequently used procedures. The Task Reference appears at the end of the book and summarizes how to accomplish tasks using the toolbar buttons, the menus, and the keyboard. Both of these features are specially designed and written so students can use the book as a reference manual after completing the course.

- **Questions, Tutorial Assignments, and Case Problems** Each tutorial concludes with meaningful, conceptual Questions that test students' understanding of what they learned in the tutorial. The Questions are followed by Tutorial Assignments, which provide students with additional hands-on practice of the skills they learned in the tutorial. Finally, each tutorial ends with three complete Case Problems that have approximately the same scope as the Tutorial Case.

- **Exploration Exercises** Unlike DOS, the Windows environment allows students to learn by exploring and discovering what they can do. The Exploration Exercises are Questions, Tutorial Assignments, or Case Problems designated by an **E** that encourage students to explore the capabilities of the computing environment they are using and to extend their knowledge using Word's on-line Help facility and other reference materials.

The CTI WinApps Setup Disk

The CTI WinApps Setup Disk bundled with the instructor's copy of this book contains an innovative Student Disk generating program designed to save instructors time. Once this software is installed on a network or standalone workstation, students can double-click the "Make Word 6.0 for Windows Student Disk" icon in the CTI WinApps group window. Double-clicking this icon transfers all the data files students need to complete the tutorials, Tutorial Assignments, and Case Problems to a high-density disk in drive A or B. Tutorial 1 provides complete step-by-step instructions for making the Student Disk.

Adopters of this text are granted the right to install the CTI WinApps group window on any standalone computer or network used by students who have purchased this text.

For more information on the CTI WinApps Setup Disk, see the section in this book called, "Read This Before You Begin."

The Supplements

■ **Instructor's Manual** The Instructor's Manual is written by the author and is quality assurance tested. It includes:
  • Answers and solutions to all the Questions, Tutorial Assignments, and Case Problems. Suggested solutions are also included for the Exploration Exercises.
  • A 3.5-inch disk containing solutions to all the Questions, Tutorial Assignments, and Case Problems.
  • Tutorial Notes, which contain background information from the author about the Tutorial Case and the instructional progression of the tutorial.
  • Technical Notes, which include troubleshooting tips as well as information on how to customize the students' screens to closely emulate the screen shots in the book.
  • Transparency Masters of key concepts.
■ **Test Bank** The Test Bank contains approximately 50 questions per tutorial in true/false, multiple choice, and fill-in-the-blank formats, plus two essay questions. Each question has been quality assurance tested by students to achieve clarity and accuracy.
■ **Electronic Test Bank** The Electronic Test Bank allows instructors to edit individual test questions, select questions individually or at random, and print out scrambled versions of the same test to any supported printer.

Acknowledgments

I would like to thank the following individuals in the College of Technology at the University of Houston for their input and support: my undergraduate and graduate students, Maryann Pringle, Sharon Lund O'Neil, and Bernard McIntyre.

My appreciation goes to the Course Technology team assigned to this project—Mark Vodnik, Cynthia Anderson, Jane Pedicini, and James Valente—for their enthusiastic attention to detail. My undying gratitude goes finally to Kathy Finnegan for her invaluable suggestions, her wordsmithing abilities, and, perhaps more importantly, her gentle spirit in the face of tremendous pressure. Thank you all for your dedication to producing a quality textbook.

Thanks to my family, Lillian, Bill, and Denise, for their steadfast love and support. Thanks also to my colleague and friend, Marionette Beyah, who never got to see the finished product, but who was beside me in spirit with her words of encouragement and humor. God bless you!

Cheryl L. Willis

Brief Contents

From the Publisher   v

Preface   vi

**Introductory Microsoft Word 6.0
for Windows Tutorials**   **W 1**

Read This Before You Begin   **W 2**

TUTORIAL 1   **Creating, Editing, Formatting,
and Printing a Document**

Requesting Information from a Supply Source   **W 3**

TUTORIAL 2   **Using Page, Paragraph, and
Font Formatting Commands**

Creating a Cover Memo and Agenda   **W 57**

TUTORIAL 3   **Creating a Multiple-Page
Document with Tables**

Developing a Travel Expense Policy Report   **W 101**

TUTORIAL 4   **Merging Documents**

Writing a Confirmation Form Letter   **W 150**

TUTORIAL 5   **Creating Reports**

Writing a Report with a Table of Contents   **W 178**

TUTORIAL 6   **Desktop Publishing with Word**

Creating a Newsletter for Enviro-Disk   **W 224**

Index   **W 273**

Task Reference   **W 283**

Contents

From the Publisher   **v**

Preface   **vi**

**Introductory Microsoft Word 6.0
for Windows Tutorials**   **W 1**

Read This Before You Begin   **W 2**

TUTORIAL 1   **Creating, Editing, Formatting,
and Printing a Document**

Requesting Information from
   a Supply Source   **W 3**

Using the Productivity Strategy   **W 4**

Using the Tutorials Effectively   **W 5**

Your Student Disk   **W 6**

Starting Word   **W 8**

Elements of the Word Screen   **W 9**

Types of Word Windows   **W 12**

Screen Check   **W 12**

Checking the Document View   W 12

Sizing the Document Window   W 13

Sizing the Word Window   W 14

Viewing the Toolbars and the Ruler   W 14

Displaying Nonprinting Characters   W 15

Checking Font and Point Size Settings   W 17

Organizing Document Windows   **W 17**

Opening a New Document   W 17

Switching Between Open Documents   W 18

Closing a Document   W 19

Creating a Document   **W 20**

Planning a Document   W 20

Entering Text   W 20

Saving a Document   **W 25**

Naming Files   W 25

Saving a Document for the First Time   W 25

Exiting Word   **W 26**

Editing a Document   **W 27**

Opening an Existing Document   W 27

Moving the Insertion Point   W 28

Inserting New Text   W 31

Deleting Text   W 32

Using Undo   W 33

Using Overtype Mode   W 34

Updating a File   W 35

Checking Spelling   W 36

Formatting a Document   **W 39**

Select, Then Do   W 39

Applying Type Styles   W 42

Removing Type Styles   W 45

Adding Bullets   W 45

Previewing and Printing a Document   **W 46**

Getting Help   **W 48**

Using Context-Sensitive Help   W 48

Using the Help Contents Window   W 49

Using Search   W 50

Printing an Envelope   **W 51**

Questions   **W 53**

Tutorial Assignments   **W 54**

Case Problems   **W 55**

TUTORIAL 2   Using Page, Paragraph, and Font Formatting Commands

Creating a Cover Memo and Agenda   **W 57**

Renaming a File   **W 60**

Moving Text Within a Document   **W 60**

Moving Text with the Move
Command ([F2])   W 61

Applying Direct Formatting Options   **W 62**

Page Setup Options   **W 63**

Changing Margins   W 63

Soft Page Breaks   W 65

Inserting Hard Page Breaks   W 65

Paragraph Formatting   **W 67**

Changing Paragraph Indentations   W 67

Using Default Tabs   W 71

Setting Custom Tab Stops   W 72

Moving Tab Stops   W 75

Moving Between Pages   W 76

Inserting Leader Characters   W 76

Using the New Line Command   W 78

Numbering Paragraphs   W 80

Adjusting Line Spacing   W 81

Aligning Paragraphs   W 82

Creating Paragraph Borders and Rules   W 85

Font Formatting   W 87

Changing Several Character Attributes
   at Once   W 89

Changing Font and Point Size Using the
   Formatting Toolbar   W 90

Inserting Special Symbols   W 91

Previewing and Printing Multiple Pages   **W 92**

Questions   **W 96**

Tutorial Assignments   **W 97**

Case Problems   **W 97**

TUTORIAL 3   **Creating a Multiple-Page
                   Document with Tables**

Developing a Travel Expense
   Policy Report   **W 101**

Creating a Table   **W 104**

Creating a Table Using the
   Table Button   W 105

Entering Text in a Table and Using
   AutoCorrect   W 107

Creating a Table Using the Insert
   Table Command   W 109

Converting Existing Text to a Table   W 110

Using the Clipboard   **W 112**

Copying and Pasting Text   W 113

Cutting and Pasting Text   W 114

Finding and Replacing Text   **W 116**

Selecting Within a Table   **W 118**

Modifying a Table Structure   **W 120**

Sorting Rows in a Table   **W 122**

Performing Mathematical Calculations in Tables   **W 124**

Inserting a Caption   **W 125**

Using Headers and Footers   **W 126**

Inserting a Header   W 127

Inserting a Footer   W 129

Using Styles   **W 131**

Applying Styles   **W 134**

Using Reveal Formats   W 135

Formatting Tables   **W 136**

Changing Column Width   W 136

Automatically Formatting Tables   W 138

Centering a Table   W 139

Questions   **W 145**

Tutorial Assignments   **W 145**

Case Problems   **W 147**

TUTORIAL 4   Merging Documents

Writing a Confirmation Form Letter   **W 150**

The Merge Process   **W 152**

Creating a Main Document   **W 153**

Creating a Data Source   **W 154**

Attaching the Data Source   W 155

Creating the Header Row   W 155

Using the Data Form   W 157

Editing a Main Document   **W 160**

Inserting Merge Field Codes   W 161

Editing the Data Source   **W 164**

Sorting Records   **W 164**

Formatting a Main Document   **W 165**

Merging Documents   **W 166**

Selecting a Data Record to Merge   **W 167**

Creating Mailing Labels   **W 169**

Formatting Labels   **W 172**

Printing Labels   W 173
Questions   W 174
Tutorial Assignments   W 174
Case Problems   W 176

TUTORIAL 5   **Creating Reports**

Writing a Report with a
    Table of Contents   W 178
Using Word's Thesaurus   W 181
Checking Grammar   W 182
Assigning Bookmarks   W 185
Formatting Sections in a Document   W 187
**Inserting Headers and Footers in a
    Multi-Section Document**   W 190
Defining Styles   W 194
    Defining a New Style by Example   W 194
    Defining a New Style Using the Style
        Command   W 196
Applying Styles   W 198
    Applying Styles Using Shortcut Keys   W 200
Modifying Styles   W 202
Transferring Data Between Documents   W 205
    Using the Clipboard to Transfer Data
        Between Documents   W 205
    Using Drag-and-Drop Between
        Documents   W 208
Adding Captions to Charts   W 210
Creating the Preface Page   W 211
    Creating a Table of Contents   W 212
    Creating a Table of Figures   W 212
Printing the Report   W 213
Creating a Customized Document Template   W 219
Questions   W 221
Tutorial Assignments   W 221
Case Problems   W 222

TUTORIAL 6   Desktop Publishing with Word

Creating a Newsletter for Enviro-Disk   W 224

Introduction to Desktop Publishing   W 225
 DTP Design Elements   W 225
Inserting a Masthead   W 227
Importing Text   W 228
Setting Mirror Margins   W 230
Creating a Banner Using WordArt   W 231
 Embedding an Object into a
  Word Document   W 233
 Editing an Embedded Object   W 234
Copying Styles Using the Organizer   W 236
Displaying the Style Area   W 238
Applying Styles Using Shortcut Keys   W 239
Activating Paste-Up Tools   W 241
Inserting Alternating Headers and Footers   W 242
Applying a Newspaper-Style Column Format   W 245
Using Outline   W 247
Inserting a Column Break   W 248
Changing Column Formatting   W 249
Inserting Word ClipArt   W 252
 Sizing Graphics   W 252
Wrapping Text Around a Picture   W 254
Inserting a Pull Quote   W 255
 Sizing a Frame   W 256
 Formatting Text in a Frame   W 257
 Positioning a Frame   W 258
Creating Drop Caps   W 259
Hyphenating a Document   W 260
Layering Text and Graphics   W 261
 Adding Color to a Graphic   W 264
 Moving an Object to the Background
  Drawing Layer   W 265
Questions   W 266
Tutorial Assignments   W 267
Case Problems   W 268

Index   W 273

Task Reference   W 283

Reference Windows

Switching Between Open Documents	**W 18**
Checking the Spelling of a Document	**W 36**
Indenting a Paragraph	**W 69**
Setting Custom Tab Stops	**W 73**
Inserting Leader Characters	**W 77**
Converting Text to a Table	**W 111**
Attaching a Template to the Current Document	**W 132**
Defining a New Style by Example	**W 195**
Defining a New Style Using the Style Command	**W 196**
Redefining a Style by Example	**W 203**
Sizing a Graphic	**W 253**

Introductory
Microsoft® Word 6.0
for Windows™ Tutorials

1 Creating, Editing, Formatting, and Printing a Document

2 Using Page, Paragraph, and Font Formatting Commands

3 Creating a Multiple-Page Document with Tables

4 Merging Documents

5 Creating Reports

6 Desktop Publishing with Word

Read This Before You Begin

To the Student

To use this book, you must have a Student Disk. Your instructor will either provide you with one or ask you to make your own by following the instructions in the section "Your Student Disk" in Tutorial 1. See your instructor or lab manager for further information. If you are going to work through this book using your own computer, you need a computer system running Microsoft Windows 3.1, Microsoft Word 6.0 for Windows, and a Student Disk. *You will not be able to complete the tutorials and exercises in this book using your own computer until you have a Student Disk.*

To the Instructor

Making the Student Disk To complete the tutorials in this book, your students must have a copy of the Student Disk. To relieve you of having to make multiple Student Disks from a single master copy, we provide you with the CTI WinApps Setup Disk, which contains an automatic Student Disk generating program. Once you install the Setup Disk on a network or standalone workstation, students can easily make their own Student Disks by double-clicking the "Make Word 6.0 Student Disk" icon in the CTI WinApps icon group. Double-clicking this icon transfers all the data files students need to complete the tutorials, Tutorial Assignments, and Case Problems to a high-density disk in drive A or B. If some of your students will use their own computers to complete the tutorials and exercises in this book, they must first get the Student Disk. The section called "Your Student Disk" in Tutorial 1 provides complete instructions on how to make the Student Disk.

Installing the CTI WinApps Setup Disk To install the CTI WinApps icon group from the Setup Disk, follow the instructions inside the disk envelope that was bundled with your book. By adopting this book, you are granted a license to install this software on any computer or computer network used by you or your students.

README File A README.TXT file located on the Setup Disk provides additional technical notes, troubleshooting advice, and tips for using the CTI WinApps software in your school's computer lab. You can view the README.TXT file using any word processor you choose.

System Requirements

The minimum software and hardware requirements for your computer system are as follows:

- Microsoft Windows version 3.1 or later on a local hard drive or a network drive.
- A 386 or higher processor with a minimum of 4 MB of RAM (6 MB or more is strongly recommended).
- A mouse supported by Windows 3.1.
- A printer supported by Windows 3.1.
- A VGA 640 x 480 16-color display is recommended; an 800 x 600 or 1024 x 768 SVGA, VGA monochrome, or EGA display is also acceptable.
- 20 MB of free hard disk space.
- Student workstations with at least 1 high-density 3.5-inch disk drive.
- If you want to install the CTI WinApps Setup Disk on a network drive, your network must support Microsoft Windows.

Creating, Editing, Formatting, and Printing a Document

OBJECTIVES

In this tutorial you will:

- Start and exit Word 6.0 for Windows
- Identify the elements of the Word screen
- Move the insertion point
- Insert and delete text
- Spell check a document
- Select text
- Bold, italicize, and underline text
- Create bulleted lists
- Open, save, and close a document
- Use Word Help
- Print a document and an envelope

Requesting Information from a Supply Source

Sweet T's, Inc.   Denise Hill is assistant director of Research and Development for Sweet T's, Inc. Sweet T's owns and operates seven Sweet Tooth Cafe restaurants in Oklahoma and northern Texas. It has also sold franchises of the Sweet Tooth Cafe to individual licensees who operate another 13 restaurants throughout the southeastern United States. The Sweet Tooth Cafe is known for food that is moderately priced and served in a casual, family dining atmosphere.

Denise works with a staff of three food specialists responsible for creating new menu items for the restaurants. She also has responsibility for finding suppliers for any specialty ingredients required in any menu item. The current supplier of the brownie in Sweet T's famous Deep Fried Brownie is about to go out of business, so Denise must locate a new supply source. Denise calls Doug Stone, a salesperson for a wholesale food distributor, who tells her about Ram Food Purveyors in Dallas, Texas. She decides to write to Ram to inquire if it can produce a brownie that meets Sweet T's specifications.

The technician from Sweet T's Information Services office has just installed Word 6.0 for Windows on Denise's computer. She has learned Windows 3.1 and is anxious to get started learning Word 6.0 for Windows.

In this tutorial you will complete Denise's task. You will also learn an efficient strategy for producing a document, and how to use the features of Word to facilitate the document production process.

Using the Productivity Strategy

A **document** is any written item, such as a letter, memo, or report. Word 6.0 for Windows is a word processing program that allows you to create, edit, format, and print documents. Your ultimate goal in using this powerful tool, however, is to increase your ability to complete high-quality work in a minimal amount of time. To do so, you also need to use a plan for producing your documents efficiently. The plan you will use throughout this book is known as the productivity strategy.

The **productivity strategy** calls for you to approach the production of each document in four separate phases: creating, editing, formatting, and printing. Furthermore, to ensure that you produce the document efficiently, you complete each phase in sequence rather than switching among the four phases.

Using this strategy, first you will create your document. **Creating** a document involves much more than typing text; it begins with planning what you want to communicate to your intended audience. Once you have planned your document, you are ready to enter text. In general, you should not make editing or formatting decisions as you are entering text. In the Sweet T's example, Denise knows that the purpose of her letter is to inquire whether Ram Food Purveyors can supply the right type of brownie. She also knows that she must provide the supplier with the specifications for the brownie and a deadline for receiving the bid proposal.

Editing is the process of inserting, deleting, and moving text. To maintain a high degree of efficiency during this phase of the productivity strategy, you make only editing changes. For example, Denise will read through her document, then insert and delete text to make it clearer. Next, she will spell check her document for spelling errors. Finally, she will proofread her document thoroughly to make sure she has found all her errors.

Next you focus on formatting your document. **Formatting** involves changing your document's appearance to make it more readable and attractive. Use of white space and boldfaced or italicized text and headings are examples of formatting options you can use to make your document easier to read and more appealing to the reader. For her letter, Denise decides to use the standard business format, which includes a date, inside address, salutation, complimentary closing, and writer's name and title. She intends to emphasize several words in the body of her letter, as well as draw attention to the specifications for the brownie.

Printing is the final phase of the productivity strategy. You need a hard copy of your document to give to your reader. You should preview your document, however, before you spend time and resources printing it. Denise intends to use the Word Print Preview feature before printing her document to check its overall appearance. She will then print her letter and an envelope.

Of course, nothing prevents you from retracing your steps. To maximize your efficiency, though, you should concentrate on completing each phase of the productivity strategy in sequence.

In this tutorial you will create the letter and accompanying envelope shown in Figure 1-1. Just as in a real work situation, your document will go through various stages of development before it reaches the final result you see in Figure 1-1. This tutorial also takes you through each phase of the productivity strategy, so that you will learn to use Word 6.0 for Windows to produce professional-looking documents as efficiently as possible.

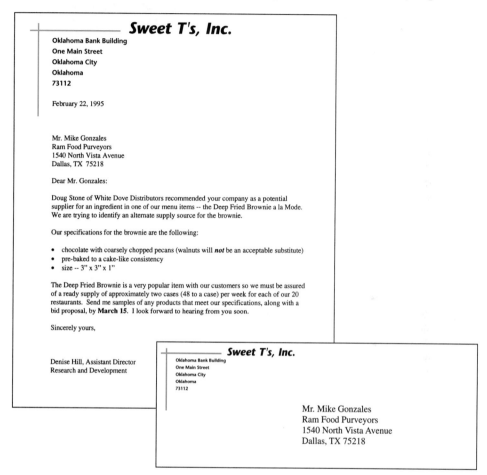

Figure 1-1
Completed letter
and envelope

Using the Tutorials Effectively

These tutorials will help you learn about Word 6.0 for Windows. These tutorials assume that you are familiar with the basics of Windows 3.1: how to control windows, how to choose menu commands, how to complete dialog boxes, and how to select directories, drives, and files. If you do not understand these concepts, please consult your instructor.

    The tutorials are designed to be used in conjunction with your instructor's discussion of the concepts covered in the tutorials. Begin by reading the tutorial to be discussed by your instructor. After reading the tutorial and listening to your instructor's lecture, complete the numbered steps, which appear on a colored background, as you work at your computer. Read each step carefully and completely before you try it.

    As you work, compare your screen with the figures in the tutorial to verify your results. It is relatively easy to change the appearance of Word's screen, so don't worry if parts of your screen are different from the figures. The important parts of the screen display are labeled in each figure. Just be sure these parts are on your screen. If you want to set up the basic Word screen used in this book, follow the procedures in the "Screen Check" section later in this tutorial.

Don't worry about making mistakes—that's part of the learning process. **TROUBLE?** paragraphs identify common problems and explain how to correct them or get back on track. Complete the suggestions in the **TROUBLE?** paragraphs *only* if you are having the specific problem described.

After you have completed a tutorial, you can do the Questions, Tutorial Assignments, and Case Problems found at the end of each tutorial. They are carefully structured so that you will review what you have learned and then apply your knowledge to new situations. When you are doing these exercises, refer to the Reference Window boxes. These boxes, which are found throughout the tutorials, provide short summaries of frequently used procedures. You can also use the Task Reference at the end of the book. It summarizes how to complete tasks using the mouse, the menus, and the keyboard.

Your Student Disk

To complete the tutorials and exercises in this book, you must have a Student Disk. The Student Disk contains all the practice files you need for the tutorials, the Tutorial Assignments, and the Case Problems. If your instructor or lab manager provides you with your Student Disk, you can skip this section and go to the next section entitled "Starting Word." If your instructor asks you to make your own Student Disk, you need to follow the steps in this section. To make your Student Disk, you need:

- A blank, formatted, high-density 3.5-inch disk
- A computer with Microsoft Windows 3.1, Word 6.0 for Windows, and the CTI WinApps icon group installed on it

  If you are using your own computer, the CTI WinApps icon group will not be installed on it. Before you proceed, you must go to your school's computer lab and find a computer with the CTI WinApps icon group installed on it. Once you have made your own Student Disk, you can use it to complete all the tutorials and exercises in this book on any computer you choose.

To make your Word Student Disk:

❶ Launch Windows and make sure the Program Manager window is open.

  TROUBLE? The exact steps you follow to launch Windows might vary depending on how your computer is set up. On many computer systems, type WIN at the DOS prompt then press [Enter] to launch Windows. If you don't know how to launch Windows, ask your instructor or technical support person.

❷ Label your formatted disk "Word 6.0 Student Disk" and place it in drive A.

  TROUBLE? If your computer has more than one disk drive, drive A is usually on top. If your Student Disk does not fit into drive A, then place it in drive B and substitute "drive B" whenever you see "drive A" in the steps throughout this book.

❸ Look for an icon labeled "CTI WinApps" like the one in Figure 1-2 or a group window labeled "CTI WinApps" like the one in Figure 1-3.

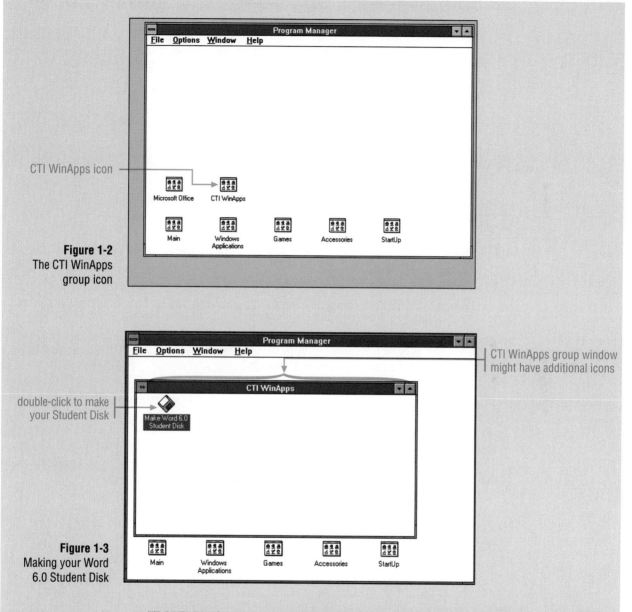

Figure 1-2
The CTI WinApps
group icon

Figure 1-3
Making your Word
6.0 Student Disk

TROUBLE? If you cannot find anything labeled "CTI WinApps," the CTI software might not be installed on your computer. If you are in a computer lab, ask your instructor or technical support person for assistance. If you are using your own computer, you will not be able to make your Student Disk. To make it you need access to the CTI WinApps icon group, which is, most likely, installed on your school's lab computers. Ask your instructor or technical support person for further information on where to locate the CTI WinApps icon group. Once you create your Student Disk, you can use it to complete all the tutorials and exercises in this book on any computer you choose.

❹ If you see an icon labeled "CTI WinApps," double-click it to open the CTI WinApps group window. If the CTI WinApps group window is already open, go to Step 5.

❺ Double-click the icon labeled **Make Word 6.0 Student Disk**. The Make Word 6.0 Student Disk window opens. See Figure 1-4.

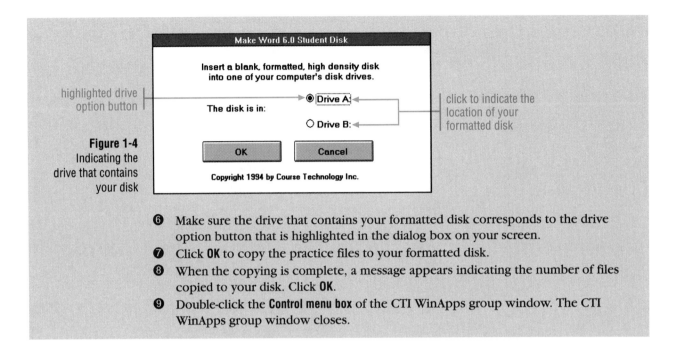

highlighted drive
option button

click to indicate the
location of your
formatted disk

Figure 1-4
Indicating the
drive that contains
your disk

⑥ Make sure the drive that contains your formatted disk corresponds to the drive option button that is highlighted in the dialog box on your screen.

⑦ Click **OK** to copy the practice files to your formatted disk.

⑧ When the copying is complete, a message appears indicating the number of files copied to your disk. Click **OK**.

⑨ Double-click the **Control menu box** of the CTI WinApps group window. The CTI WinApps group window closes.

Now the files you need to complete the Word tutorials and exercises are on your Student Disk. Your next step is to start Word.

Starting Word

You are now ready to create Denise's letter, so let's learn how to start Word. Although there are a variety of ways to start Word, this tutorial assumes that Word is launched from the Microsoft Office group window within the Program Manager window.

To start Word:

❶ Make sure Windows is launched and the Program Manager window is open. The Microsoft Office group icon should be visible in the Program Manager window.

TROUBLE? If you don't see the Microsoft Office group icon, ask your instructor or technical support person for help finding the icon. Perhaps Word has not been installed on the computer you are using.

❷ Double-click the **Microsoft Office group icon** in the Program Manager window. The Microsoft Office group window opens. See Figure 1-5.

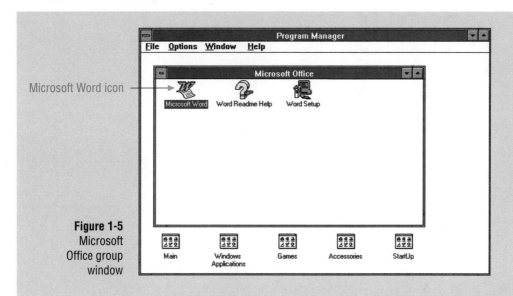

Microsoft Word icon

Figure 1-5
Microsoft
Office group
window

TROUBLE? Don't worry if the Microsoft Office group window contains more program-item icons than shown in Figure 1-5.

❸ Double-click the **Microsoft Word icon** in the Microsoft Office group window.

Word displays a title screen briefly, then the Word screen appears. After starting Word, you might see a Word feature called "Tip of the Day" on your screen. The Tip of the Day provides useful information about different Word features and commands. If you do not see the Tip of the Day, your instructor or technical support person has deactivated this feature.

❹ If the Tip of the Day dialog box appears, read the tip, then click **OK** to close the dialog box. To deactivate this feature, click the **Show Tips at Startup check box** to clear it before clicking OK.

Elements of the Word Screen

Because you are familiar with the Windows screen, or interface, you can already identify several elements of the Word screen: the Word window Control menu box, the title bar, the Word window sizing buttons, the menu bar, the workspace, the mouse pointer, and the scroll bars. These appear as blue labels in Figure 1-6. In addition, you notice a few new elements: the document window Control menu box, the document window Restore button, the Standard toolbar, the Formatting toolbar, the ruler, the insertion point, the end mark, the document view buttons in the horizontal scroll bar, and the status bar. These appear as red labels in Figure 1-6.

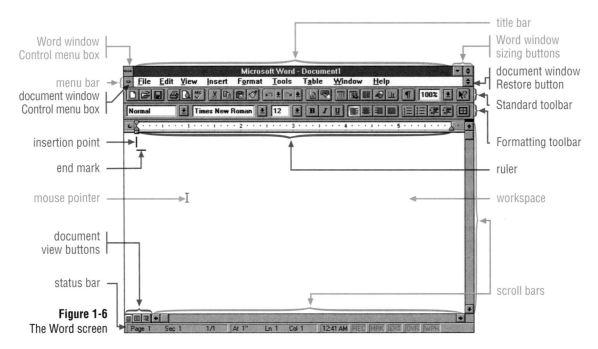

Figure 1-6
The Word screen

If your screen doesn't look like Figure 1-6, going through the next sections of this tutorial should resolve this. Just continue with the tutorial for now.

Figure 1-7 describes the function of each element of the Word screen. You need to become familiar with these elements to take full advantage of Word's features. You will learn to use all of them as you work through the tutorials.

Screen Element	Function
Word window Control menu box	Allows you to size, move, and close the Word window, as well as switch to other applications
Title bar	Identifies the current application (i.e., Word) and the name of the current document
Word window sizing buttons	The Minimize button reduces the Word application to an icon; the Restore button restores the Word window to its standard size
Document window Control menu box	Allows you to size, move, and close the document window
Menu bar	Contains all the Word commands
Document window Restore button	Restores the document window to its standard size
Standard toolbar	Contains buttons that represent some of Word's most often used commands
Formatting toolbar	Contains buttons that represent Word's most often used font and paragraph formatting features
Ruler	Allows you to adjust margins and indents quickly, set tabs, and adjust column widths
Document view buttons	Allow you to view a document in different ways
Scroll bars	Allow you to see different parts of the document
Status bar	Gives information about the location of the insertion point
Workspace	Area where text and graphics are entered
Insertion point	Flashing vertical line that marks the point where characters will be inserted or deleted
End mark	Identifies the end of a document
Mouse pointer	Changes shape depending on its location on the screen

Figure 1-7
Functions of the
Word screen
elements

If you want, you can take time now to browse through each of Word's menus.

Types of Word Windows

The Word screen is made up of two types of windows: an application window and a document window. Because both windows are maximized and share the same title bar and borders, they appear as one window. The application window, known as the **Word window**, opens automatically when you start Word. The **document window** opens within the Word window and will contain your document.

If you're not sure whether both the Word window and the document window are maximized, compare the shape of your screen's sizing buttons to the right of the title bar (the Word window sizing buttons) and to the right of the menu bar (the document window sizing button) with those in Figure 1-6. If the shapes are different on your screen, the next section gives you the information you need to solve this problem.

Screen Check

The appearance of the Word screen is easily changed. This ability to customize the appearance of the screen is an advantage in the business world, but it can pose problems in the academic world. Business people like Denise usually don't have to share a computer and so don't worry that another user will change the way the Word screen looks. To follow along with the tutorials as easily as possible, conduct a screen check each time you begin a new Word session. This section of the tutorial will help you cope with changes in the appearance of the Word screen from session to session.

Checking the Document View

The document view buttons in the horizontal scroll bar allow you to change the editing view you see on the screen (Figure 1-8). **Normal view** is the default view; you do most of your creating and editing of Word documents in normal view. You use **page layout view** to display your document as it will look when printed. **Outline view** allows you to create a topic outline of your document or to reorganize the sections of your document.

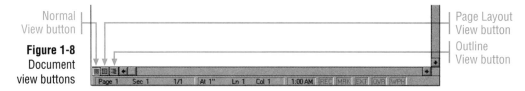

Normal
View button

Page Layout
View button

Outline
View button

Figure 1-8
Document
view buttons

By default, Word displays the document view used by the last person opening Word, so you must know how to switch to normal view before you begin these tutorials. Let's practice that now.

To change document views:

❶ Position your pointer on the **Page Layout View button** 回 in the horizontal scroll bar.

You might notice a Word feature called a "ToolTip" as you move the pointer over the button. The ToolTip feature displays the button name and corresponding status bar message for any button on any toolbar when the pointer is positioned over a button (without clicking).

TROUBLE? If you do not see the ToolTip, the feature has been deactivated. Ask your instructor or technical support person how to activate this feature, if you want to see the ToolTips.

❷ Click 🖿. Notice that the Page Layout View button appears lighter to indicate that it is now activated. The document view changes—now a vertical ruler appears on the left side of the screen, and double-headed arrows appear at the bottom of the vertical scroll bar. See Figure 1-9.

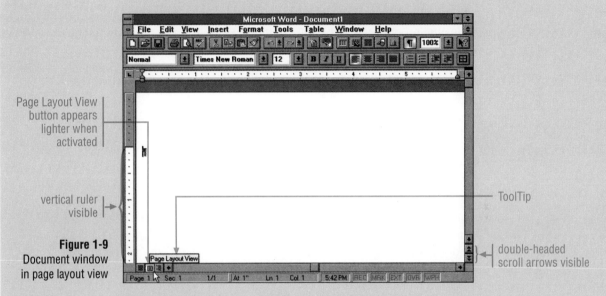

Page Layout View button appears lighter when activated

vertical ruler visible

ToolTip

double-headed scroll arrows visible

Figure 1-9
Document window in page layout view

❸ Click **View** on the menu bar. Notice that the Page Layout command has a bullet in front of it to indicate that it is activated.

❹ Click **Normal** on the View menu. The vertical ruler and double-headed arrows in the vertical scroll bar disappear. Also notice that the Normal View button in the horizontal scroll bar is lighter to indicate that it is once again activated.

Unless otherwise directed, use normal view when completing these tutorials. If the Normal View button is not selected, you can either click it or choose Normal from the View menu to reset the screen to normal view.

Sizing the Document Window

Unless you are instructed otherwise, the document window you are working in should be maximized. You can use either the document window Restore button or the document window Control menu box to change the size of the document window (see Figure 1-6). Whenever you start a new Word session to work on the tutorials in this book, make sure the document window is maximized.

Sizing the Word Window

The Word window should also be maximized unless otherwise stated. You can use the Word window sizing buttons or the Word window Control menu box to change the size of the Word window. Whenever you start a new session of Word, make sure the Word window is maximized (see Figure 1-6).

Viewing the Toolbars and the Ruler

The procedures in the tutorials instruct you to use the toolbars—the Standard toolbar and the Formatting toolbar—and the ruler whenever possible, because they allow you to speed up your work (Figure 1-6). Because the Word screen is easily changed, the toolbars and the ruler might not always be displayed when you start a Word session. You need to know how to display the toolbars and the ruler in case they have been removed from the screen.

To deactivate and activate the toolbars:

❶ Click **View**. The View menu opens. Notice that the Ruler command has a check mark in front of it to indicate that it is activated.

   TROUBLE? If the Ruler command doesn't have a check mark in front of it, click Ruler to display it on the screen, then repeat Step 1.

❷ Click **Toolbars...**. The Toolbars dialog box appears with Word's available toolbars listed. See Figure 1-10. Notice that the check boxes for both the Standard toolbar and the Formatting toolbar have been activated. Also, note the Show ToolTips check box. If this box is selected, the ToolTips feature has been activated.

activated toolbars

Figure 1-10
Toolbars dialog
box

ToolTips activated

❸ Click the **Standard check box** to clear it, then click **OK** or press **[Enter]**. The Standard toolbar disappears from the Word screen, but the Formatting toolbar is still visible.

You can also remove or display toolbars by using the shortcut Toolbar menu. To display the shortcut Toolbar menu, point to any visible toolbar, then click the *right* mouse button. Let's practice activating a toolbar with the shortcut Toolbar menu now.

To use the shortcut Toolbar menu:

❶ Point anywhere on the Formatting toolbar, then click the **right mouse button.** A menu appears containing all of Word's available toolbars, with a check mark in front of Formatting to indicate that the Formatting toolbar is displayed. See Figure 1-11.

TROUBLE? If you do not see the shortcut Toolbar menu, perhaps you did not click the *right* mouse button. Repeat Step 1.

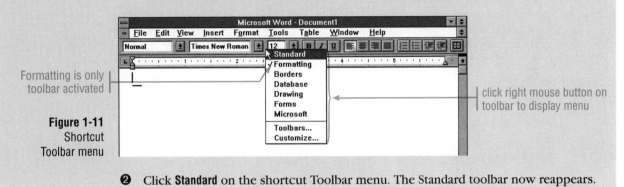

Formatting is only toolbar activated

click right mouse button on toolbar to display menu

Figure 1-11
Shortcut
Toolbar menu

❷ Click **Standard** on the shortcut Toolbar menu. The Standard toolbar now reappears.

Now let's practice deactivating and activating the ruler using keyboard commands.

To deactivate and activate the ruler using keyboard commands:

❶ Press **[Alt][v]** to display the View menu.

❷ Press **[r]** to deactivate the Ruler command. The ruler disappears from the Word screen.

❸ Press **[Alt][v]**. The View menu opens again. Notice that the Ruler command does not have a check mark in front of it. The ruler is deactivated.

❹ Press **[r]**. The ruler appears once again.

As you complete these tutorials, the Standard and Formatting toolbars should be the only toolbars visible on your screen, unless otherwise instructed. The ruler should also be visible.

Displaying Nonprinting Characters

Word allows you to display paragraph marks, tabs, spaces, and all other nonprinting characters on your screen by activating the Show/Hide ¶ button on the Standard toolbar. To help you recognize the format of your document as you are working in it, and to avoid accidentally deleting one of these characters, work with the Show/Hide ¶ button activated.

To activate the Show/Hide ¶ button:

❶ Click the **Show/Hide ¶ button** ¶ on the Standard toolbar. A paragraph mark appears in the workspace of the document. The Show/Hide ¶ button now appears lighter to indicate that the button has been clicked—in other words, that the command is activated. See Figure 1-12.

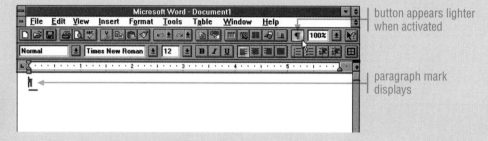

Figure 1-12
Show/Hide ¶
button activated

button appears lighter when activated

paragraph mark displays

> **TROUBLE?** If the paragraph mark in your workspace disappeared when you clicked ¶, the Show/Hide ¶ command had already been activated; by clicking the button, you *deactivated* the command. Click ¶ one more time to activate the command.

❷ Press **[Tab]**. A nonprinting character (→) appears to mark the location of the tab inserted into your document.

❸ Type **This is my first Word document.** A nonprinting character (•) appears to mark the location of the spaces inserted into your document. See Figure 1-13.

space indicators

tab character

Figure 1-13
Screen showing
nonprinting
characters

paragraph mark

❹ Click ¶ on the Standard toolbar. The nonprinting characters are no longer displayed in the workspace.

You can also activate the nonprinting characters through the Tools Options command.

❺ Click **Tools** then click **Options...**.

❻ Click the **View tab**, if necessary, then click the **All check box** in the Nonprinting Characters section.

❼ Click **OK** or press **[Enter]**. The nonprinting characters appear once again and the Show/Hide ¶ button is activated. Leave the Show/Hide ¶ button activated throughout these tutorials so you can see any special marks you insert.

Checking Font and Point Size Settings

Notice the term "Times New Roman" and the number "12" on the Formatting toolbar. These terms represent the shape (font) and size (point) of the letters used to create the documents shown in the figures throughout the tutorials. If the font or point size settings are different on your screen, ask your instructor or technical support person to adjust these settings for you. (By default, Word uses a 10-point font size in new documents; ask your instructor or technical support person to change the default setting to 12 if your screen shows 10 for the point size.)

In summary, each time you start a new Word session, conduct a screen check by asking yourself the following questions:

- Is the Word window in normal view?
- Is the document window maximized?
- Is the Word window maximized?
- Are only the Standard and Formatting toolbars and the ruler visible?
- Is the Show/Hide ¶ button activated?
- Is the font set to Times New Roman and the point size set to 12?

If you can't answer "yes" to all of these questions, adjust the Word screen appropriately.

Organizing Document Windows

Word makes it easy for you to open more than one document at a time—so easy, in fact, that you might not know it has happened. You need to know how to keep track of your open documents, as well as how to close them.

Opening a New Document

Currently you have one document window open; it is titled Document1. Within that document window, you create your document. You can have as many documents open at one time in Word as your computer's memory will allow. When you open a new document, it is displayed in a new document window. Word automatically assigns the new document a name—the word "Document" followed by a number. The Window menu contains a list of all open or minimized Word documents.

If the document name in your title bar has a different number, you have accidentally created a new document. Don't worry about it now; just continue with the tutorial.

Now let's practice opening two new documents.

To open a new document:

❶ Click the **New button** 🗋 on the Standard toolbar. Notice the change in the title bar. It now reads "Document2." Document1 is still open but is not visible—it is open behind Document2.

❷ Type **This is my second Word document.**

❸ Click **File** then click **New....** The New dialog box appears. See Figure 1-14. The Template section contains a listing of Word's predefined document templates. You will learn about document templates later in this book.

Figure 1-14
New dialog box

❹ Click **OK** or press **[Enter]** to open a new document. Notice the change in the title bar. Now it reads "Document3." Document1 and Document2 are still open but not visible.

❺ Type **This is my third Word document.**

Switching Between Open Documents

Although you can have many documents open at one time, you can work in only one document at a time. This document is called the **active document.** To work in another open document, you must first make it the active document.

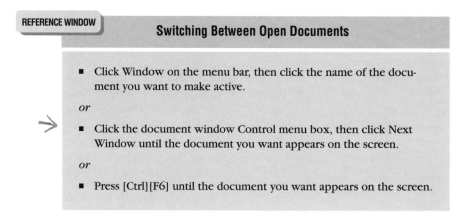

REFERENCE WINDOW

Switching Between Open Documents

- Click Window on the menu bar, then click the name of the document you want to make active.

or

- Click the document window Control menu box, then click Next Window until the document you want appears on the screen.

or

- Press [Ctrl][F6] until the document you want appears on the screen.

Let's practice switching between open documents.

To switch between the open documents:

❶ Click **Window** to display the Window menu. Three document names are listed at the bottom of the Window menu, and a check mark is in front of Document3, the active document. See Figure 1-15.

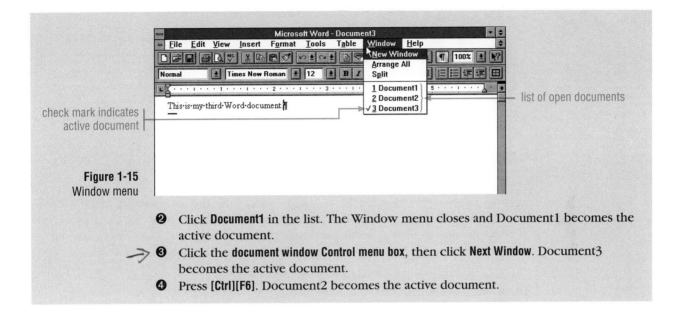

check mark indicates
active document

Figure 1-15
Window menu

list of open documents

❷ Click **Document1** in the list. The Window menu closes and Document1 becomes the active document.

❸ Click the **document window Control menu box**, then click **Next Window**. Document3 becomes the active document.

❹ Press **[Ctrl][F6]**. Document2 becomes the active document.

If you ever lose sight of a document you have been working on, open the Window menu to see if your document is listed at the bottom of the menu, or try one of the other techniques to switch between open documents.

Closing a Document

Even though you can have several documents open at one time in Word, you should generally close your documents once you no longer need them. The more windows that are open, the more memory is used and the slower the performance of your computer. When you close a document, you remove that document from your computer's memory.

Let's practice closing a document without saving changes.

To close a document without saving changes:

❶ Switch to Document1.

❷ Click **File** then click **Close**. The message, "Do you want to save changes to Document1?" appears.

❸ Click **No** to indicate that you do not want to save any changes to the document. Document2 is now the active document.

❹ Click **Window** in the menu bar. Notice that Document1 is not listed.

❺ Close the Window menu by clicking outside the menu.

❻ Double-click the **document window Control menu box**. The message, "Do you want to save changes to Document2?" appears.

TROUBLE? If you mistakenly double-click the Word window Control menu box, click Cancel to return to your document without closing Word. Then repeat Step 6.

❼ Click **No**. Document2 closes.

❽ Click **Window**. Notice that Document2 is not listed. Document3 is now the active document.

❾ Close the Window menu. Document3 is the only document remaining open at this point.

TROUBLE? If Document3 is not the only document remaining open at this point, use the previous set of steps to close all open documents except Document3 without saving changes.

Creating a Document

The initial phase of the productivity strategy, creating, requires you to do a great deal of planning. Although you might be tempted to just start typing, you must organize your thoughts first. Having a clear picture of what you need to say and how to say it will greatly improve the quality of your writing and help contribute to your success. Word is a powerful word processing program, but it cannot compensate for poorly planned writing.

Planning a Document

Denise decides that she will set the stage for her request in the opening paragraph of her letter, describe the specifications of the brownie in the second paragraph, and close with a request for a bid proposal in the last paragraph. With her writing plan for the body of the letter in mind, she also plans to enter the standard parts of a letter: the date, inside address, salutation, complimentary closing, and her name and title. During this phase of the productivity strategy, Denise is concerned only with typing the text of her letter as she has planned it, and not with editing or formatting the letter.

Entering Text

Each Word document is based on a **document template,** a set of predefined features. Unless you specify otherwise, new documents are assigned the features of the Normal template—8.5 x 11-inch print orientation, single spacing, 1.25-inch left and right margins, 1-inch top and bottom margins, tabs set at every 0.5 inch, and text aligned at the left margin only. These standard features of a document are called **default settings.**

The status bar, located at the bottom of the screen, is an extremely valuable feature when you are entering text because it keeps you informed of the location of the insertion point. Figure 1-16 describes the purpose of each element of the status bar.

This section of the status bar:	Indicates:
Page 1	Page number where the insertion point is located
Sec 1	Section number where the insertion point is located
1/1	Number of pages from the beginning of the document to the insertion point, followed by the total number of pages in the document
At 1"	Position of the insertion point as measured from the top edge of the page
Ln 1	Position of the insertion point as measured from the top margin of the page
Col 1	Position of the insertion point as measured from the left margin of the page
Time	Current time as determined by the computer's clock

Figure 1-16
Status bar elements

Denise doesn't want to change Word's default document settings, but she does want to start the date 2.5 inches from the top edge of the paper to allow room for the company letterhead. The "At" section of the status bar indicates that the insertion point is currently located 1 inch from the top edge of the paper. To insert a blank line in a document, press [Enter]. Each time you press [Enter], a paragraph mark is displayed (if the Show/Hide ¶ button is activated).

Denise must open a new document and then move the insertion point 2.5 inches from the top edge of the paper.

To insert blank lines:

❶ Click the **New button** ☐ on the Standard toolbar (or click **File**, click **New...**, then click **OK** or press **[Enter]**). A new document titled Document4 appears. Document 3 is still open, just not visible.

❷ Make sure the "At" section of the status bar displays 1".

TROUBLE? If the "At" section does not display 1", you have inadvertently inserted blank lines into your document. Press [Backspace] to remove the blank lines.

❸ Press **[Enter]** eight times. Notice the change in the status bar. The "At" section, which is the position from the top edge of the paper, is now 2.5"; the "Ln" section, the position from the top margin of the page, now reads "Ln 9."

TROUBLE? If the "Ln" section displays 9 but the "At" section does not display 2.5", ask your instructor or technical support person to change the default font to Times New Roman 12 point. If the default font or its size cannot be changed, continue with the tutorial, keeping in mind that your screen, and eventually your printed document, will look different from the figures shown in this tutorial.

Denise has moved the insertion point so that she has 2.5 inches of blank space at the top of her document, and now she is ready to type the date. In the following steps, you will make an intentional error by entering an incorrect date. This is so you can practice correcting errors in text as you type.

To type the date:
❶ Type **February 22, 1985**. Notice the change in the "Col" section of the status bar. The "Col" indicator in the status bar changes as you move the insertion point to the right. See Figure 1-17.

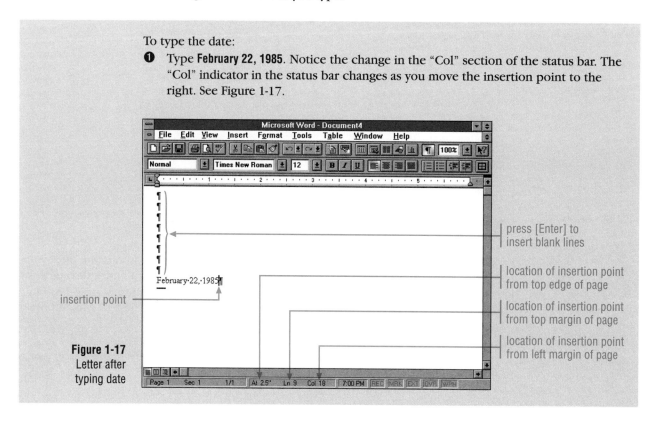

Figure 1-17
Letter after typing date

Denise notices that she typed 1985 instead of 1995. Because she discovers this typing error shortly after making it, she can press [Backspace] up to and including the error and then type the correct text. Pressing [Backspace] deletes characters or spaces to the left of the insertion point. There are other ways to correct errors, but for now let's use this method to correct your typing errors.

To correct an error using [Backspace]:
❶ Make sure the insertion point is after the "5" in 1985.
❷ Press **[Backspace]** twice to delete the "5" and then the "8."
❸ Type **95**. The date is now correct.

Now Denise is ready to type the inside address. She needs to move the insertion point to the left margin and to insert three blank lines before the inside address.

To insert blank lines then type the inside address:

❶ Press **[Enter]** one time to move the insertion point to the left margin, then press **[Enter]** three more times to insert three blank lines after the date.

❷ Type **Mr. Mike Gonzales** (the first line of the inside address).

❸ Press **[Enter]**.

❹ Continue to enter the remaining three lines of the inside address, as shown in Figure 1-18. Press **[Enter]** at the end of each short line in the inside address to move the insertion point to the left margin of the next line. Make sure you press **[Enter]** at the end of the last line of the inside address as well.

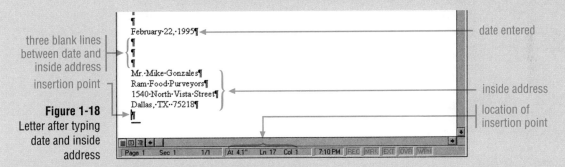

three blank lines between date and inside address

insertion point

Figure 1-18
Letter after typing date and inside address

date entered

inside address

location of insertion point

You have now typed the inside address of the letter. Next add a blank line after the inside address, then type the salutation.

❺ Press **[Enter]** to insert a blank line after the inside address.

❻ Type **Dear Mr. Gonzales:** then press **[Enter]** twice to leave a blank line between the salutation and beginning of the body of the letter.

Now you are ready to begin typing the body of the letter. As you type the letter, however, you do not have to press [Enter] at the end of the line as you did when you typed the date, inside address, and salutation. As you are entering text, if a word does not fit completely on the line, Word automatically moves it to the beginning of the next line for you. This feature is known as **word wrap**.

To type the body of the letter:

❶ Type the first paragraph of the body of the letter, as shown in Figure 1-19. Remember—do not press [Enter] at the end of each full line. Let Word do the work for you. Notice that some lines inserted at the top of the letter are now no longer in view.

blank lines at top of document are no longer in view

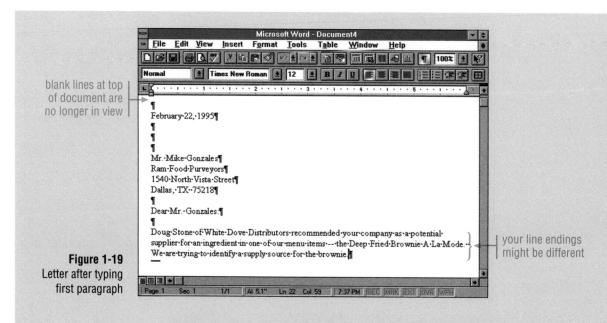

your line endings might be different

Figure 1-19
Letter after typing first paragraph

TROUBLE? If your lines wrap differently from those shown in Figure 1-19, it could be because you have a printer selected that is different from the one used to prepare this tutorial. Don't worry; just continue with the tutorial.

❷ Press **[Enter]** to end the first paragraph, then press **[Enter]** again to insert a blank line between the first and second paragraphs.

❸ Finish typing the rest of the letter, as shown in Figure 1-20, *including the three deliberate typographical errors in the last paragraph.* Press **[Enter]** twice at the end of each paragraph to insert a blank line between paragraphs.

type **ofa** leaving no space between "f" and "a"

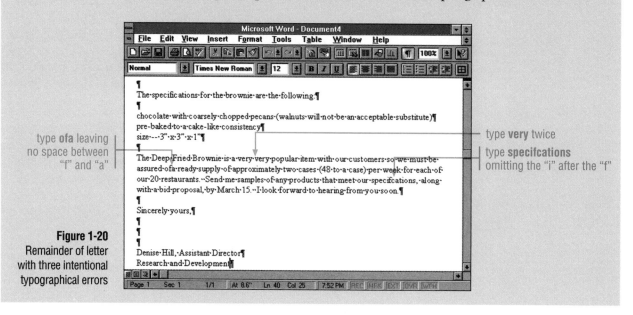

type **very** twice

type **specifcations** omitting the "i" after the "f"

Figure 1-20
Remainder of letter with three intentional typographical errors

Denise has finished entering the text of her letter, and now she is ready to save her work.

Saving a Document

While you were creating Denise's document, it was not stored permanently to disk. A default feature of Word, AutoSave, automatically saves changes made to a document every specified number of minutes to a temporary file in case of a power failure. The changes are not saved to the permanent file, however, until you save the document. It is a good idea to save your work to disk at least every 15 minutes or when you finish something you wouldn't want to do again. When you save a document, it is preserved permanently on the disk in its own file with its own filename.

Naming Files

Word's filenames can be any legal filename; that is, they can contain from one to eight characters and no spaces. The extension "DOC" is added automatically to Word document files. Each filename must be unique, should be descriptive of the file's content, and should follow a naming scheme.

Before you save your work, you need to understand the file naming scheme used in this book, which was designed to help you and your instructor recognize the origin and content of documents. You will create many files, but some files have already been created for you and are stored on your Student Disk. As shown in Figure 1-21, you will be working with four categories of files. Those files provided for you on the Student Disk are for use in the Tutorial Cases, Tutorial Assignments, and Case Problems. The filenames of any files used in Tutorial Cases begin with C; Tutorial Assignments begin with T; and Case Problems begin with P. However, all files that you are instructed to save throughout these tutorials will have a filename that begins with S (for "saved").

File Category	Description
Tutorial Cases	The files you use to work through each tutorial
Tutorial Assignments	The files that contain the documents you need to complete the Tutorial Assignments at the end of each tutorial
Case Problems	The files that contain the documents you need to complete the Case Problems at the end of each tutorial
Saved Document	Any document that you save

Figure 1-21
Types of tutorial files

In the file naming convention used in these tutorials, the second character of the filename identifies the number of the tutorial to which the file relates. The last six characters of the filenames represent a description of the document's content—a word or an abbreviation that helps to identify the document. Thus, the filename S1RAM would represent a file you saved in Tutorial 1 that has something to do with Ram Food Purveyors.

Saving a Document for the First Time

The first time you save a document after it has been created, you must tell Word the filename that you want to give your document and where you want the document saved.

Let's save the work you have completed so far and name the document S1RAM.

To save the document for the first time:

❶ Make sure your Student Disk is in drive A.

❷ Click the **Save button** 🖫 on the Standard toolbar (or click **File** then click **Save** or **Save As...**). The Save As dialog box appears with the default filename doc4.doc highlighted in the File Name text box.

❸ In the File Name text box, type **s1ram**. *Do not press [Enter]*. Because the default filename doc4.doc was highlighted, typing s1ram automatically replaces the selected text. Word automatically adds the extension "DOC" to the filename when you complete the dialog box. You can type the filename using uppercase or lowercase letters.

You want to save this document to your Student Disk, not the hard drive, so you must change the destination, or target drive, information.

❹ Click the **Drives list box down arrow**. A list of available target drives appears.

❺ Click the letter of the drive in which you put your Student Disk. This tutorial assumes that your Student Disk is in drive A. Notice that the Directories section of the dialog box also changes to reflect the change in the target drive. See Figure 1-22.

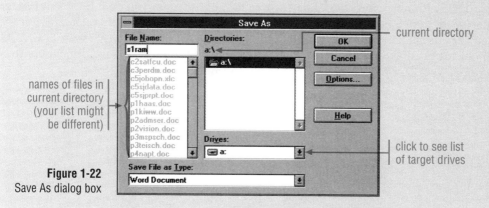

Figure 1-22
Save As dialog box

❻ Click **OK** or press **[Enter]** to save the document. Notice that the title bar has changed to reflect the new filename, S1RAM.DOC.

Now that Denise has created her letter and saved it, she decides to take a break before she begins editing her letter to Ram Food Purveyors. First, she needs to exit Word.

Exiting Word

You can exit Word by double-clicking the Word window Control menu box, or by choosing Exit from the File menu.

To exit Word:

❶ Double-click the **Word window Control menu box** (or click **File** then click **Exit**). Be sure not to double-click the document window Control menu box. The message, "Do you want to save changes to Document3?" appears because Document3 is still open.

❷ Click **No**. You do not need to save Document3.

❸ Double-click the **Microsoft Office group window Control menu box** to close it. You return to the Program Manager.

❹ At the Program Manager, either exit Windows or start another application.

If you want to take a break and resume the tutorial at a later time, you can do so now. When you want to resume the tutorial, start Word and place your Student Disk in the disk drive. Remember to complete the screen check procedure described earlier in this tutorial. Then continue with the tutorial.

Editing a Document

Editing a document involves changing its content by inserting, deleting, or moving text. The purpose of editing is to refine a document so that its meaning is clear and it is free of errors. The most efficient way to edit a document is first to make changes in content and then to check for spelling and typographical errors.

Opening an Existing Document

To resume work on the letter, you must first open the file that contains that document. You can either click the Open button on the Standard toolbar or choose the Open command from the File menu to display the Open dialog box, in which you specify the file you want to open.

You can also open a document that you have worked on recently from the File menu. The four most recently closed documents are listed at the bottom of the File menu. See Figure 1-23. (Your list might include other filenames.) Just click the name of the document on which you want to work, and it will open.

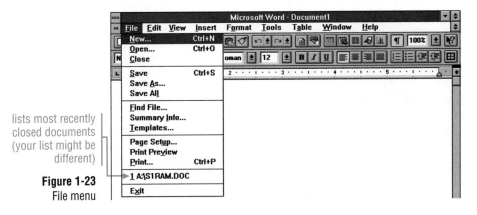

lists most recently closed documents (your list might be different)

Figure 1-23
File menu

Let's open the file S1RAM, which you saved on your Student Disk.

To open the S1RAM document:

❶ If necessary, start Word and conduct the screen check of your Word screen as described in the "Screen Check" section earlier in this tutorial.

❷ Click the **Open button** 📂 on the Standard toolbar (or click **File** then click **Open...**). Word displays the Open dialog box.

❸ Click the **Drives list box down arrow**. The list of available drives appears.

❹ Click the letter of the drive containing your Student Disk. Notice that the Directories section of the dialog box changes to reflect the selected drive. Scroll through the list of files until s1ram.doc appears.

❺ Click **s1ram.doc**. The name of the selected file now appears in the File Name text box. See Figure 1-24.

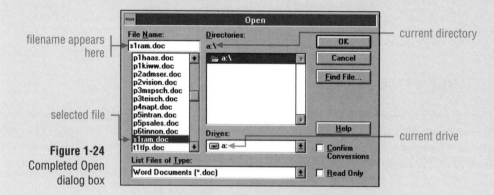

filename appears here

selected file

Figure 1-24
Completed Open
dialog box

current directory

current drive

TROUBLE? If you can't find a file named S1RAM.DOC, make sure the Drives section indicates the location of your Student Disk. If the Drives section indicates the correct drive name, perhaps you accidentally saved the file to the hard drive. If you are working on the same computer as you were when you saved the document, check drive C. If you still cannot locate your file, check with your instructor or technical support person.

❻ Click **OK** or press **[Enter]**. The document S1RAM.DOC opens with the insertion point at the top of the document.

After reading through her letter, Denise decides to make a few changes to its content. Before she can make these changes, however, she must move the insertion point to the location in the document where the revisions will be made.

Moving the Insertion Point

The fastest way to move the insertion point to a new location in the window you are currently viewing is to move the mouse pointer to the new location, then click the mouse button. The mouse pointer takes the shape of an I-beam I when it is in the workspace of the Word window to aid you in the exact placement of the insertion point.

Keyboard Techniques

Skilled keyboarders might find it more efficient to move the insertion point with keyboard shortcuts rather than with the mouse, because they do not have to take their hands off the keyboard. The basic keyboard movement keys are the arrow keys: [→], [←], [↑], [↓]. To move the insertion point further with the keyboard, however, you need to use the keyboard movement techniques listed in Figure 1-25. To perform a movement that involves two keys, hold down the first key listed while pressing the second key listed. For instance, hold down [Ctrl] while pressing [End] to move the insertion point to the end of the document.

To move the insertion point:	Press:
Left or right one character at a time	[←] or [→]
Up or down one line at a time	[↑] or [↓]
Left or right one word at a time	[Ctrl][←] or [Ctrl][→]
Down one paragraph at a time	[Ctrl][↑] or [Ctrl][↓]
To the previous screen	[PgUp]
To the next screen	[PgDn]
To the top of the screen	[Ctrl][PgUp]
To the bottom of the screen	[Ctrl][PgDn]
To the beginning of the previous page	[Alt][Ctrl][PgUp]
To the beginning of the next page	[Alt][Ctrl][PgDn]
To the beginning of the current line	[Home]
To the end of the current line	[End]
To the top of the document	[Ctrl][Home]
To the bottom of the document	[Ctrl][End]

Figure 1-25
Keyboard movement
techniques

Let's practice moving the insertion point using the keyboard. Look at the status bar to determine the location of the insertion point before you begin. Because you just opened the document, the insertion point should be at the top of the document.

To change the location of the insertion point using keyboard techniques:

❶ Press **[Ctrl][End]** to move to the end of the document. Notice that the status bar reflects the change in the location of the insertion point.

  TROUBLE? If the insertion point didn't move to the end of the document, perhaps you released [Ctrl] before you pressed [End]. Try again; this time continue to hold down [Ctrl] while you press [End].

❷ Press **[Ctrl][Home]**. The insertion point moves to the top of the document.

❸ Press **[Ctrl][PgDn]**. Notice that you see the same text on the screen, but the insertion point moves to the last line on the screen.

❹ Press **[↓]** until the insertion point is in the first paragraph of the body of the letter.

⑤ Press **[Ctrl][→]** once. Word moves the insertion point forward one word. Practice moving forward a word at a time a few more times.

⑥ Press **[End]**. The insertion point moves to the end of the current line.

⑦ Press **[Home]**. The insertion point moves to the beginning of the current line.

⑧ Press **[Ctrl][↓]** once. The insertion point moves to the next paragraph. To Word, a paragraph is any string of characters that ends with a paragraph mark, including a paragraph mark on a line by itself.

⑨ Press **[Ctrl][Home]**. The insertion point moves to the beginning of the document.

Mouse Techniques

Now let's practice moving the insertion point with the mouse by using the point-and-click method. The insertion point is at the top of the document, but Denise wants to move it in front of the word Street in the inside address.

To move the insertion point using the point-and-click method:

❶ Move the pointer so that the I-beam is in front of the "S" in Street. The insertion point is still at the top of the document. See Figure 1-26.

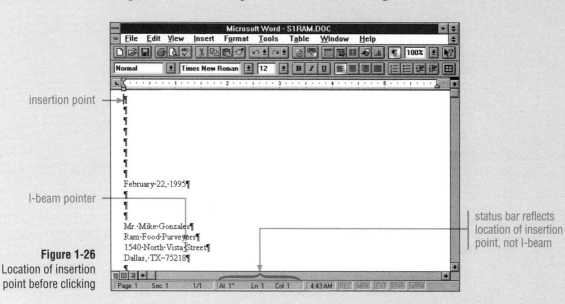

insertion point

I-beam pointer

status bar reflects location of insertion point, not I-beam

Figure 1-26
Location of insertion point before clicking

❷ Click the mouse button. Move the mouse pointer out of the way so that you can see the insertion point in its new location. Notice the change in the status bar.

The point-and-click method of moving the insertion point with the mouse is useful when the part of the document you need to move to is visible on the screen. If you can't see the place in your document to which you want to move, you must use the scroll bars first to move the new location into view, then click the I-beam at the point where the revision needs to be made.

Word's vertical and horizontal scroll bars contain the same elements as Windows' scroll bars—scroll arrows and a scroll box. Let's practice using the scroll bars. Take note of the status bar to determine the current location of the insertion point.

To scroll through a document:

❶ Click the **down arrow** at the bottom of the vertical scroll bar several times. Notice that the location of the insertion point does not change. You can use the down arrow and the up arrow on the vertical scroll bar to scroll through your document line by line.

❷ Click once below the scroll box in the vertical scroll bar. When you click below or above the scroll box, you scroll one window of text at a time.

❸ Drag the scroll box to the bottom of the vertical scroll bar to move quickly through the document. Although you can see the end of your document on the screen, you cannot see the insertion point.

❹ Move the I-beam anywhere in the last line of text you can see on the screen, then click. Now the location of the insertion point changes.

❺ Drag the scroll box in the horizontal scroll bar all the way to the right. You lose sight of your document. Drag the scroll box back to the left edge of the horizontal scroll bar. Your document comes back into view.

You can use the scroll bars to bring different parts of your document into view. However, until you click the mouse pointer, the insertion point does not move to a new location.

Inserting New Text

Now that Denise knows how to move within her document and change the location of the insertion point quickly, she can modify her document. She sees several changes she wants to make. First, she decides to insert the letter "n" and the word "alternate" before the word "supply" in the last sentence of the first paragraph.

To insert new text into previously created text, move the insertion point and type in the new text. Word's default typing preference mode is **Insert mode**; that is, as new characters are inserted into previously typed text, Word moves the existing text to the right and adjusts the line endings to accommodate the changes.

To insert the new text in the first paragraph:

❶ Place the insertion point in the first paragraph of the body of the letter, immediately after the "a" in "identify a..."

❷ Type **n** and press **[Spacebar]**, then type **alternate**. As you type the new text, the existing text moves to the right. See Figure 1-27.

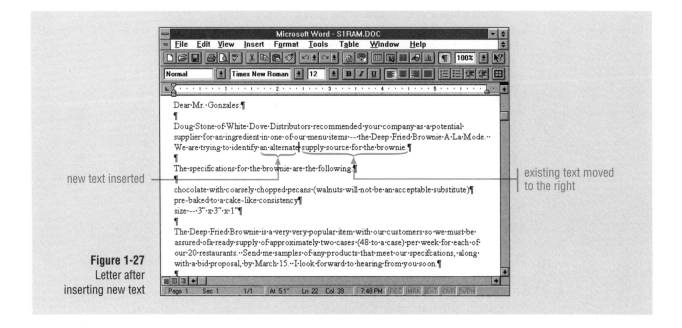

new text inserted

existing text moved to the right

Figure 1-27
Letter after
inserting new text

Deleting Text

Thus far, you have been correcting your errors by backspacing over them. Backspacing deletes the character or space to the left of the insertion point. To delete a space or character to the *right* of the insertion point, you press [Del]. Denise notices that she capitalized the words "A La" in A La Mode, but they should be lowercase. Let's delete the capital A and capital L and replace them with lowercase letters.

To use [Del] to delete the text:

❶ Place the insertion point directly in front of the "A" in A La.

❷ Press **[Del]** three times to remove the "A," the space, and the "L." Notice that the text closes up after the characters are deleted.

❸ Type **a** then press **[Spacebar]** and type **l**. The correction is inserted, and the existing text moves to the right. See Figure 1-28.

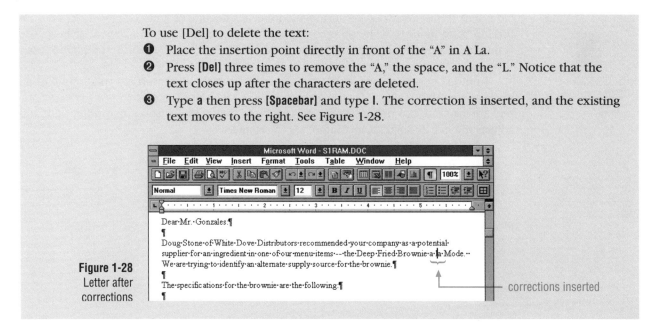

Figure 1-28
Letter after
corrections

corrections inserted

Deleting text one character at a time is inefficient if you have several characters to delete. Figure 1-29 describes other keyboard deletion techniques you can use.

To delete:	Press:
The character to the right of the insertion point	[Del]
The character to the left of the insertion point	[Backspace]
Text from the insertion point to the end of the word	[Ctrl][Del]
The word to the left of the insertion point	[Ctrl][Backspace]

Figure 1-29
Keyboard deletion
techniques

Denise wants to delete the word "The" in the sentence beginning "The specifications..." and change it to "Our."

To delete the word "The":
❶ Place the insertion point in front of "The" at the beginning of the second paragraph.
❷ Press **[Ctrl][Del]**. Notice that the word "The" and the space after it are deleted.

Using Undo

Sometimes Word makes it so easy to delete text that you might delete something unintentionally. In such a case, you could use another feature of Word, the Undo command. If you accidentally delete text, you can click the Undo button on the Standard toolbar or choose Undo from the Edit menu. The Standard toolbar also contains a Redo button, which redoes the previously undone action. The text you deleted reappears in its original location. The word or words that follow Undo on the Edit menu change to reflect the type of action that Word can undo at that point (for instance, "Undo Typing"). Note that some actions cannot be undone at any time. In that case, "Can't Undo" appears dimmed in the Edit menu to indicate that the command is not currently available for use.

Denise has just deleted the word "The" at the beginning of the second paragraph. Let's practice using the Undo feature to reinsert the deleted word.

To undo the text deletion:
❶ Click the **Undo button** 🔄 on the Standard toolbar (or click **Edit** then click **Undo Delete Word**). The deleted word is recovered.

Now try reversing the undo action to delete the word "The" again.

❷ Click the **Redo button** 🔄 on the Standard toolbar (or click **Edit** then click **Redo Delete Word**). Your previous undone action is reversed. "The" is deleted again.

Now you can insert the word "Our" in place of "The."

❸ Type **Our** then press **[Spacebar]**. The sentence is corrected. See Figure 1-30.

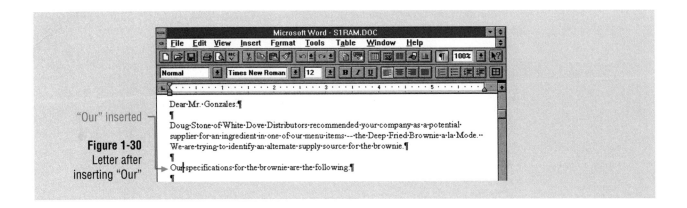

"Our" inserted

Figure 1-30
Letter after
inserting "Our"

You can also undo more than just your last action. Clicking the down arrow next to the Undo button displays a list of all actions that can be reversed. You then select the action to be undone, and that action is undone as well as all subsequent actions. The Redo button has a similar list of all actions that can be redone.

Using Overtype Mode

As you learned earlier, Word's default typing preference is Insert mode. You can deactivate Insert mode by pressing [Ins] or by double-clicking the dimmed OVR indicator in the status bar. The Insert key acts as a **toggle switch;** in other words, you can activate and deactivate Insert mode by pressing the same key.

When you deactivate Insert mode, you overwrite existing text as you type new text. This mode of typing is called **Overtype mode.** When you activate Overtype mode, the abbreviation OVR changes from dimmed to bolded in the status bar.

Let's use Overtype mode to correct an error in Denise's letter. She notices that the address of Ram Food Purveyors is incorrect—it should be 1540 North Vista Avenue instead of Street. She wants to type Avenue over Street.

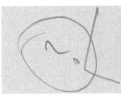

To type the word Avenue over the word Street:
❶ Place the insertion point in front of the "S" in Street in the inside address.
❷ Press **[Ins]**. In the status bar, OVR appears darker to remind you that you have changed to Overtype mode. See Figure 1-31.

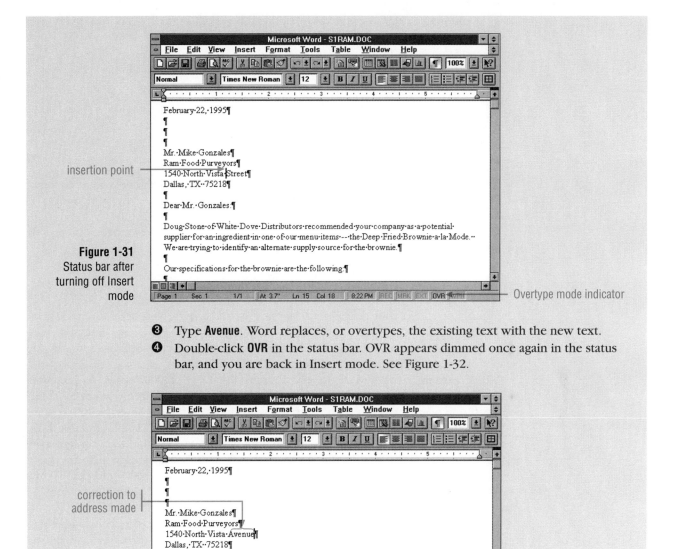

Figure 1-31
Status bar after
turning off Insert
mode

insertion point

Overtype mode indicator

❸ Type **Avenue**. Word replaces, or overtypes, the existing text with the new text.
❹ Double-click **OVR** in the status bar. OVR appears dimmed once again in the status
   bar, and you are back in Insert mode. See Figure 1-32.

Figure 1-32
Address after
correction

correction to
address made

OVR is dimmed

Updating a File

You have now made several changes to Denise's letter, but these changes are not automatically saved. You must instruct Word to update your file to reflect any changes made since
you last saved your document. Once a Word document is saved and given a name, all you
have to do to save again is click the Save button on the Standard toolbar or choose Save
from the File menu. The Save As dialog box will not appear.

As mentioned earlier, the AutoSave feature saves changes to a temporary file just in case of a power failure. The changes are not saved to the permanent file, however, until you save the document in the usual manner.

To update the file:
❶ Click the **Save button** 🖫 on the Standard toolbar (or click **File** then click **Save**). Notice that the Save As dialog box does not appear.

If you wanted to save both the original file and the file with the most recent changes, you would choose the Save As command from the File menu, then give a different filename to the most recent version of your document.

Denise has finished revising the content of her document. Now she must correct any spelling and typographical errors.

Checking Spelling

After you have edited your document to get the wording right, you need to check it for misspelled words and typographical errors. Proofing a document for spelling and typographical errors can be tedious. Word's Spelling command considerably reduces the amount of time you spend on this part of the editing process.

Word contains a standard dictionary of approximately 130,000 words. As you spell check a document, Word compares each word in your document with the words in its dictionary. If one of your words doesn't match a word in its dictionary letter for letter, Word highlights the misspelled word in your document and opens the Spelling dialog box. Correctly spelled words would still be highlighted if Word did not find them in its dictionary. Examples of words that might not be in Word's standard dictionary include proper names, specialized vocabulary, foreign words, and acronyms. If you use a word consistently that Word doesn't recognize, you can add it to a custom dictionary. The Spelling command also points out instances of repeated or doubled words within your document.

A word of caution: don't rely solely on the Spelling command to catch all your errors. It does not catch grammatical and syntax errors. You should always proofread your documents to make the final decisions about their correctness.

REFERENCE WINDOW

Checking the Spelling of a Document

- Click the Spelling button on the Standard toolbar (or click Tools then click Spelling...).
- Change the spelling or ignore Word's suggestion for each flagged word.
- Click OK or press [Enter] when the spell check is finished.

Recall that you made some intentional typing mistakes in the last paragraph of Denise's letter. Let's use the Spelling command to locate and correct these errors. If you made other mistakes, Word will stop at additional places in your document.

To check the spelling of your document:

➊ Press **[Ctrl][Home]** to move the insertion point to the top of the document. Word checks your document from the location of the insertion point to the end of the document.

➋ Click the **Spelling button** 📝 on the Standard toolbar (or click **Tools** then click **Spelling...**). The Spelling dialog box appears. See Figure 1-33. The word "Gonzales" is not found in Word's dictionary, which is typical for most proper nouns. Notice that the word "Gonzales" is highlighted in the text and also appears in the Not in Dictionary text box of the dialog box. Word has no suggested correct spellings.

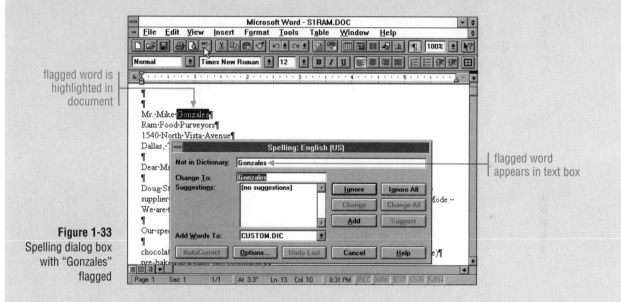

flagged word is highlighted in document

flagged word appears in text box

Figure 1-33
Spelling dialog box with "Gonzales" flagged

Denise knows that this is the correct spelling, so she wants to tell Word to ignore this word as well as all other instances of "Gonzales" in her letter.

➌ Click **Ignore All** in the Spelling dialog box. Word will not stop at the next instance of "Gonzales" in the salutation.

Word continues to check the spelling in the document and next flags the occurrence of a repeated word "very." The repeated word is highlighted in the document and flagged in the Spelling dialog box. Notice that the text box in the Spelling dialog box changes to Repeated Word instead of Not in Dictionary, and that the Change button is now a Delete button. See Figure 1-34.

repeated word flagged in document

indicates repeated word

Figure 1-34
Spelling dialog box with "very" flagged

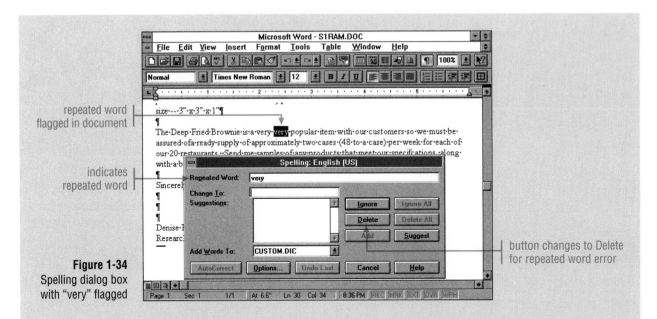

button changes to Delete for repeated word error

Denise decides to delete the second occurrence of the word "very."

❹ Click **Delete** in the Spelling dialog box.

Word edits your document by deleting the second instance of "very," then stops at another typographical error, "ofa." As shown in Figure 1-35, Word's suggestions for correcting "ofa" are not appropriate, so you must edit this word manually.

error highlighted in document

Word's first suggestion highlighted in Change To text box

list of suggested corrections

Figure 1-35
Spelling dialog box with "ofa" flagged

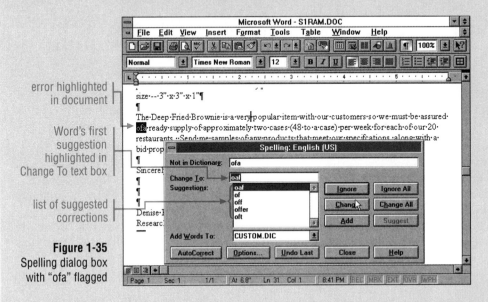

❺ Click after the highlighted word "oaf" in the Change To text box to remove the highlighting.

❻ Press [Backspace] twice, then type f and press [Spacebar], then type a. The Change To text box should now contain the correct text, "of a."

❼ Click **Change** in the Spelling dialog box to instruct Word to insert the correct text in the document.

Word moves to the next misspelled word, "specfcations." Notice that the Change To text box contains the correct spelling. If you accept the suggested spelling, Word edits your text for you by replacing the misspelled word in your document with the correct spelling.

❽ Click **Change** to accept Word's suggested spelling.

Word finds no more spelling errors (unless you made additional errors), and a message box appears. You're finished checking the document for spelling errors, so let's exit Spelling and save the corrections you've made.

To exit Spelling and save changes:
❶ Click **OK** or press [Enter].
❷ Click the **Save button** 🖫 on the Standard toolbar (or click **File** then click **Save**) to save the changes you have made.

Denise proofreads her letter one last time, looking for any errors that the spell check would not catch. The content of her letter is correct and free from errors, and she has saved all of the changes she has made so far. Now she's ready to format her document.

If you want to take a break and resume the tutorial at a later time, you can do so now. Follow the procedure for exiting Word. When you want to resume the tutorial, start Word and place your Student Disk in the disk drive. Remember to complete the screen check procedure described earlier in this tutorial. Then open the file S1RAM.DOC and continue with the tutorial.

Formatting a Document

Formatting is the process of controlling how your printed document looks. The purpose of formatting is to improve the readability and attractiveness of your document so that the reader can concentrate on your message. To implement this phase of the productivity strategy efficiently, you should format your document only after you have created and edited the text.

Select, Then Do

When you want to format, you must first indicate to Word the portion of your document you want formatted. You give Word this information by selecting the text you want to change. To **select** text means to highlight it. You can select one character, the whole document, or any amount of text in between. Once you have selected the text you want to format, you then issue the commands to change the highlighted text. Simply stated, the process is "select, then do."

You can select text with either the mouse or the keyboard. Because the mouse is the most efficient way to select text, this book focuses on mouse techniques. The **selection bar** is the area located in the left margin of the document screen. It is one way you select a line or a paragraph of text. The I-beam pointer changes to ↗whenever it passes into the selection bar.

The mouse technique most frequently used to select small amounts of text is the click-and-drag technique: you click and hold the I-beam in front of the first character to be selected, then drag the pointer across all the text you want selected. The selected text is highlighted. Figure 1-36 summarizes the various techniques for selecting text.

To select:	Then:
A word	Double-click in the word
A sentence	Press [Ctrl] and click within the sentence
A line	Click in the selection bar next to the line
Multiple lines	Click and drag in the selection bar next to lines
A paragraph	Double-click in the selection bar next to the paragraph
Multiple paragraphs	Click and drag in the selection bar next to the paragraphs
Entire document	Triple-click in the selection bar or press [Ctrl] and click
Non-standard block of text	Click at beginning of block, then press [Shift] and click at end of block

Figure 1-36
Selection techniques

Selected text is extremely sensitive to change, so be careful. Word immediately carries out whatever command you issue after you have selected text. If you select text and then press [Enter], for instance, Word replaces your highlighted text with a paragraph mark. If you want your replaced text back, just click the Undo button on the Standard toolbar or select Undo from the Edit menu.

Once you become more familiar with Word and working with selected text, you will see that selecting and replacing text can be a very useful editing tool. For example, earlier you deleted the word "The" and typed the word "Our" to replace it. You could also select the word "The" then simply type "Our" to both delete the selected text and insert the new text in one step.

It is best to deselect text as soon as you can. To deselect highlighted text, you click anywhere off the selected text in the workspace or press any of the arrow keys.

Let's apply the principle of "select, then do" by practicing with the first sentence of Denise's letter.

To select the first sentence in the letter:
❶ Place the insertion point anywhere within the first sentence of the first paragraph of the body of the letter.

❷ Press and hold **[Ctrl]** and click within the first sentence. The entire first sentence plus the period and the spaces following are selected. The selected text appears highlighted. See Figure 1-37.

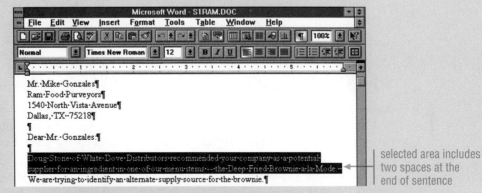

Figure 1-37
Letter with first sentence highlighted

selected area includes two spaces at the end of sentence

TROUBLE? If the entire first sentence is not selected, make sure the insertion point is visible within the first sentence, then press [Ctrl] while you click the left mouse button.

Now let's practice the "do" part of the principle: issuing a command to Word. Let's intentionally make an error, then undo it. If you type something rather than issue a formatting command after you select text, Word will replace your highlighted text with your typing. The principle here is "typing replaces selection." Let's try it.

❸ Press **[Enter]**. Your selection disappears and is replaced with a paragraph mark. See Figure 1-38.

illustrates "typing replaces selection"

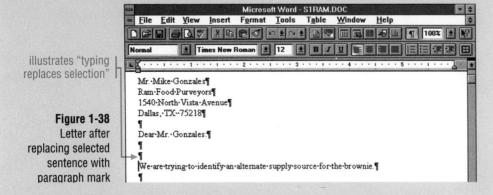

Figure 1-38
Letter after replacing selected sentence with paragraph mark

Don't worry that your sentence disappeared. Word carried out your command. You can recover your selected text by reversing the last command.

❹ Click the **Undo button** on the Standard toolbar (or click **Edit** then click **Undo Typing**). The text returns to its original location and is still highlighted.

To reduce the risk of error, it is always a good idea to deselect highlighted text as soon as possible after you are finished working with it.

To deselect the first sentence:

❶ Click in the workspace outside the selected area or press one of the arrow keys. The highlighting is removed from the first sentence.

Now that you have learned how to select text, you are ready to format Denise's document.

Applying Type Styles

One common formatting technique is to add emphasis to words by changing the style of the printed type. The three most popular type styles are **bold**, *italic*, and <u>underline</u>. Because these three type styles are used so often, they each have a button on the Formatting toolbar.

To add, or **apply**, these type styles to text, follow the "select, then do" principle. Select the text you want to change, then click the appropriate type style button on the Formatting toolbar. The type style is applied only to the selected text.

Denise wants to emphasize several words in her letter so that Mr. Gonzales will pay particular attention to them. She wants to italicize "not" in the first specification.

To italicize the word "not":

❶ Double-click **not** in the first specification ("walnuts will not be...") to select it. When you double-click a word, you select the word and the space after it.

Now let's issue the command to italicize the word you've selected.

❷ Click the **Italic button** *I* on the Formatting toolbar. Notice that the Italic button appears lighter to indicate that the italic type style is in effect, or activated, for the highlighted text. See Figure 1-39.

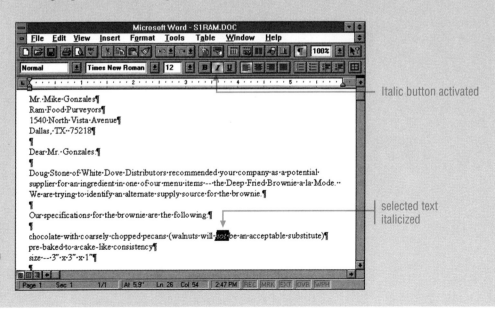

Figure 1-39
Letter with "not"
italicized

You are essentially "pressing" the Italic button to activate that type style. By selecting the text first, though, you instruct Word to start and end the italic type style with the selected text.

❸ Click anywhere to deselect the highlighted text so that you can see the change in the type style of "not."

Next Denise wants to emphasize the date by which she needs the bid proposal from Mr. Gonzales. She decides to bold "March 15."

To bold the text "March 15":

❶ Click and hold the I-beam in front of the "M" in March, drag across and through March 15, then release the mouse button.

TROUBLE? If you have difficulty highlighting March 15, deselect the text by clicking in the workspace or pressing one of the arrow keys. Then start over. The insertion point serves as an anchor for whatever you want to select. As long as you do not release the mouse button, you can reduce or expand the amount of text you have highlighted. Once you have selected the text, you are ready to give a formatting command.

❷ Click the **Bold button** B on the Formatting toolbar. The Bold button appears lighter to indicate it has been applied to the selected text.

❸ Deselect the text to see the effect of the bold type style. See Figure 1-40.

Figure 1-40
Letter with
"March 15" bolded

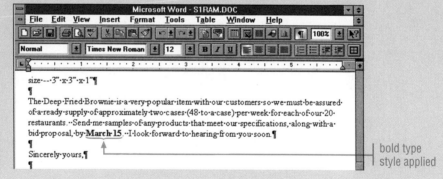

bold type
style applied

You can apply more than one type style to selected text. Denise wants the word "not," which she italicized in the first specification, to really stand out, so she decides to bold it, too. Let's do that now.

To apply more than one type style to the word "not":

❶ Double-click **not** in the first specification. Notice that the Italic button I becomes lighter because the word "not" has been italicized. The appearance of the button on the Formatting toolbar changes to reflect the format applied to the selected text.

❷ Click the **Bold button** B on the Formatting toolbar. Notice that the Bold button also becomes lighter. Both type styles have now been applied to the word.

❸ Deselect the text to see the effect of adding the bold type style to the italicized text.

❹ Click the **Save button** 🖫 on the Standard toolbar (or click **File** then click **Save**) to save the changes you have made so far.

Denise wants to emphasize "the Deep Fried Brownie a la Mode" in the first paragraph, so she decides to underline it. Although she could use the click-and-drag method to select the text, she decides to try a selection technique that gives her more control over what she wants to select.

Let's use the shift-click technique to highlight "the Deep Fried Brownie a la Mode" in the first paragraph before you underline it.

To underline the text:
❶ Place the insertion point in front of the "t" in the word "the" in the first sentence of the first paragraph.
❷ Move the I-beam after the "e" in Mode. Just move the I-beam to the end of the block—do not drag the mouse pointer over the text. See Figure 1-41.

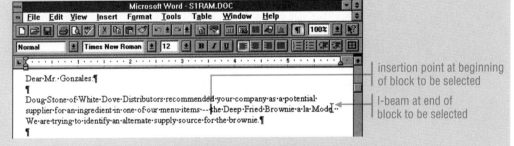

Figure 1-41
Preparing to use
the shift-click
selection technique

insertion point at beginning of block to be selected

I-beam at end of block to be selected

❸ With the I-beam after the "e" in Mode, press **[Shift]** then click. Just the block of text, "the Deep Fried Brownie a la Mode," is highlighted.

Now that you have selected the text, you are ready to underline it.

❹ Click the **Underline button** 🖳 on the Formatting toolbar to underline the selected text. The Underline button is activated. See Figure 1-42.

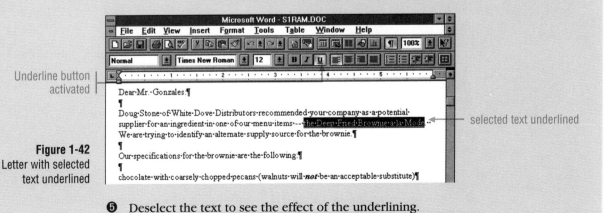

Underline button
activated

Figure 1-42
Letter with selected
text underlined

selected text underlined

❺ Deselect the text to see the effect of the underlining.

Now you have seen how the shift-click technique gives you more control over the block of text you need to select.

Removing Type Styles

Denise changes her mind about the underlining and wants to remove it. She knows that to remove a type style format, such as bold, italic, or underline, all she has to do is select the formatted text she wants to change, then click the button of the type style she wants to remove. Let's try it.

To remove the underlining:

❶ Use the shift-click method again to select "the Deep Fried Brownie a la Mode." Notice that the Underline button ⓤ becomes lighter to indicate that it is activated for the selected text.

❷ Click ⓤ and notice that the button is deactivated.

❸ Deselect the text to see that the underlining is removed.

The type style buttons are toggle switches; you turn the type styles on and off with the same button.

Adding Bullets

Another way to format documents is to add special characters—often heavy dots—to call attention to a particular passage or list of items. These characters are called **bullets**. The Bullets button on the Formatting toolbar makes it easy for you to add or remove these special characters because it also acts like a toggle switch. To add a bullet to selected text, simply click the Bullets button; to remove a bullet from selected text, click the Bullets button again to deactivate the feature.

Denise decides to emphasize the three specifications for the brownie by placing a bullet in front of each of them. She could select each specification individually and then click the Bullets button, but the more efficient procedure would be to select all three specifications at once, then format the entire selection with the bullets. She decides to use the selection bar to highlight all three specifications.

To apply bullets to the list of specifications:

❶ Move the I-beam into the selection bar next to the first specification, "chocolate..." The pointer changes to ⇗ when you move it into the selection bar.

❷ Press and drag the pointer down until the last specification, "size ...," is highlighted.

❸ Click the **Bullets button** ▤ on the Formatting toolbar. A special character, the rounded bullet, appears in front of each item. Notice that the button appears lighter to indicate that it is activated.

❹ Deselect the text to view the bullets. See Figure 1-43.

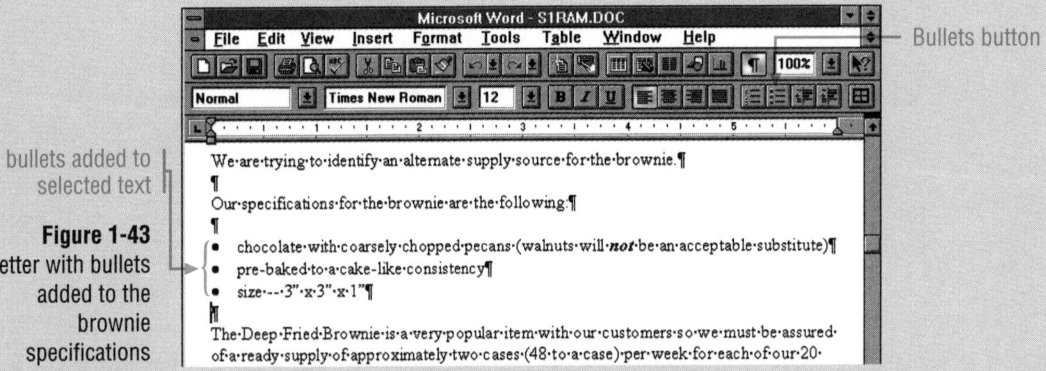

bullets added to
selected text

Figure 1-43
Letter with bullets
added to the
brownie
specifications

TROUBLE? If your bullets look different from the ones in the figure, that's okay. Continue
with the tutorial.

❺ Click the **Save button** 🖫 on the Standard toolbar (or click **File** then click **Save**) to
save the changes you have made so far.

Denise is now finished with three of the four phases of the productivity strategy. She
began by entering the text, keeping in mind her plan for organizing her letter as she
typed. Then she edited her letter by making changes in content and correcting any errors
she found during proofreading, including spell checking her document. Next she used the
various techniques for selecting text with the mouse to format her document so that it is
more readable and attractive. Now she is ready to print her document.

Previewing and Printing a Document

During the first three phases of the production strategy, you typically use only Word's normal editing view. Now it is time to see a printed version of your document.

It is not necessary to actually print a hard copy of your document to see how it will
look when printed. Rather, you can preview your printed document on screen. You can
use the Print Preview button on the Standard toolbar to see a miniaturized view of your
document as it would look printed. You can also choose Print Preview from the File
menu. Then you can either edit the document while in print preview or return to your
document to make adjustments. If the document needs no modifications, you can print it
directly from the Preview window. Previewing your document before actually printing it
saves time and resources.

To preview then print the document:
❶ Make sure your printer is on and contains paper.
❷ Click the **Print Preview button** 🔍 on the Standard toolbar (or click **File** then click **Print
Preview**). The Preview window opens and displays a reduced version of your document. See Figure 1-44.

Print Preview toolbar

Print button

letter appears miniaturized so entire page can be viewed

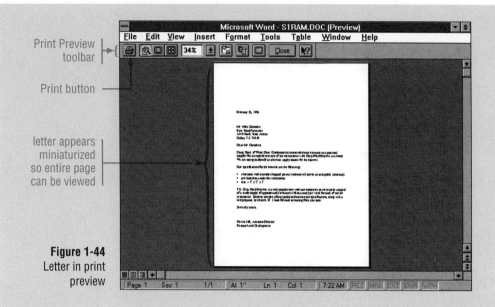

Figure 1-44
Letter in print preview

The letter looks evenly balanced on the page, both vertically and horizontally, so Denise decides to print the letter. However, she wants to check the print settings first. To do so, she needs to choose the Print command from the File menu instead of clicking the Print button on the toolbar. The Print button sends the document directly to the printer; the Print command displays the Print dialog box in which you can modify the print settings. Both the Print button and the Print command are also available from the document window.

❸   Click **File** then click **Print...**. The Print dialog box appears. See Figure 1-45. Notice that the Print dialog box provides options for printing all the pages in your document, the current page only, or selected pages that you specify. You can also choose to print multiple copies of your document.

prints entire document

prints page containing insertion point

prints specified range of pages

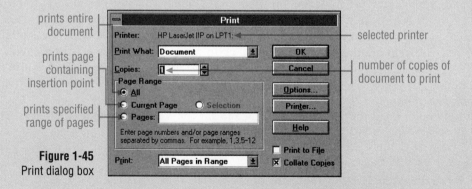

selected printer

number of copies of document to print

Figure 1-45
Print dialog box

Always check the Printer section of the dialog box to make sure that it shows the correct printer.

TROUBLE? If the correct printer is not selected, click Cancel in the Print dialog box. Click File, click Print..., then click Printer.... Select the correct printer from the list of available printers. If you change a document's printer after formatting a document, the way your document displays and prints might be different from the way you intended.

❹ Click **OK** or press **[Enter]**. A message appears briefly in the status bar letting you know that your document is being sent to the printer. A printer icon also appears briefly in the time slot of the status bar along with the number of pages sent to the printer. To cancel a print job from within Word, double-click the printer icon in the status bar.

Once your letter prints, it should look similar to Figure 1-1 without the Sweet T's letterhead.

TROUBLE? If your document hasn't printed yet, check the status of your document in Windows Program Manager by pressing [Alt][Tab] until the Print Manager title bar appears. Remove your document from the print queue before returning to your document, then send the document to print again. If it still doesn't print, check with your instructor or technical support person.

❺ Click the **Close button** on the Print Preview toolbar to return to the document.

Getting Help

Although the tutorials in this book will help you learn a great deal about Word's operations, you might want to explore a topic not taught yet or refresh your memory about a procedure already covered. In any case, you need to be able to find your own answers to word processing questions that might arise in the future.

Word's on-line Help system gives you quick access to information about Word's features, commands, and procedures. You can get help by using context-sensitive Help as you work, by looking up a topic in Word Help Contents, or by using the Help Search feature.

Using Context-Sensitive Help

Context-sensitive Help allows you to find out information about menu commands, buttons, toolbars, rulers, or other screen elements as you are working with them in your document. You click the Help button on the Standard toolbar or press [Shift][F1] to change the pointer to the Help pointer ▯. Then you click the screen item you want to know about and the related Help topic appears automatically. Most dialog and message boxes also have a Help button, which you can click to get information about that specific feature's options. Once you have initiated context-sensitive Help, you can also use it to find out what function a key combination performs—just press the key combination and information is displayed about that command.

Denise noticed the Full Screen command on the View menu and wonders what it does. She decides to use context-sensitive Help to find out.

To use context-sensitive Help to learn about the Full Screen command:
❶ Click the **Help button** ▯ on the Standard toolbar. The mouse pointer changes to ▯.
❷ Click **View** then click **Full Screen**. The Word Help window appears and displays the topic, "Full Screen command (View menu)."
❸ Read the information in the topic window, using the scroll bar to view the entire topic if necessary.

Denise is ready to exit Word Help.

❹ Double-click the **Word Help window Control menu box** (or click **File** then click **Exit** in the Word Help window).

Using the Help Contents Window

If you want general information about Word's features, you should open the Word Help Contents window, which serves as a table of contents for all topics in on-line Help. You can even have Word demonstrate some of its features for you. To access the Help Contents window, you press [F1] or choose Contents from the Help menu. From this window you can move to topics of interest by clicking the appropriate **hot topic,** a solid underlined word or phrase.

Denise is interested in finding out more about Outline view. She decides to look it up using the Help Contents window.

To use the Help Contents window to find information about Outline view:

❶ Press **[F1]** (or click **Help** then click **Contents**). The Word Help Contents window appears in front of the document and becomes the active window. See Figure 1-46.

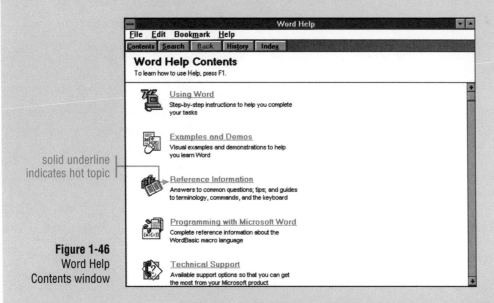

solid underline
indicates hot topic

Figure 1-46
Word Help
Contents window

❷ Click the **Reference Information** hot topic, then click **Definitions** in the General Reference Information section. Notice that the pointer changes to a hand when placed over a topic. An alphabetical listing of terms opens. The dotted underlined words are known as *hot words*. To see a definition of a hot word, simply click it.

Because you're looking for information on Outline view, you need to move to the topics that begin with the letter "O."

❸ Click the **O button** then click the **outline view** hot word. A definition of Outline view appears in a separate window. See Figure 1-47.

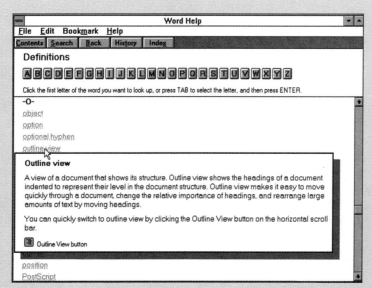

Figure 1-47
Definition of
outline view

④ Read the information then press **[Esc]** to dismiss the definition window.

Denise now has a better understanding of outline view and is ready to exit Help.

⑤ Close the Word Help Contents window.

Using Search

You can let Word do the leg work for you by using the Search feature of Word Help. You access the Search dialog box by double-clicking the Help button on the Standard toolbar or choosing the Search for Help on command from the Help menu.

Denise decides to use the Search feature to find information about printing envelopes, because she needs a printed envelope in which to send her completed letter to Ram Food Purveyors.

To search in Word Help for information on printing envelopes:
① Double-click the **Help button** ▶? on the Standard toolbar. The Search dialog box appears.
② Type **e** in the "search for" text box. The list of topics shown changes to those topics starting with "e."
③ Type **nv** after the "e" in the "search for" text box. The list of topics shown changes to those starting with "env" and the topic "envelopes" is now highlighted.
④ Click **Show Topics** or press **[Enter]**. Several related topics appear in the lower half of the window. See Figure 1-48.

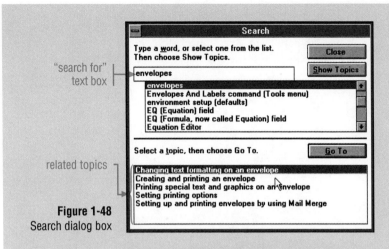

"search for"
text box

related topics

Figure 1-48
Search dialog box

❺ Click **Creating and printing an envelope**, then click **Go To** or press **[Enter]**. The How To
window for Creating and Printing Envelopes appears.

❻ Maximize the How To window. How To windows have their own button bars,
including an On Top button, which keeps the window visible so you can return to
your document and still see the procedures for completing the task.

❼ Read the information about creating envelopes, double-click the **How To window
Control menu box**, then double-click the **Help Contents window Control menu box** (or click
File then click **Exit** in the Help Contents window) to close the window and return
to the document.

Now that Denise has read the information about creating and printing envelopes, she
decides to print the envelope for her letter to Mr. Gonzales.

Printing an Envelope

Envelopes have always been difficult to address on computers and, until recently, almost
impossible to print on ordinary printers. It was generally easier just to type the address on
an envelope using a typewriter rather than spend time figuring out how to do it on a computer. Word now makes it extremely easy to address the envelope, but you must still have
a printer capable of printing envelopes. *Before you attempt this section of the tutorial,
check with your instructor or technical support person to determine whether your
printer can print envelopes.*

Denise inserts an envelope into the envelope feeder of her printer and is now ready
to print her envelope.

To print an envelope:
❶ Insert an envelope into the envelope feeder on your printer. Check with your
instructor or technical support person to make sure your printer can print
envelopes before continuing. If your printer doesn't have an envelope feeder or
you don't have an envelope, try printing the address on a regular sheet of paper.

❷ Click **Tools** then click **Envelopes and Labels....** The Envelopes and Labels dialog box appears with the Envelopes tab displayed. See Figure 1-49. Notice that the address for Mr. Gonzales appears automatically in the Delivery Address box.

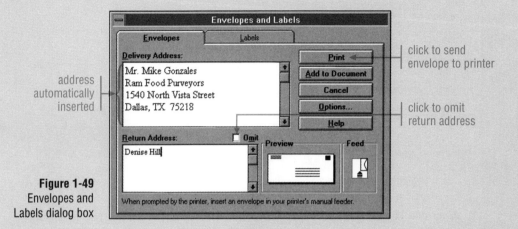

Figure 1-49
Envelopes and Labels dialog box

The information in your Return Address box will vary, depending on who installed Word on your computer. Generally in a business situation, the Omit check box would be selected because a company's return address is already printed on the envelope. However, you will enter your name and address in the Return Address box so that you can distinguish your printed envelope from those of other students.

❸ If the Omit check box is selected, click the box to clear it.

❹ Select any text that appears in the Return Address box, then type your name and address.

Ask your instructor or technical support person about your printer's ability to print envelopes before completing the next step. If your printer cannot print envelopes, click Cancel in the dialog box instead of completing the next step.

❺ Click **Print**. Because you have inserted your name and address in the Return Address box, Word wants to know if you want to change the default so that your name and address will automatically appear as the return address.

❻ Click **No**. A printing message appears briefly in the status bar.

❼ Save the changes you have made.

TROUBLE? If your envelope didn't print, your printer might not be able to print envelopes. Check with your instructor or technical support person to determine what to do next.

Your envelope should look like the envelope in Figure 1-1 except that your name and address will appear where the Sweet T's, Inc. preprinted address appears.

Now that Denise has printed both her letter and her envelope, she decides to close her document and exit Word.

To close the document and exit Word:

❶ Double-click the **document window Control menu box** (or click **File** then click **Close**). Notice the difference in the menu bar of the Word window—just the File and Help menus are available on the menu bar. Also, the status bar is blank. See Figure 1-50. When you have no other documents open, Word displays this window, known as the Nil menu screen.

only File and Help menus available

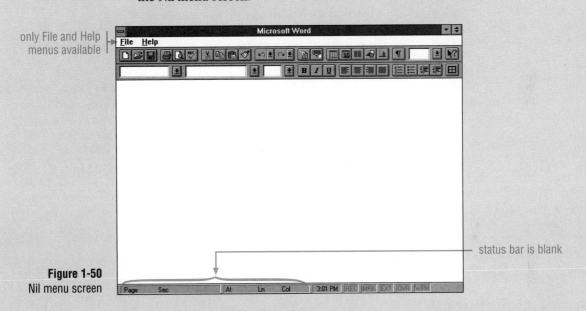

status bar is blank

Figure 1-50
Nil menu screen

You could create a new document or open an existing document if you wanted to continue to work in Word, but in this case you will exit Word.

❷ Double-click the **Word window Control menu box** (or click **File** then click **Exit**). You return to the Program Manager. The Microsoft Office group window is still open.

TROUBLE? If you are asked to save changes to any documents other than S1RAM.DOC, click No.

❸ Double-click the **Microsoft Office group window Control menu box** to close this window.

❹ Exit Windows.

Denise has completed all phases of her productivity strategy—creating, editing, formatting, and printing—and is now is ready to mail her letter.

Questions

1. List and briefly describe the four phases of the productivity strategy.
2. Describe the differences between the Word window and the document window.
3. What are the six questions you should answer at the beginning of each new Word session to determine whether your Word screen is arranged properly?
4. How do you display the shortcut Toolbar menu?

5. What is the difference between an open document and an active document?
6. Describe two methods for switching between open documents.
7. What are default settings for a Word document?
8. In the status bar, what do the following indicate about the location of the insertion point?
   a. At 7.2"
   b. Ln 20
   c. Col 29
9. Which key do you press to insert a blank line in your document?
10. What is the difference between using [Backspace] and [Del] to correct errors?
11. Which keyboard command moves the insertion point to the top of the document?
12. Describe the difference between the insertion point and the I-beam.
13. What is the difference between Insert mode and Overtype mode?
14. What types of errors will the Spelling command discover?
15. Explain the principle of "select, then do." Give examples.
16. Where is the selection bar located?
17. What is the purpose of the print preview feature?
18. What is the difference between a dotted underscored word and a solid under-scored word in a Word Help topic window?

Use Word Help to answer Questions 19 through 22:

E   19. How do you open a file in Word that was created by another application?

E   20. What is the purpose of the Summary Info dialog box?

E   21. How would you check the spelling of just one word in a document?

E   22. How do you modify the format of a bullet?

Tutorial Assignments

Start Word, if necessary, and make sure your Student Disk is in the disk drive. Conduct a screen check, then open T1TFP.DOC and complete the following:

1. Change the date to October 5, 1995.
2. Use the selection bar to select the inside address, then insert your name and address.
3. Change the salutation appropriately.
4. Move the insertion point into the last paragraph and change the date, March 15, to October 31. Bold and italicize the date.
5. Remove the applied type styles from "not" in the last brownie specification.
6. Spell check and proofread for additional errors.
7. Save the letter as S1TFP.DOC to your Student Disk.
8. Preview the letter.
9. Print the letter and an envelope, if your printer has the capability to print envelopes.
10. Save the changes, if necessary.

 E   11. Apply bullets to the brownie specifications, but change the shape of the bullet to ⇒. Save the document as S1TFP2.DOC.
12. Print the document.

E   13. Use Word Help to look up how to remove bullets. Then print the Help Topic on "Adding or removing bullets or numbers in a list."

Case Problems

1. A Confirmation Letter to Haas Petroleum

Lillian May coordinates off-campus credit offerings for Western Hills Community College in Colorado Springs, Colorado. She has worked for several years with Fred Maxwell, Human Resources director at Haas Petroleum, to schedule academic classes for Haas employees at their site. She needs to write a letter confirming next semester's schedule. To save time, she uses the document she wrote last year, making a couple of changes.

Open P1HAAS.DOC from your Student Disk and complete the following:

1. Change the date to today's date.
2. Save the document as S1HAAS.DOC.
3. Insert the course description shown in Figure 1-51 one blank line below the course description for GOVT 2301.

Figure 1-51

> CSCI 1301. Introduction to Computer Information Systems. (3-0) Tuesday, 5-8 p.m.
>
> This course is designed to teach you computer concepts by providing a general knowledge of mainframes and microcomputers, their functions, and applications.

4. Delete the entire course description for PSYC 1301.
5. Edit the wording of the letter to make it appropriate for next semester.
6. Bold the course abbreviation and number for each course description.
7. Italicize each course name.
8. Remove the underlining from days and times in GOVT 2301 and ENGL 1302.
9. Spell check the document and proofread for all errors.
10. Save the changes.
11. Preview the letter.
12. Print the letter.
13. Print an envelope, if your printer supports printing envelopes. Include your name and address in the return address. Save the changes.
14. Close the document.

2. A Response to a High School Student

As program manager for KIWW, a radio station in your home town, you often receive requests from local high school students interested in radio and television. Marcus Vincente wrote to you asking for sources of information about radio or television for a research paper he has to write.

Open P1KIWW.DOC from your Student Disk and complete the following to respond to his request:

1. Insert seven blank lines at the top of the document.
2. Save the document as S1KIWW.DOC.
3. Type today's date then insert three blank lines after the date.
4. Insert the names of the three books shown in Figure 1-52 and insert a blank line after the sentence "Check with your school librarian for the following books."

Figure 1-52

> Handbook of American Popular Culture
> Les Brown's Encyclopedia of Television
> The Encyclopedia of Television Series, Pilots, and Specials, 1937-1973

5. Move to the end of the document, type your name, press [Enter], then type Program Manager.
6. Spell check the document and proofread for all errors.
7. Save your changes.
8. Format your document to improve its readability and appearance by italicizing the names of books and adding rounded bullets to the list of books.
9. Save your changes.
10. Preview then print your document.
11. Remove the bullets from the list of books, then print the letter again. Save the document as S1KIWW2.DOC.
12. Close the document.

3. Inquiring About a Sweet Tooth Cafe Franchise

You are interested in opening a Sweet Tooth Cafe franchise in your area. Write a letter to Jocelyn Titus, president of Sweet T's, requesting information about franchising and convincing her of the need for a Sweet Tooth Cafe in your town. Her address is Oklahoma Bank Building, One Main Street, Oklahoma City, OK 73112.

1. Plan your letter then type it.
2. Save the document as S1SWEET1.DOC.
3. Correct all errors, including spelling.
4. Save your changes.
5. Format your document to improve its readability and appearance.
6. Save your changes.
7. Preview then print your document.
8. Close the document.

Using Page, Paragraph, and Font Formatting Commands

Creating a Cover Memo and Agenda

CASE

Seattle Area Teachers Federal Credit Union Marcus Jenkins recently was hired by the Seattle Area Teachers Federal Credit Union as an administrative assistant to the president of the credit union, Michael Brown. The credit union provides financial services for its approximately 10,000 members, all of whom are employees or former employees of school districts within greater metropolitan Seattle.

Michael is responsible for the daily operations of the credit union and its staff. However, overall policy decisions are made by the Board of Directors, who are elected from the credit union's membership. Part of Marcus's new job is to develop the agenda for the monthly meetings of the board, along with a cover memo announcing the meeting and outlining the agenda for the board members. Because this is his first attempt at completing these documents, Marcus asks Michael to review them and make corrections. Michael suggests that Marcus submit his draft free of any formatting so that Michael can concentrate on the wording.

In this tutorial you will edit, format, and print the cover memo and agenda for Marcus. Marcus decides to use the productivity strategy to complete his assignment. He will first create a draft of the cover memo and agenda, then edit the document to include any additions or corrections Michael wants to make. Marcus will next format the cover memo and agenda and finally print his document.

Before creating the first draft of his cover memo and agenda, Marcus reviews the files from several previous meetings to see how his predecessor had created these documents. He notes that the content of the various cover memos and the order of the items on the agendas remain essentially the same from meeting to meeting. He also notices that occasionally more information is included in the memo than just the announcement of the meeting, and that the agenda items are sometimes rearranged. Marcus then creates a draft cover memo and agenda, which he submits to Michael, using basically the same wording as previous cover memos and the same order of agenda items, changing only the dates. As Michael requested, Marcus submits an unformatted document for his review.

Michael returns the draft of the cover memo and agenda with his edits. He attaches notes with additional information he wants inserted in the memo and some suggestions for reordering and formatting the agenda (shown in Figure 2-1). Marcus looks over his comments and is ready to begin editing the document.

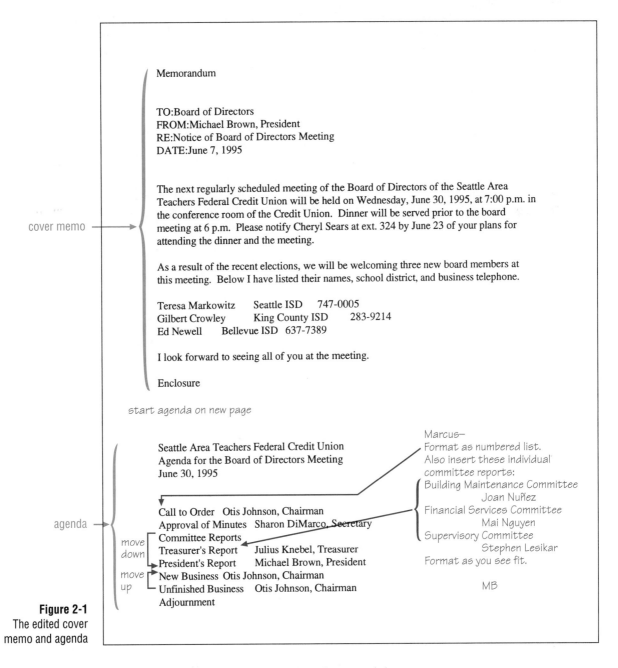

Figure 2-1
The edited cover memo and agenda

Let's begin by opening Marcus's unformatted document.

To open the document containing the cover memo and agenda:

❶ Start Word, if necessary, and conduct the screen check as described in Tutorial 1.

❷ Insert your Student Disk in the disk drive, then open the file C2SATFCU.DOC from your Student Disk. If you do not remember how to open an existing file, refer to Tutorial 1. After C2SATFCU.DOC is open, scroll through the document to become familiar with it.

Before Marcus begins making changes to the document, he decides to save the file with a new name. He wants to keep the original version intact in case he needs it later. To do so, he must rename the file.

Renaming a File

You rename a file using the Save As dialog box, which you used in Tutorial 1 to name a document when saving it for the first time.

To rename the file:

❶ Click **File** then click **Save As....** The Save As dialog box appears. The file's current name, "c2satfcu.doc," appears highlighted in the File Name text box.

❷ Type **s2satfcu** in the File Name text box. The new filename replaces the previous filename.

❸ Make sure the Drives list box displays the name of the drive containing your Student Disk.

❹ Click **OK** or press **[Enter]**. Word adds the extension "DOC" automatically to the filename.

Marcus saved the file he will work in as S2SATFCU.DOC, and he still has the original version of the file. Now he can begin editing the document.

Moving Text Within a Document

In the process of editing a document, you might want to rearrange the content by changing the location of an entire block of text. One of the advantages of word processing is that you can move text quickly and easily from its original location to another without retyping it. Word allows you to move text from one location in a Word document to another location in the *same document,* or to a *different Word document,* or to a *different application program,* such as a spreadsheet program. Furthermore, for each type of move you want to make, Word provides a variety of ways to make it.

The easiest method for moving text short distances within the same document involves the feature known as **drag-and-drop**, so named because you simply *drag* selected text to its new spot in your document and then *drop* it in place by releasing the mouse button.

Michael suggested a change in the order of the agenda items, and Marcus decides to use the drag-and-drop feature to relocate the Committee Reports agenda item after the President's Report agenda item and before the New Business agenda item.

To move the agenda items using drag-and-drop:

❶ Click in the selection bar next to Committee Reports to select that line (Ln 37), including the paragraph mark at the end of the line.

TROUBLE? If you don't remember how to use the selection bar or the other techniques for selecting text, refer to Tutorial 1.

❷ Move the mouse pointer over the selected text. Notice that the shape of the pointer changes to ⬉.

❸ Press and continue to hold down the mouse button. The drag-and-drop pointer ⬉ appears. Use the dashed insertion point of the pointer to help guide you as you drag the selected text to its new location.

❹ Drag the selected text to its new location so that the dashed insertion point is in front of the "N" in New Business. See Figure 2-2.

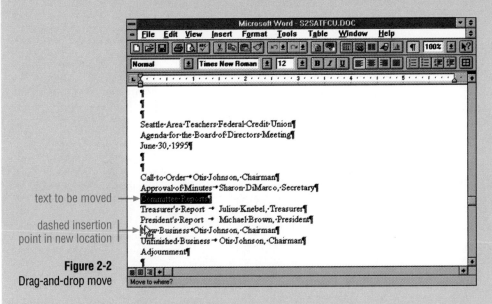

text to be moved

dashed insertion
point in new location

Figure 2-2
Drag-and-drop move

❺ Release the mouse button. The selected text is moved to its new location and is still highlighted.

❻ Deselect the highlighted text.

TROUBLE? If the move did not work, click the Undo button ⬚ on the Standard toolbar (or click Edit then click Undo Move). Repeat the steps above, making sure that you do not release the mouse button until the dashed insertion point is in front of the "N" in New Business.

Moving Text with the Move Command ([F2])

The keyboard equivalent for the drag-and-drop feature is the Move command ([F2]). Marcus also needs to move the Unfinished Business agenda item before New Business, but this time he decides to use the Move command.

To move the agenda item using the Move command:

❶ Click in the selection bar next to Unfinished Business to select that line, including the paragraph mark.

❷ Press **[F2]**. Notice that the status bar displays the message "Move to where?"

❸ Place the insertion point in front of the "N" in New Business. Notice that the insertion point changes to a dashed vertical line.

❹ Press **[Enter]**. Unfinished Business is moved above New Business. See Figure 2-3.

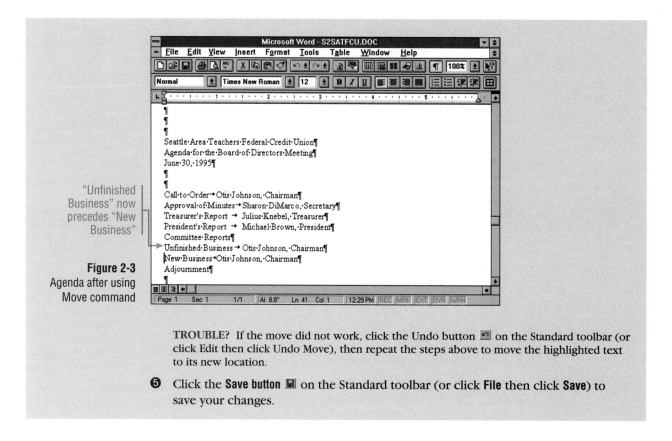

"Unfinished Business" now precedes "New Business"

Figure 2-3
Agenda after using
Move command

TROUBLE? If the move did not work, click the Undo button ◘ on the Standard toolbar (or click Edit then click Undo Move), then repeat the steps above to move the highlighted text to its new location.

❺ Click the **Save button** ◘ on the Standard toolbar (or click **File** then click **Save**) to save your changes.

Marcus is ready to move to the next phase of the productivity strategy: formatting the document.

Applying Direct Formatting Options

Word divides its formatting options into three groups: document-level or page setup commands, paragraph-level commands, and character-level or font commands. To work efficiently, start with decisions that affect the entire document (page setup decisions), then move to decisions about paragraph formatting options, and finally make decisions about font formatting options. By starting with those options that affect your entire document and moving to more specific formatting choices, you eliminate retracing your steps. You can apply individual formatting options directly to specific elements of your document by selecting the element and then choosing the appropriate formatting command, or you can apply several formatting options at once through the use of Word's styles. In this tutorial you will use direct formatting; in Tutorial 3 you will learn about using styles to apply formatting to a document.

Both the cover memo and the agenda require a great deal of formatting, so Marcus decides to begin by making the changes that affect the overall appearance of the document.

Page Setup Options

Word's page setup features govern the size of your document's text area—in other words, how many lines of text will fit on a page. Setting margins is a page formatting decision that affects the size of the available text area. Two other factors affecting your document's text area are paper size (8.5 x 11 or 8.5 x 14) and page orientation (tall or wide). The default page orientation is tall, or **portrait**, but you can change it to wide, or **landscape**. You can make changes to the margins, paper size, or page orientation by choosing Page Setup from the File menu.

Changing Margins

Word uses a default width of 1.25 inches for the left and right margins, and a default width of 1 inch for the top and bottom margins. Any changes to the margins affect the entire document, not just the current page. The area that remains after allowing for the margin settings is called the **available text area** (Figure 2-4).

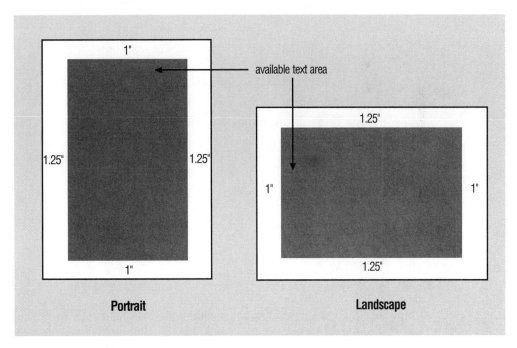

Figure 2-4
Available text area

The ruler, displayed below the Formatting toolbar on the Word screen, shows the length of the typing line, given the width of the current left and right margins. For instance, the default left and right margin settings of 1.25 inches provide a typing line of 6 inches (8.5 - 1.25 - 1.25 = 6). The numbers on the ruler scale indicate distances in inches from the left margin *not* from the left edge of the paper; therefore, the scale starts with 0. The tick marks on the ruler scale indicate increments of ⅛ inch.

To create a more balanced frame of white space around the text, making the document more attractive to the reader, Marcus wants to increase the top margin to 1.5 inches and the left and right margins to 1.75 inches.

To change the top, left, and right margins:

❶ Press **[Ctrl][Home]** to move to the beginning of the document.

❷ Click **File** then click **Page Setup...**. The Page Setup dialog box appears. From this dialog box, you can also change paper size and orientation, and paper source. The Preview section allows you to preview any changes you make to the page setup.

> TROUBLE? If you do not see the Page Setup dialog box with the Margins tab displayed, as shown in Figure 2-5, click the Margins tab at the top of the dialog box.

Marcus wants to increase the top margin to 1.5 inches.

❸ Click the **Top text box up arrow** until it reads 1.5". Notice that the Preview section changes as you change the value for the top margin.

Next, Marcus wants to change the left and right margin settings to 1.75 inches. This setting is not available in the list of settings, so he needs to type 1.75 in the Left and Right text boxes.

❹ Press **[Tab]** twice to highlight the Left text box.

❺ Type **1.75**. Note that you do not have to type the quotation mark to indicate inches; this is the assumed measurement.

❻ Press **[Tab]** once to highlight the Right text box. The Preview section now changes to reflect the new left margin setting.

❼ Type **1.75**. Figure 2-5 shows the completed Page Setup dialog box.

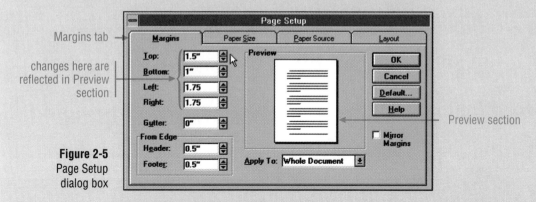

Figure 2-5
Page Setup
dialog box

❽ Click **OK** or press **[Enter]** to return to your document. The ruler changes to reflect the new length of the typing line based on the new left and right margin settings (8.5 - 1.75 - 1.75 = 5). Also, notice the changes in the status bar, which now indicates that the first line begins 1.5 inches from the top of the page and that the document has two pages (as indicated by 1/2, meaning page 1 of 2). The increased top margin forced the text of the document onto a second page.

❾ Click the **Save button** 🖫 on the Standard toolbar (or click **File** then click **Save**) to save your changes.

Now that Marcus has made changes to the document's margins, he needs to adjust where the pages end within his document.

Soft Page Breaks

When you enter enough text to fill up a page, Word automatically starts a new page for you. To indicate the start of a new page, a row of dots appears across the page. This row of dots is called a **soft page break** because as you insert and delete text, the position of the soft page break can change. The status bar also changes to indicate the increase or decrease in the number of pages in the document.

Because his document has increased to two pages, Marcus must see where the second page starts. Michael wants the agenda to appear on a page by itself.

To view the soft page break in the document:

❶ Drag the vertical scroll box to the bottom of the scroll bar to move quickly to the end of your document. Notice the row of dots across the page. See Figure 2-6. This is Word's indication that you have filled one page of text and started another.

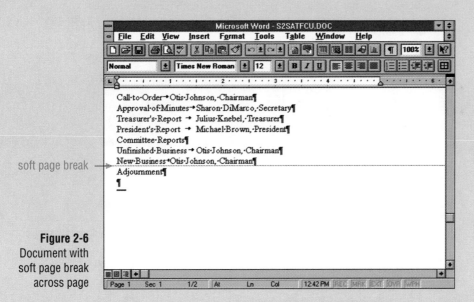

soft page break

Figure 2-6
Document with
soft page break
across page

TROUBLE? Depending on the type of monitor or printer that you're using, the soft page break might occur in a different location. Just continue with the tutorial.

❷ Place the insertion point in the line of text directly *below* the soft page break. Notice the status bar. After the soft page break, the insertion point is located on page 2 of your document.

❸ Press [↑] to move the insertion point up one line of text, directly *above* the soft page break. The status bar now shows that the insertion point is on page 1.

Because the soft page break does not fall at the beginning of the agenda, Marcus must force the agenda to appear on a page by itself. He will do so by inserting a hard page break.

Inserting Hard Page Breaks

At times you might want to force a page to end at a particular spot in your document. To start a new page, you must insert a **hard page break**, also called a **manual page break**.

You can insert a hard page break by pressing [Ctrl][Enter] or by choosing Break from the Insert menu.

A hard page break is indicated by a row of dots across the page, like those used for a soft page break, but the words "Page Break" appear in the center of the row of dots. To delete a hard page break, select the page break then press [Del].

Let's insert a hard page break so that the agenda appears on a page by itself.

To insert the hard page break:

❶ Place the insertion point in front of the "S" in Seattle in the first line of the agenda heading (Ln 32).

TROUBLE? If the first line of the agenda title in your document does not fall at the same point, perhaps you accidentally pressed [Enter] and inserted extra blank lines. Or, perhaps you have not changed the point size from 10 to 12. Ask your instructor or technical support person to do this for you. The line variation might also be due to the selection of a printer different from the one used in this book. Continue with the tutorial, keeping in mind this difference between your screen and the figures in this tutorial; use any line number indications as a point of reference.

❷ Press **[Ctrl][Enter]**. The status bar indicates that the insertion point is on page 2. See Figure 2-7.

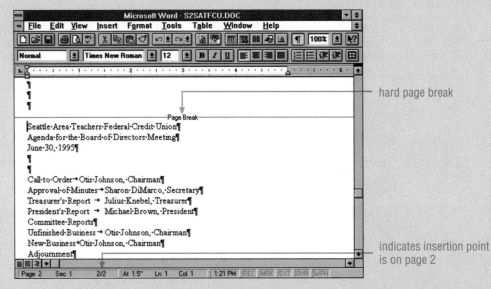

Figure 2-7
Screen after inserting hard page break

hard page break

indicates insertion point is on page 2

TROUBLE? If you do not see a hard page break across your page, perhaps you did not hold down [Ctrl] while you pressed [Enter]. Click the Undo button 🔄 on the Standard toolbar (or click Edit then click Undo Page Break), then repeat Step 2.

❸ Press [↑] to move the insertion point to the hard page break. Notice that the status bar changes to indicate that the insertion point is on page 1, Ln 32. Even though you have not filled page 1 completely with text, inserting a hard page break forced one page to end and another to begin.

❹ Click the **Save button** 💾 on the Standard toolbar (or click **File** then click **Save**) to save your changes.

Marcus has completed making the document-level formatting decisions.

If you want to take a break and resume the tutorial at a later time, you can close the current document then exit Word by double-clicking the Control menu box in the upper-left corner of the screen. When you want to resume the tutorial, start Word, place your Student Disk in the disk drive, then complete the screen check procedure described in Tutorial 1. Open the file S2SATFCU.DOC then continue with the tutorial.

■   ■   ■

Now Marcus moves to the next group of formatting decisions: paragraph formatting options.

Paragraph Formatting

Paragraph formatting includes a wide variety of features such as paragraph indentations, tabs, numbered paragraphs, line spacing, paragraph alignment, paragraph borders, and rules. Some of the most often used paragraph formatting features are available on the Formatting toolbar; others are available only through the Paragraph command and the Borders and Shading command on the Format menu.

Remember that Word defines a paragraph as any amount of text that ends with a paragraph mark (¶). Word stores the paragraph formatting options that have been applied to a paragraph in the paragraph mark at the end of that paragraph. If you accidentally delete a paragraph mark, immediately click the Undo button or choose Undo from the Edit menu to restore the paragraph mark and any paragraph formatting changes that you might have made.

To make paragraph formatting changes, you first select the paragraph or paragraphs to be changed and then choose the paragraph formatting options you want to apply to the selection. To select a *single* paragraph, all you need to do is position the insertion point anywhere in that paragraph. Once you have selected a paragraph, you can make the necessary paragraph formatting changes. To make changes to *multiple* paragraphs, you can select the paragraphs and then apply paragraph formatting options. As you can see, the principle of "select, then do" pertains to formatting, too.

Marcus will begin formatting the paragraphs in his document by changing paragraph indentations.

Changing Paragraph Indentations

You might want to call attention to certain paragraphs within your document by indenting them from the left or right margin, or both, thus changing the length of your typing line. As you learned previously, changing margins is one way to change the length of the typing line; however, changing margins is a document-level option that affects the entire document, rather than just a paragraph. Word provides four ways to indent paragraph text from the margins without adjusting the entire document's margins—first-line indents, left indents, right indents, and hanging indents—as shown in Figure 2-8. The text in Figure 2-8 describes the different types of indents.

This is an example of a paragraph in which the first line is indented from the left margin. You can create this type of indent by moving only the *first-line indent marker* on the ruler.

This is an example of a paragraph in which all lines are indented from the left margin. You can create this type of indent by moving the *rectangle* below the left indent marker.

This is an example of a hanging indent, that is, a paragraph in which all lines except the first line are indented from the left margin. You can create this type of indent by moving only the *left indent marker* on the ruler.

This is an example of a paragraph in which all lines are indented from the right margin. You can create this type of indent by moving the *right indent marker* on the ruler.

Figure 2-8
Samples of
Word's indents

As usual, Word gives you a variety of ways to apply these features. You can create all these indents using the ruler or the Paragraph command on the Format menu. You can also use the Formatting toolbar to create left indents and hanging indents.

The ruler allows you to change paragraph indents quickly through the use of the indent markers (Figure 2-9). By default the indent markers are even with the left and right margins. The top triangle at the left end of the ruler, called the **first-line indent marker**, controls the amount of indentation from the left margin for the *first line* of a selected paragraph. The bottom triangle at the left end of the ruler, called the **left indent marker**, controls the amount of indentation from the left margin for *all* lines in the selected paragraph *except* the first line. The **rectangle** below the left indent marker controls the amount of indentation from the left margin for *all* lines in the selected paragraph, including the first line. The triangle at the right end of the ruler, called the **right indent marker**, controls the amount of indentation from the *right* margin for all lines in the selected paragraph. Any changes to the indentation level affect only the paragraph with the insertion point or any selected paragraphs. If you indent a paragraph and do not like the indentation you have chosen, you can click the Undo button and start again.

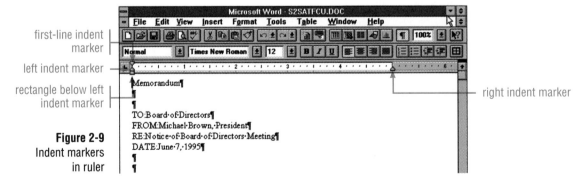

first-line indent
marker

left indent marker

rectangle below left
indent marker

right indent marker

Figure 2-9
Indent markers
in ruler

You change the indent level for a paragraph by following the "select, then do" principle: select the appropriate paragraph or paragraphs to be changed and then drag the appropriate indent marker to a new position on the ruler.

REFERENCE WINDOW   **Indenting a Paragraph**

- Select the paragraph or paragraphs to be indented.

- Point to the indent marker you want to change and drag it to its
  new location on the ruler scale.

To indent:	*Do the following:*
Only the first line	Drag the first-line indent marker
All lines but the first line	Drag the left indent marker
All lines	Drag the rectangle under the left indent marker
All lines from the right margin	Drag the right indent marker

or

- Select the paragraph or paragraphs to be indented.

- Click Format then click Paragraph…. If necessary, click the Indents
  and Spacing tab in the Paragraph dialog box.

- From the Indentation section of the Paragraph dialog box, do one
  or more of the following:

  • In the Left text box, select or type the distance that you want to
  indent the paragraph from the left margin.

  • In the Right text box, select or type the distance that you want to
  indent the paragraph from the right margin.

  • In the Special section, select First Line, then select or type the
  negative or positive distance that you want to indent the first line
  of the paragraph from the *left indent*.

  • In the Special section, select Hanging, then select or type the negative or positive distance that you want to hang text after the first
  line.

- Click OK or press [Enter].

Marcus wants to try indenting the first line of each paragraph of the body of the memo by 0.5 inch, to see if this improves the appearance of the memo. He'll do so by changing the first-line indent marker. Because he's not sure if this is the format he wants, Marcus decides to indent just the first paragraph to see the results.

To indent the first line of the first paragraph:
❶ Place the insertion point anywhere in the first paragraph of the body of the memo, which begins "The next regularly…"
❷ Point to the first-line indent marker (top triangle), then click and drag it to the right 0.5 inch. The first line of the first paragraph is indented, but the remaining lines of the paragraph do not change. See Figure 2-10. Also notice that the other paragraphs in the memo were not affected by the change.

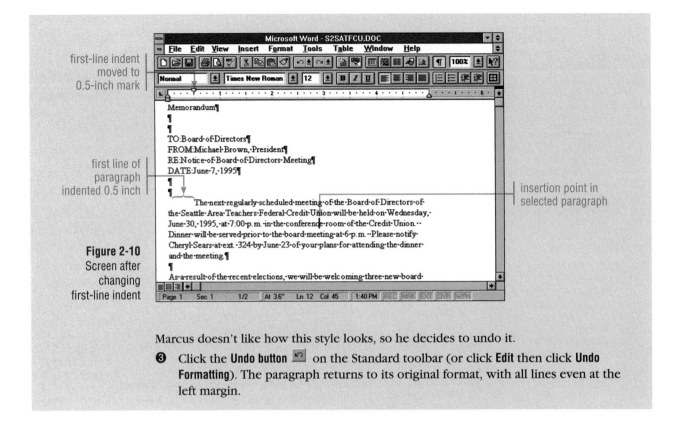

first-line indent moved to 0.5-inch mark

first line of paragraph indented 0.5 inch

insertion point in selected paragraph

Figure 2-10
Screen after changing first-line indent

Marcus doesn't like how this style looks, so he decides to undo it.

❸ Click the **Undo button** 🔄 on the Standard toolbar (or click **Edit** then click **Undo Formatting**). The paragraph returns to its original format, with all lines even at the left margin.

Next Marcus decides to indent *all* lines of the paragraph 1 inch from the left margin. He could drag the rectangle to move both the first-line indent and the left indent to the 1-inch mark on the ruler, or he could use the Increase Indent button on the Formatting toolbar. Whenever you click the Increase Indent button, both the first-line and left indent markers move to the next tab stop to the right on the ruler. (You learn about tab stops in the next section.) You can just as easily "unindent" selected paragraphs by clicking the Decrease Indent button on the Formatting toolbar. Each time you click the Decrease Indent button, the first-line and left indent markers move to the previous tab stop to the left.

Marcus decides to use the Increase Indent button on the Formatting toolbar to indent all of the paragraphs of the body of the memo and the enclosure notation to the 1-inch mark on the ruler.

To indent the paragraphs using the Increase Indent button:

❶ Use the selection bar to select all the paragraphs in the body of the memo, from the first paragraph in the body of the memo ("The next regularly...") through Enclosure.

Next, let's make an intentional error and move the indentation too far to the right.

❷ Click the **Increase Indent button** 🔲 on the Formatting toolbar three times. The selected paragraphs move to the right. Notice that the first-line and left indent markers have moved to the 1.5-inch mark on the ruler—half an inch too far to the right of where Marcus wants them.

❸ Click the **Decrease Indent button** 🔲 on the Formatting toolbar. All selected paragraphs move to the left 0.5 inch. Notice that the first-line and left indent markers have moved to the 1-inch mark on the ruler.

❹ Deselect the highlighted text and then scroll through the document. The body of the memo is indented to the 1-inch mark, but the rest of the document remains at the left margin. See Figure 2-11.

first-line and left
indent markers

paragraphs indented

Figure 2-11
Paragraphs
indented 1 inch
from the left margin

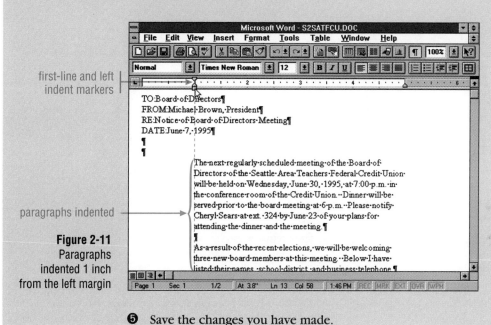

❺ Save the changes you have made.

Next, to improve the appearance of the memo, Marcus wants to align the information vertically after the memo headings (TO:, FROM:, RE:, and DATE:) at the 1-inch mark on the ruler. This will match the indentation of the paragraphs in the body of the memo. To make this paragraph formatting change, Marcus will use Word's default tab settings.

Using Default Tabs

A **tab stop** is a predefined stopping point along your document's typing line. Each time you press [Tab], the insertion point moves to the next tab stop. If the Show/Hide ¶ option is activated, a tab character (→) appears on the screen at the point where you pressed [Tab]. Word's default tabs are set every 0.5 inch. To delete a tab character, you place the insertion to the left of the → then press [Del], or place the insertion point to the right of the → then press [Backspace].

Tabs are useful for aligning text or numerical data vertically in columns. Marcus will insert tabs to align the information after the memo headings.

To align the information after the memo headings by inserting tabs:

❶ Place the insertion point after the colon in the first memo heading (TO:).

❷ Press **[Tab]** twice. Notice that two tab characters appear and that the text aligns vertically under the 1-inch mark on the ruler. See Figure 2-12.

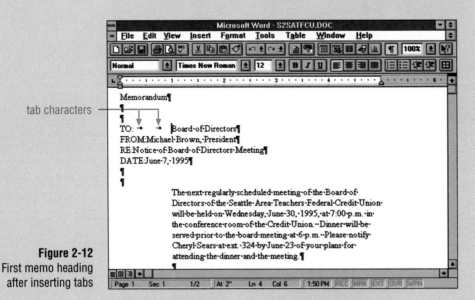

Figure 2-12
First memo heading after inserting tabs

TROUBLE? If you don't see the tab characters on your screen, you need to activate the Show/Hide ¶ option by clicking the Show/Hide ¶ button 🔳 on the Standard toolbar.

❸ Place the insertion point after the colon in the second memo heading (FROM:), then press **[Tab]** twice. The text aligns vertically at the 1.5-inch mark instead of at the 1-inch mark.

Marcus wants all the information to align at the 1-inch mark, so he must delete one of the tabs.

❹ Press **[Backspace]** once. The second tab character is deleted, and the text aligns vertically at the 1-inch mark.

❺ Place the insertion point after the colon in the third memo heading (RE:), then press **[Tab]** twice.

❻ Place the insertion point after the colon in the fourth memo heading (DATE:), then press **[Tab]** twice.

Because you inserted tabs between the headings and the information that follows them, the information aligns vertically.

Marcus now wants to format the information in the memo about the three new board members so that the three columns of information are more balanced on the page. To do so, he needs to set custom tab stops.

Setting Custom Tab Stops

Sometimes you might want to set tab stops at locations other than those of the default settings. In other words, you might want to customize the tab stops. Word allows you to set custom tabs using different alignment tab styles, namely, left, right, centered, or decimal (Figure 2-13). The default tab style, which you just used, is **left-aligned**, meaning that text at that tab stop is positioned even at the left and extends to the right from the tab stop. The **centered** tab aligns text evenly on either side of the tab stop, while the **right-aligned** tab creates text that is positioned even at the right and extends to the left from the tab stop. With **decimal-aligned** tabs, a number aligns at the decimal point, but text aligns to the right. You can use the tab alignment selector on the left side of the ruler or the Tabs command on the Format menu to set custom tabs.

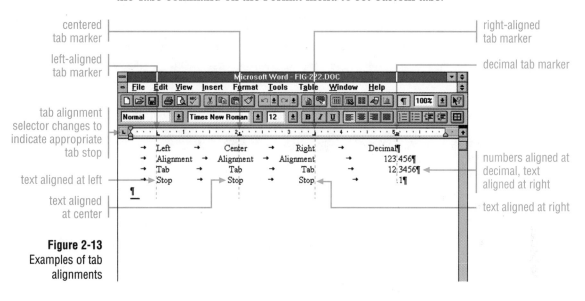

Figure 2-13
Examples of tab alignments

Setting Custom Tab Stops

- Select the paragraph or paragraphs for which you want to set custom tab stops.
- Click the tab alignment selector on the ruler until the appropriate icon for the tab alignment appears.
- Click at the point in the ruler where you want to set the custom tab stop.

or

- Click Format then click Tabs…. The Tabs dialog box appears.
- Type the position where you want to set the custom tab stop in the Tab Stop Position text box.
- Click the appropriate tab alignment option in the Alignment section.
- Click Set.
- Repeat the above steps for each additional tab stop to be set.
- Click OK or press [Enter].

Originally, Marcus entered the information about the board members by inserting a tab between each column of information, that is, between the board member's name and the school district, and between the school district and the telephone number. Now he wants to set a centered tab stop for the column containing the school districts, and a right-aligned tab stop for the column containing the telephone numbers.

To set the centered and right-aligned tab stops using the ruler:

❶ Select the three lines of information in the memo about the new board members ("Teresa Markowitz..." through "...637-7389").

❷ Click the **tab alignment selector** on the ruler until the **centered tab button** ⬆ appears.

❸ Move the tip of the mouse pointer below the 2.75-inch mark on the ruler, then click to set the centered tab at that point. A centered tab marker is inserted into the ruler. See Figure 2-14. Notice that the text *after* the first tab character in each of the selected lines shifts to the location of the centered tab stop.

centered tab marker at 2.75-inch mark

tab alignment selector changes to centered tab button

text centered at tab stop

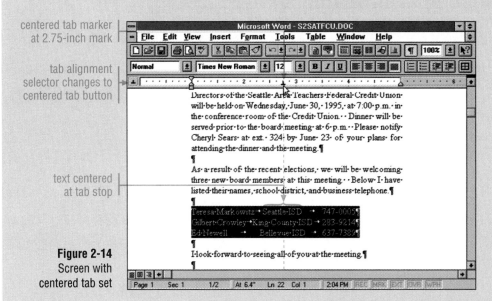

Figure 2-14
Screen with
centered tab set

Now Marcus wants to set a right-aligned tab stop for the last column of information.

❹ Click the **tab alignment selector** on the ruler until the **right-aligned tab button** ⬇ appears.

Marcus decides to set the tab at the 4.75-inch mark on the ruler, but he wants to make sure he gets the tab exactly in place.

❺ Press and hold **[Alt]**, move the mouse pointer to the 4.75-inch mark (approximately) on the ruler, then press and hold down the mouse button. As you do, the ruler indicates the exact distances from the left and right indents.

❻ When the ruler indicates that you are exactly 3.75" from the left indent, release [Alt] and the mouse button. A right-aligned tab marker is inserted into the ruler. The text after the second tab character in each of the selected lines moves to the new tab stop, and the default tabs between the centered tab marker and the right-aligned tab marker on the ruler are cleared. See Figure 2-15.

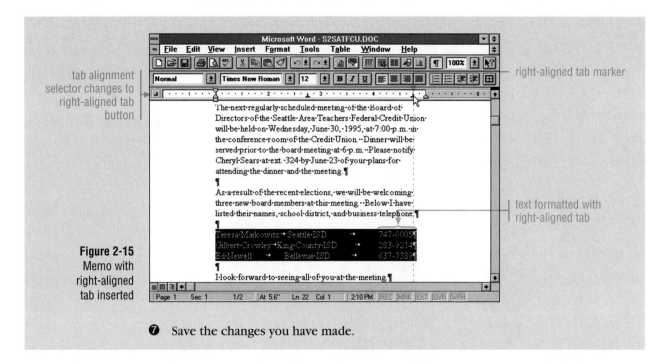

tab alignment
selector changes to
right-aligned tab
button

right-aligned tab marker

text formatted with
right-aligned tab

Figure 2-15
Memo with
right-aligned
tab inserted

❼   Save the changes you have made.

Marcus notices that the second column containing the names of the school districts is too close to the first column. He decides to move the second column to the right so that it looks evenly centered between the first and third columns.

Moving Tab Stops

You can adjust the location of a custom tab stop simply by dragging its marker to a new location on the ruler. Marcus will drag the right-aligned and centered tab markers to improve the format of the three columns.

To move the right-aligned and centered tab stops using the ruler:

❶   Select the information in the memo about the three new board members, if it is not already selected.

❷   Point to the right-aligned tab marker (at the 4.75-inch mark) in the ruler, then click and drag it to the 5-inch mark, on top of the right indent marker. The selected text adjusts to the new setting.

❸   Point to the centered tab marker (at the 2.75-inch mark) in the ruler, then click and drag it to the 3.25-inch mark. If necessary, continue to adjust the centered tab marker on the ruler until the items look evenly centered between the board members' names and their telephone numbers.

❹   Deselect the highlighted text.

❺   Save the changes you have made.

You can clear a custom tab stop just as easily as you can change its location. Simply point to the custom tab stop you want to remove, drag it down below the ruler, then release the mouse button.

Marcus decides that, to make the agenda easier to read, he will separate each agenda item from its presenter with a series of dots, called leader characters. To do so he needs to move to the second page of the document.

Moving Between Pages

Word's Go To command, which is available by pressing [F5] or choosing Go To from the Edit menu, allows you to move to a specified location in your document. Marcus will use the Go To command to move to page 2 so that he can insert the leader characters in the agenda items.

To move to page 2:

❶ Press **[F5]**. The Go To dialog box appears. See Figure 2-16.

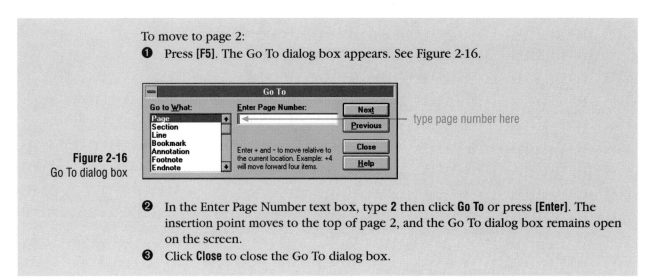

Figure 2-16
Go To dialog box

❷ In the Enter Page Number text box, type **2** then click **Go To** or press **[Enter]**. The insertion point moves to the top of page 2, and the Go To dialog box remains open on the screen.

❸ Click **Close** to close the Go To dialog box.

When formatting the rest of the document, you can use the Go To command to move between the two pages.

Now Marcus can insert the leader characters.

Inserting Leader Characters

Leader characters are repeated characters that help guide the reader's eye from one column of text formatted with tabs to another. Word provides you with three choices of leader characters: dots, dashed lines, or solid lines. The leader character you choose is inserted into the space preceding the designated tab stop.

Inserting Leader Characters

- Select the paragraph or paragraphs for which you want to set custom tab stops, or select the paragraph or paragraphs containing the existing tab stops.
- Click Format then click Tabs.... The Tabs dialog box appears.
- In the Tab Stop Position text box, type the position where you want to set the custom tab stop (if necessary).
- Select the appropriate type of tab alignment option from the Alignment section (if necessary).
- Select the appropriate type of leader character from the Leader section.
- Click Set then click OK or press [Enter].

Marcus originally entered the agenda items with a tab between the agenda item and the presenter's name. Now he will insert leader characters between the two columns. In addition, he will right-align the names of the presenters at the right indent (the 5-inch mark).

To insert leader characters in the agenda items:

❶ Select all the agenda items, beginning with Call to Order and ending with Adjournment.

❷ Click **Format** then click **Tabs...**. The Tabs dialog box appears.

❸ Type **5** in the Tab Stop Position text box to set the location of the custom tab stop at the same position as the right indent.

❹ Click the **Right radio button** in the Alignment section to right-align text typed at this tab.

❺ Click the **2 radio button** (dot leaders) in the Leader section.

❻ Click **Set**. A tab is set at the position you have indicated in the Tab Stop Position text box with the options you have chosen in the Tabs dialog box. Dot leaders will be inserted in the blank space leading up to the right-aligned tab set at the 5-inch mark. See Figure 2-17.

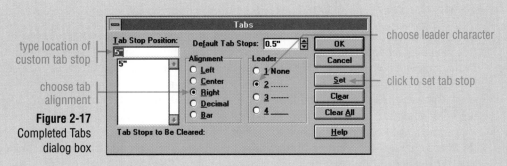

Figure 2-17
Completed Tabs
dialog box

❼ Click **OK** or press [Enter]. A right-aligned tab marker appears in the ruler at the 5-inch mark (on top of the right indent). Dot leaders appear in the tab space leading up to the names of the presenters, and the names of the presenters are right-aligned at the 5-inch mark. All default tabs to the left of the right-aligned tab stop at the 5-inch mark are cleared (for the selected paragraphs).

8 Deselect the highlighted text. See Figure 2-18.

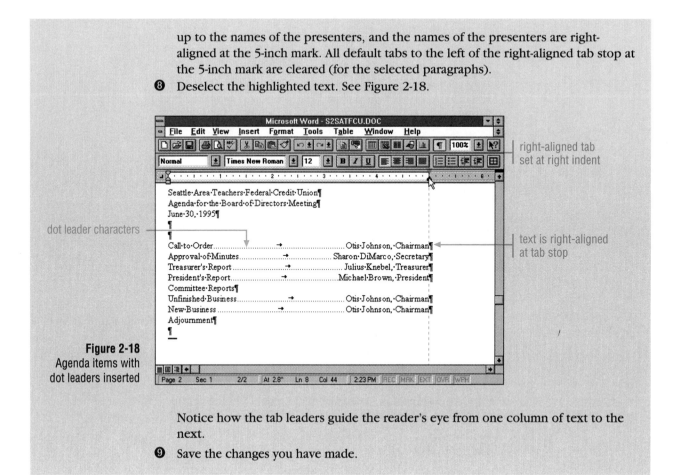

Figure 2-18
Agenda items with
dot leaders inserted

Notice how the tab leaders guide the reader's eye from one column of text to the next.

9 Save the changes you have made.

Marcus reviews the changes Michael requested (Figure 2-1) and notes that Michael wants to add three new agenda items (under Committee Reports), and he wants the list of agenda items to be numbered. However, the new items Marcus needs to insert under Committee Reports should not be numbered—only the main item (Committee Reports) should be numbered. To format the list in this way, Marcus will use Word's New Line command when entering the new agenda items.

Using the New Line Command

As you learned in Tutorial 1, Word treats any block of text that ends with a paragraph mark (¶), including a paragraph mark on a line by itself, as a paragraph. Because of the way Word formats paragraphs, treating a series of short lines as a single paragraph rather than several paragraphs is sometimes desirable. If you want to start a new *line*, but you do not want to start a new *paragraph*, use the **New Line command**, [Shift][Enter]. Word will insert a new line mark (↵) on the screen to indicate the use of the New Line command.

To format the agenda items in the numbered list as Michael requested, Marcus needs the line Committee Reports and the three new committee agenda items to be treated as *one paragraph* rather than as four short paragraphs. Therefore, when he types the new agenda items, Marcus must end all but the last item (Supervisory Committee) with a new line mark (↵).

To enter the new agenda items with new line marks:

❶ Place the insertion point after the "s" in the agenda item Committee Reports and before the paragraph mark.

❷ Press **[Shift][Enter]**. A new line mark (↵) is inserted after Committee Reports and Unfinished Business is forced to the next line.

> **TROUBLE?** If you inserted a paragraph mark instead of a new line mark, you did not hold down [Shift] while you pressed [Enter]. Press [Backspace] to delete the paragraph mark, then repeat Step 2.

Now let's enter the three new individual committee report items Michael wants inserted. You will separate the committee name from the presenter's name with a tab. When you do, the dot leaders will automatically be inserted because the Committee Reports paragraph mark stores the leader characters as part of its format.

❸ Type **Building Maintenance Committee** then press **[Tab]**. Pressing [Tab] inserts a tab character (→) and moves the insertion point to the next tab stop. The dot leaders are also inserted.

❹ Type **Joan Nunez** then press **[Shift][Enter]**.

❺ Type **Financial Services Committee** then press **[Tab]**.

❻ Type **Mai Nguyen** then press **[Shift][Enter]**.

❼ Type **Supervisory Committee** then press **[Tab]**.

❽ Type **Stephen Lesikar**. *Do not press [Enter]* because there is a paragraph mark already following Stephen Lesikar, signifying the end of the paragraph. The paragraph consists of the text "Committee Reports" through "Stephen Lesikar," even though the text appears on different lines. See Figure 2-19.

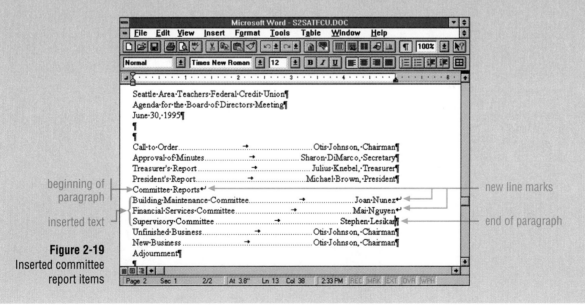

Figure 2-19
Inserted committee report items

Now Marcus can number the agenda items, as Michael requested, so that the order of presentation in the meeting is clear.

Numbering Paragraphs

Adding numbers to a group of paragraphs is another paragraph formatting option that might make your document easier to understand. To create a numbered list of paragraphs, you select the paragraphs you want to number and then click the Numbering button on the Formatting toolbar. Although you can use the Numbering button to apply or remove this option to selected paragraphs, you must choose Bullets and Numbering from the Format menu to reformat the numbers.

Marcus will use the Numbering button to number the agenda items.

To add numbers to the list of agenda items:

❶   Select all the agenda items, from Call to Order through Adjournment.

❷   Click the **Numbering button** 📋 on the Formatting toolbar. Each paragraph in the selected text is numbered consecutively.

❸   Click within the numbered list to deselect the highlighted text. Notice the indent markers in the ruler for the numbered paragraphs. See Figure 2-20.

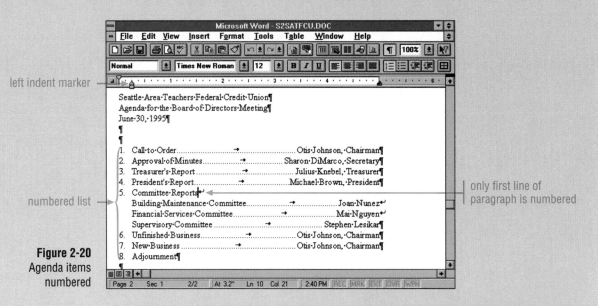

left indent marker

numbered list

only first line of paragraph is numbered

Figure 2-20
Agenda items
numbered

Using the Numbering button formats the paragraphs as hanging indents, with the first-line indent marker at the left margin and the left indent marker at the 0.25-inch mark. For example, look at agenda item 5, Committee Reports. Notice that the individual committee report items were not numbered because Word did not consider them separate paragraphs, but they were indented because a hanging indent causes all lines of a paragraph except the first line to be indented.

Marcus wants the agenda items to start at the 0.5-inch mark instead of the 0.25-inch mark. Because of the change to the left indent, the agenda items moved to the point of the indent at the 0.25-inch mark instead of to the first default tab stop at the 0.5-inch mark. Marcus must adjust the amount of the hanging indent for the numbered agenda items.

To adjust the hanging indent for the numbered list:

❶ Select all the agenda items again.

❷ Click **Format** then click **Bullets and Numbering...**. The Bullets and Numbering dialog box appears. Notice that the Numbered tab is selected.

Marcus needs to modify the numbering options.

❸ Click **Modify...**. The Modify Numbered List dialog box appears.

❹ In the Number Position section, click the **Distance from Indent to Text up arrow** until it reads 0.5". See Figure 2-21. The Preview section changes to reflect the change in the value for the hanging indent.

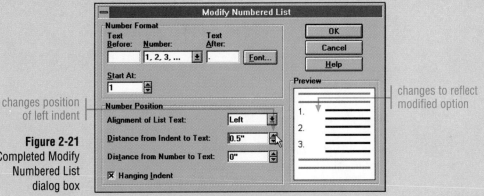

changes position of left indent

changes to reflect modified option

Figure 2-21
Completed Modify
Numbered List
dialog box

❺ Click **OK** or press **[Enter]**. The amount of the left indent is changed, and the agenda items start at the 0.5-inch mark on the ruler.

❻ Deselect the highlighted text.

❼ Save the changes you have made.

Viewing the numbered list, Marcus decides that it would look better if he added more space between the lines of text in the list. This will help to distinguish the items from each other.

Adjusting Line Spacing

The default line spacing in Word documents is single spacing. Sometimes, however, you might want to use 1.5 spacing or double spacing. Because these options do not appear on the Formatting toolbar, the quickest way to apply line spacing options is through shortcut key combinations. The shortcut key combination for single spacing is [Ctrl][1]; for 1.5 spacing, [Ctrl][5]; and for double spacing, [Ctrl][2]. Other line spacing options are available when you choose Paragraph from the Format menu. Changes in line spacing affect only the selected paragraph or paragraphs.

Marcus wants to double space the agenda items to make them stand out more. He'll use the Paragraph command on the Format menu to do so.

To double space the agenda items using the Paragraph command:
❶ Select all the agenda items from Call to Order through Adjournment.
❷ Click **Format** then click **Paragraph...** to display the Paragraph dialog box.
❸ Click the **Line Spacing list box down arrow**. The list of line spacing options appears. See Figure 2-22.

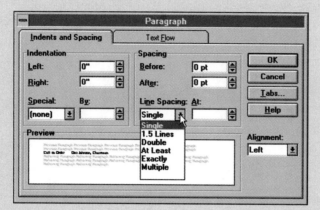

Figure 2-22
Line spacing
options on Indents
and Spacing tab

❹ Click **Double** in the list of line spacing options. Notice that the Preview section changes to reflect the new line spacing setting.
❺ Click **OK** or press **[Enter]**. The agenda items are now double-spaced.
❻ Deselect the highlighted text.

Marcus also decides to double space the memo headings on the first page, to make them stand out more. This time, he'll use the shortcut key combination.

To double space the memo headings using the shortcut key combination:
❶ Place the insertion point at the top of page 1.
❷ Select the four lines of the memo headings (TO:, FROM:, RE:, DATE:).
❸ Press **[Ctrl][2]**. Notice that only the selected area is affected by the paragraph format change to double spacing.
❹ Deselect the highlighted text.
❺ Save the changes you have made.

Next, Marcus wants to change how text aligns in some of the paragraphs in his document.

Aligning Paragraphs

Paragraph alignment involves specifying how you want the text within a paragraph to align horizontally in relation to its left and right *indents*. Remember, initially the left and right indents are located at the same point as the left and right *margins*. With **left alignment**, the paragraph text is set even with the left indent and ragged at the right; with **centered alignment**, the paragraph text is positioned evenly between the left and right indents; with **right alignment**, the lines of text within a paragraph are set even at the right indent and ragged at the left; and with **justified alignment**, the paragraph text at both the left and right indents is even. Left alignment is the default alignment setting.

Buttons for each of these alignment options appear on the Formatting toolbar. Alternatively, you can apply the different alignment options by using shortcut key combinations: [Ctrl][l] for left alignment, [Ctrl][e] for centered alignment, [Ctrl][r] for right alignment, or [Ctrl][j] for justified alignment. You can also choose the Paragraph command from the Format menu and then select the appropriate alignment option from the Paragraph dialog box.

Marcus wants to apply centered alignment to the memo title Memorandum and to the three-line agenda title, because titles are often centered on the page so that they stand out. He also wants to justify the text in the body of the memo, for a more formal appearance.

To apply centered alignment to the memo title:

❶ Place the insertion point anywhere within the paragraph, Memorandum. Remember that because of the way Word defines a paragraph, you merely position the insertion point anywhere within the paragraph to select it and Word will apply any paragraph formatting changes to the entire paragraph.

❷ Click the **Center button** ≣ on the Formatting toolbar. The text is centered between the left and right indents, and the Center button appears lighter to indicate that it is activated for the selected text. See Figure 2-23.

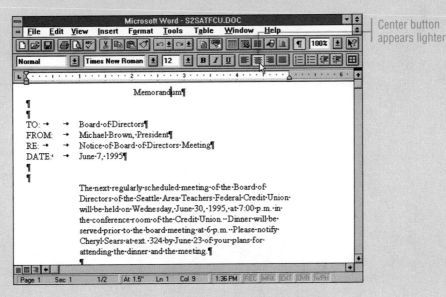

Figure 2-23
"Memorandum"
centered

Now Marcus needs to center the three lines of the agenda title. Because each line of the agenda title is a separate paragraph, he must first select all three paragraphs.

To apply centered alignment to the paragraphs of the agenda title:

❶ Move to page 2.

❷ Use the selection bar to select the three lines of the agenda title.

❸ Press **[Ctrl][e]**, the shortcut key combination for centered alignment. Notice that the Center button on the Formatting toolbar appears lighter, and the three paragraphs that you selected are centered.

❹ Deselect the highlighted text. See Figure 2-24.

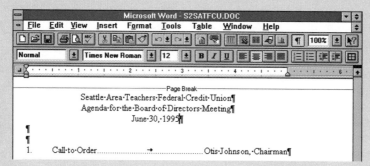

Figure 2-24
Agenda title
lines centered

Next Marcus decides to justify all paragraphs in the body of the memo to give the memo a more formal appearance. He decides to use the shortcut editing and formatting menu to do so.

To justify all paragraphs in the body of the memo using the shortcut menu:

❶ Move to page 1, then use the selection bar to select all the paragraphs in the body of the memo from "The next regularly scheduled..." through "...at the meeting."

❷ Click the **right mouse button**. The shortcut editing and formatting menu appears. See Figure 2-25.

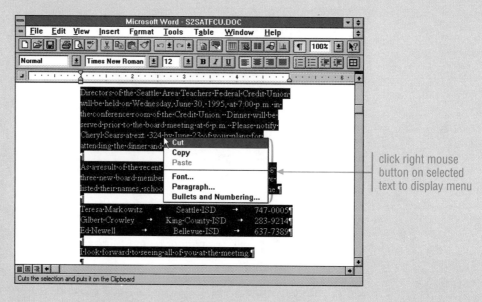

click right mouse
button on selected
text to display menu

Figure 2-25
Shortcut editing and
formatting menu

❸ Click **Paragraph...**. The Paragraph dialog box appears.

❹ Click the **Indents and Spacing tab**, if necessary. Notice that the Alignment section on the right side of the dialog box currently shows "Left" as the alignment.

❺ Click the **Alignment list box down arrow**. The list of alignment options appears.

❻ Click **Justified**. The Preview section changes to reflect the new alignment option.

❼ Click **OK** or press **[Enter]**.

❽ Deselect the highlighted text.

❾ Scroll through the memo to see the effect of justifying the body of the memo. Notice that only those lines that take up a full line of typing are affected by justification.

❿ Save the changes you have made.

Marcus is pleased with how the agenda looks, but he wants to emphasize its three-line title by putting a border around it. He also wants to separate the memo headings from the memo text by inserting a rule from the left margin to the right margin.

Creating Paragraph Borders and Rules

Applying borders and rules to paragraphs is another paragraph formatting technique. A **border** is a box that you use to frame text or graphics. A **rule** is a horizontal or vertical line that you use to enhance the appearance of your document. You can add borders and rules using either the Borders and Shading command on the Format menu or the Borders toolbar.

Marcus decides to put a shadow border, also called a drop shadow, around the three-line title of the agenda. Remember that each line of the title is actually a paragraph.

To create a border around the agenda title lines:

❶ Move to page 2.

❷ Select the three lines of the agenda title from "Seattle Area..." through "...1995."

❸ Click **Format** then click **Borders and Shading...**. The Paragraph Borders and Shading dialog box appears.

❹ Click the **Borders tab**, if necessary. The Border section allows you to preview changes you make.

❺ Click the **Shadow icon** in the Presets section. Notice the change in the Border section.

Next Marcus needs to decide on the thickness of the line style. The choices are given in point sizes, with 1 point equal to $\frac{1}{72}$".

❻ In the Line section, under Style, click **¾ pt** (if it's not already selected). Figure 2-26 shows the completed Paragraph Borders and Shading dialog box.

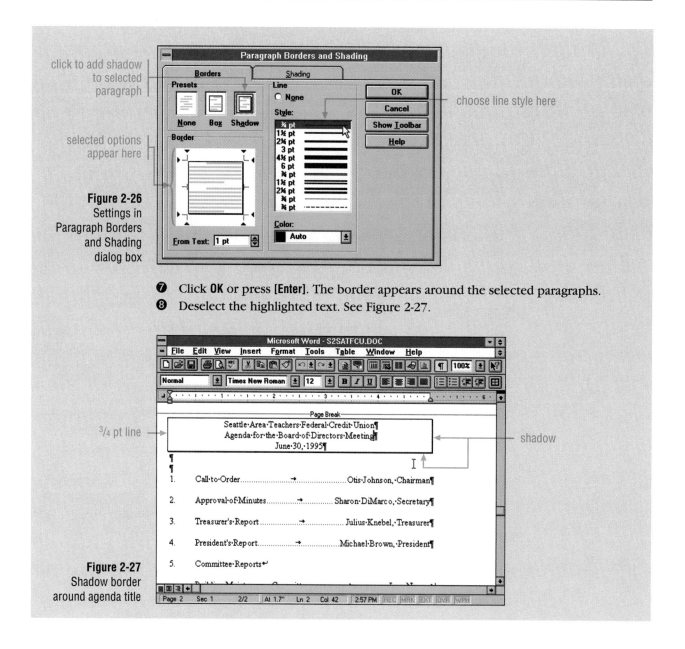

click to add shadow
to selected
paragraph

selected options
appear here

Figure 2-26
Settings in
Paragraph Borders
and Shading
dialog box

choose line style here

❼ Click **OK** or press **[Enter]**. The border appears around the selected paragraphs.
❽ Deselect the highlighted text. See Figure 2-27.

³/₄ pt line

shadow

Figure 2-27
Shadow border
around agenda title

Marcus follows basically the same procedure to add a rule between the date line in the memo headings and the body of the memo, except this time he'll use the Borders toolbar.

To insert a rule below the memo headings:
❶ Move to page 1.
❷ Place the insertion point in front of the first paragraph mark below the date of the memo. Even though this line has no text on it, Word considers it a paragraph.
❸ Click the **Borders button** ⊞ on the Formatting toolbar. The Borders toolbar appears. See Figure 2-28.

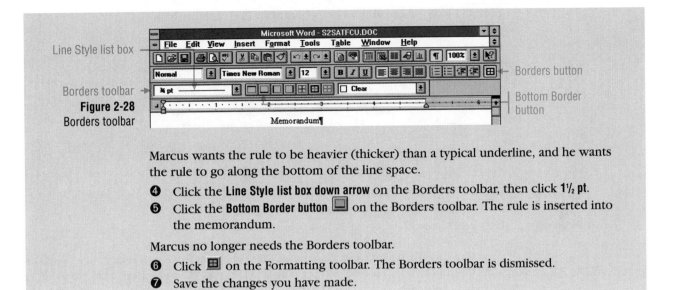

Line Style list box

Borders toolbar

Figure 2-28
Borders toolbar

Borders button

Bottom Border
button

Marcus wants the rule to be heavier (thicker) than a typical underline, and he wants the rule to go along the bottom of the line space.

❹ Click the **Line Style list box down arrow** on the Borders toolbar, then click **1½ pt**.

❺ Click the **Bottom Border button** 🔲 on the Borders toolbar. The rule is inserted into the memorandum.

Marcus no longer needs the Borders toolbar.

❻ Click ⊞ on the Formatting toolbar. The Borders toolbar is dismissed.

❼ Save the changes you have made.

To remove a border or rule, select the paragraph or paragraphs to be changed. Choose Borders and Shading from the Format menu, then click the None radio button in the Line section of the Paragraph Borders and Shading dialog box. You can also click the No Border button on the Borders toolbar to remove a border or rule from a selected paragraph.

Marcus has now completed the paragraph formatting phase for his document.

If you want to take a break and resume the tutorial at a later time, you can close the current document then exit Word by double-clicking the Control menu box in the upper-left corner of the screen. When you want to resume the tutorial, start Word, place your Student Disk in the disk drive, then complete the screen check procedure described in Tutorial 1. Open the file S2SATFCU.DOC, press [Shift][F5], Word's Go Back command, to return to your last point in the document, then continue with the tutorial.

Next, Marcus begins the final stage of formatting: font-level formatting.

Font Formatting

A **font** is the general shape of the characters in your document. A **character** is any letter, number, punctuation mark, or symbol that you enter in your document. Font formatting involves choices about how the individual characters in your document appear on the screen and in print. These different choices are known as **character attributes**. Font formatting changes are made through the Formatting toolbar or the Font command on the Format menu. You can change the font type, the size of the characters, the style of the characters, the space between characters, the vertical position of characters, and even the color of the characters. In Tutorial 1 you learned how to change the type style of characters using the Bold, Italic, and Underline buttons on the Formatting toolbar. In this tutorial you will also use the Formatting toolbar and the Font command to make font-level formatting changes.

The available choices of fonts are listed in the Font list box. A partial listing of the available fonts is shown in Figure 2-29.

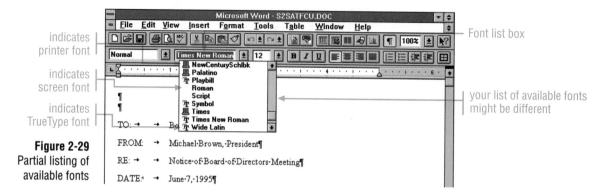

Font list box

your list of available fonts might be different

Figure 2-29
Partial listing of available fonts

The fonts with a printer icon in front of them represent **printer fonts**—that is, fonts that are built into your selected printer. These printer fonts are limited, however, to just those sizes your printer is capable of producing. The fonts in the list with no icon beside them are **screen fonts** only; if you choose a screen font, the way your document appears on your screen might be different from the way it looks when it is printed. The fonts in the list with double "Ts" in front of them are TrueType fonts, a special type of font that is available only in Windows 3.1. **TrueType fonts** work with every printer, including dot matrix printers, and any size can be specified. Word provides you with several TrueType fonts. Figure 2-30 illustrates each TrueType font available in Word. Although all these different fonts are available to you, you should limit to two or three the number of different fonts you use in any one document.

Figure 2-30
Example of TrueType fonts available in Word

The size of a font is measured in **points**; there are 72 points in an inch. The larger the point size of a font, the larger the font will be displayed and printed. The Font Size list box shows the sizes available for the font you have selected. Available point sizes vary depending on the font selected. The basic TrueType fonts are available, however, in sizes ranging from 4 points to 127 points. Figure 2-31 illustrates various font sizes.

This is Arial 12 point

This is Arial 24 point

This is Arial 36 point

Figure 2-31
Various font sizes

Another character attribute that you can change is type style. You have already used the bold, italic, and underline type styles, but Word provides other effects in the Font dialog box, such as strikethrough, all caps, small caps, and color (if you print on a color printer). The Character Spacing tab also provides you with the option to decrease or increase the space between characters and create superscript or subscript characters.

Marcus wants to change several character attributes of the memo title, Memorandum.

Changing Several Character Attributes at Once

Marcus wants to make the title Memorandum stand out from the rest of the memo text. He decides to change the font type of the memo title to the TrueType font Arial, make its size 14 point, make its font style bold and all caps, and expand the amount of space between each character. He decides to use the Font dialog box to change all these character attributes at once.

To change the character attributes at one time:

❶ Select the memo heading **Memorandum**. Because you are now changing font formats, you must select all the characters you want to change; you cannot simply click the insertion point in the paragraph.

❷ Click **Format** then click **Font....** The Font dialog box appears.

The Font list box displays the available font types in alphabetical order.

❸ Scroll up the list of fonts, then click **Arial**. Notice that the Preview section changes to reflect the new font choice.

TROUBLE? If you cannot locate Arial at the top of your font list, then perhaps your system is using a previous version of Windows. Ask your instructor or technical support person which font to use instead of Arial.

❹ Click **Bold** in the Font Style list box. The Preview section changes to reflect the new type style choice.

❺ Click **14** in the Size list box. The Preview section changes to reflect the new point size.

❻ Click the **All Caps check box** in the Effects section. Figure 2-32 shows the completed settings on the Font tab of the Font dialog box.

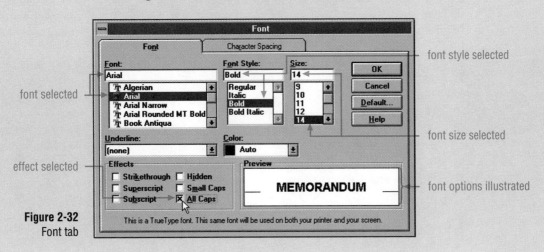

Figure 2-32
Font tab

Next, Marcus wants to increase the spacing between characters, so he needs to move to the Character Spacing tab of the Font dialog box.

❼ Click the **Character Spacing tab**, then click the **Spacing list box down arrow** to display the available spacing options.

❽ Click **Expanded**. An additional 1 point of space will be inserted between each character of the selected text. See Figure 2-33.

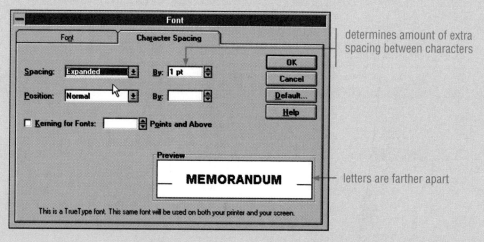

determines amount of extra spacing between characters

letters are farther apart

Figure 2-33
Character
Spacing tab

❾ Click **OK** or press **[Enter]**. All the character attribute changes you made are applied to the title Memorandum.

❿ Deselect the highlighted text, then save the changes you have made.

Next, Marcus wants to change the agenda's title to make it stand out more from the list of agenda items.

Changing Font and Point Size Using the Formatting Toolbar

Marcus decides to change the font and enlarge the type size of the agenda's title lines. He decides to change the font to Arial and the point size to 14 using the Formatting toolbar. He also wants to bold the title lines.

To change the font and point size of the agenda's title lines using the Formatting toolbar:

❶ Move to page 2.

❷ Select the three lines of the agenda title.

❸ Click the **Font list box down arrow** on the Formatting toolbar to open the font list. At the top of the list, Word keeps track of the fonts used most recently in a document.

❹ Click the **Arial**. The selected text changes to reflect the new font choice.

❺ Click the **Font Size list box down arrow** on the Formatting toolbar to open the Font Size list.

❻ Click **14**. The selected text changes to reflect the new point size choice.

❼ Click the **Bold button** **B**. The selected text changes to reflect the new type style choice.

❽   Deselect the highlighted text. See Figure 2-34.

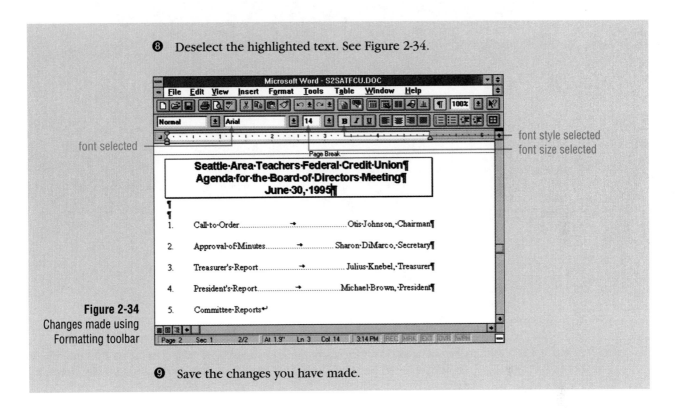

Figure 2-34
Changes made using
Formatting toolbar

font selected

font style selected
font size selected

❾   Save the changes you have made.

Marcus decides to insert the tilde (~) above the second "n" in Nuñez, the last name of one of the presenters on the agenda.

Inserting Special Symbols

Word provides an easy way to insert special symbols called **character sets** in your documents. The character sets available depend on the selected printer; you choose them using the Symbol command on the Insert menu. Each character set has a variety of available characters or symbols. Once you have selected a character, it is placed in your document at the insertion point. To delete an inserted symbol, you must first select it and then press [Del].

The (normal text) character set contains the symbol with the tilde above the letter "n," which is the symbol Marcus wants to insert in this document.

To insert the tilde above the "n" in Nunez:
❶   Move the insertion point to page 2, if necessary.
❷   Select the second "n" in Nunez, the last name of the presenter for the Building Maintenance Committee report. Only the "n" should be highlighted.
❸   Click **Insert** then click **Symbol...**. The Symbol dialog box appears and the Symbols tab is selected.
❹   Click the **Font list box down arrow** to display the available character sets. Scroll up, then click **(normal text)** at the top of the list. The (normal text) character set is displayed.
❺   Click the **ñ symbol** to select it. (You will find it in the last row.) The symbol "ñ" now appears much bigger. See Figure 2-35.

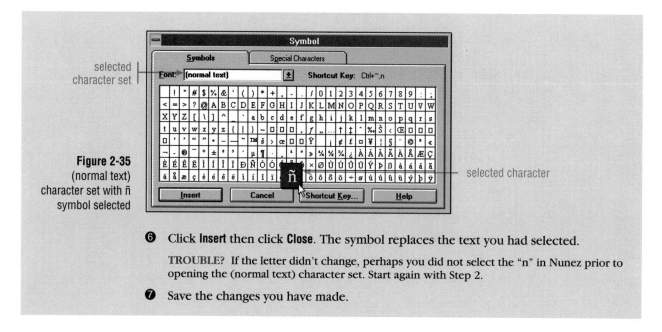

Figure 2-35
(normal text)
character set with ñ
symbol selected

selected character set

selected character

❻ Click **Insert** then click **Close**. The symbol replaces the text you had selected.

   TROUBLE? If the letter didn't change, perhaps you did not select the "n" in Nunez prior to opening the (normal text) character set. Start again with Step 2.

❼ Save the changes you have made.

Marcus has completed all the formatting changes he needs to make to the memo and agenda. He is now ready to print his document—the final stage of the productivity strategy.

Previewing and Printing Multiple Pages

Now you are ready to print a copy of Marcus's memo and agenda. Before you do, you'll first spell check the document and correct any errors. Then, you'll view the document in print preview to see how it will look when printed. One of the options in print preview, Multiple Pages, allows you to view several pages of your document side by side.

To spell check the document:

❶ Press **[Ctrl][Home]** to move to the beginning of the document.

❷ Click the **Spelling button** on the Standard toolbar (or click **Tools** then click **Spelling...**). Follow the procedures described in Tutorial 1 for performing a spell check.

❸ Save your changes if necessary.

Now you can preview and print the document.

To preview both pages at the same time, then print the document:

❶ Click the **Print Preview button** on the Standard toolbar (or click **File** then click **Print Preview**).

   TROUBLE? If two pages are already displayed in print preview, skip to Step 4.

❷ Click the **Multiple Pages button** on the Print Preview toolbar.

❸ Drag the mouse pointer across two of the page icons to indicate that you want to view two pages side by side, then release the mouse button. Both pages of your document appear in the Preview window. See Figure 2-36.

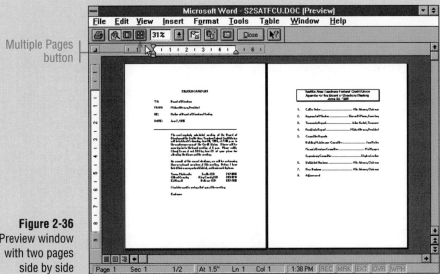

Multiple Pages button

Figure 2-36
Preview window with two pages side by side

❹ Click the **Print button** 🖨 on the Print Preview toolbar if you are satisfied with the appearance of your document. Otherwise, click **Close**, return to your document to make changes, then repeat Steps 1 through 4. Your final document should look like Figure 2-37.

❺ Click the **Close button** on the Print Preview toolbar to return to your document.

❻ Close the document and exit Word.

MEMORANDUM

TO: Board of Directors

FROM: Michael Brown, President

RE: Notice of Board of Directors Meeting

DATE: June 7, 1995

The next regularly scheduled meeting of the Board of Directors of the Seattle Area Teachers Federal Credit Union will be held on Wednesday, June 30, 1995, at 7:00 p.m. in the conference room of the Credit Union. Dinner will be served prior to the board meeting at 6 p.m. Please notify Cheryl Sears at ext. 324 by June 23 of your plans for attending the dinner and the meeting.

As a result of the recent elections, we will be welcoming three new board members at this meeting. Below I have listed their names, school district, and business telephone.

Teresa Markowitz	Seattle ISD	747-0005
Gilbert Crowley	King County ISD	283-9214
Ed Newell	Bellevue ISD	637-7389

I look forward to seeing all of you at the meeting.

Enclosure

Figure 2-37
Marcus's final
document
(page 1 of 2)

Seattle Area Teachers Federal Credit Union
Agenda for the Board of Directors Meeting
June 30, 1995

1.   Call to Order .... Otis Johnson, Chairman

2.   Approval of Minutes............................ Sharon DiMarco, Secretary

3.   Treasurer's Report................................... Julius Knebel, Treasurer

4.   President's Report...................................Michael Brown, President

5.   Committee Reports

      Building Maintenance Committee ....Joan Nuñez

      Financial Services Committee ....Mai Nguyen

      Supervisory Committee .... Stephen Lesikar

6.   Unfinished Business.................................... Otis Johnson, Chairman

7.   New Business... Otis Johnson, Chairman

8.   Adjournment

Figure 2-37
Marcus's final
document
(page 2 of 2)

Marcus is pleased with his final document. He gives it to Michael for distribution to the board members.

Questions

1. Explain the purpose of Word's drag-and-drop feature. What is another way to accomplish the same purpose?
2. Explain the uses of a new line mark.
3. What command do you choose to rename an existing file?
4. Explain the differences among page setup, paragraph formatting, and font formatting.
5. What would the length of your typing line be if you changed your left and right margins both to 1 inch?
6. Explain the difference between a soft page break and a hard page break.
7. What different methods can you use to move quickly between pages in a document?
8. What is the difference between portrait page orientation and landscape page orientation? What command do you choose to change page orientation?
9. What are Word's four types of indent formats? How do you create them using the indent markers on the ruler?
10. Describe the effect of the following paragraph alignment options:
    a. Left
    b. Centered
    c. Right
    d. Justified
11. What are the shortcut keyboard combinations for the following line spacing options?
    a. Single spacing
    b. 1.5 spacing
    c. Double spacing
12. Explain the difference between an indent and a tab.
13. What are the four types of tab alignments? How do you set tabs using the ruler?
14. What is the difference between paragraph alignment and tab alignment?
15. What are the three types of leader characters? How do you set leader characters?
16. What is the difference between a border and a rule? How do you create a border around a paragraph?
17. Describe the different types of character attributes.
18. If you wanted to print a word so that it appeared 1.5 inches high, what point size would you apply to the selected word?
19. What are the advantages of using TrueType fonts rather than printer fonts?
20. What is a character set?

Use Word Help to find the answers to the following questions:

E 21. What is the keyboard equivalent command to indent all lines of a paragraph to the next tab stop?

E 22. How do you remove the numbers from a numbered list of items?

E 23. How do you change the number format of a numbered list of items?

E 24. What is the keyboard equivalent command to remove all font formatting from selected text?

E 25. What is the procedure for inserting a vertical bar between tabbed columns of information?

Tutorial Assignments

Start Word, if necessary, and conduct a screen check. Open T2SATMIN.DOC from your Student Disk, then complete the following:

1. On the line after the Attendance section heading, type the names given below of the members in attendance. Press [Tab] once after the name in the first column, then type the name in the second column.

Joan Nuñez	Michael Brown
Gilbert Crowley	Sharon DiMarco
Otis Johnson	Julius Knebel
Stephen Lesikar	Teresa Markowitz
Ed Newell	Mai Nguyen

2. Insert new line marks so that the Committee Reports section (from Committee Reports through the Supervisory Committee) is all one paragraph.
3. Move the President's report after the Treasurer's report.
4. Change the top margin to 1.5 inches and the side margins to 1 inch.
5. Center the three-line heading.
6. Indent the names of the members in attendance 1 inch from the left margin.
7. Insert a left-aligned tab so that the second column of the members in attendance starts at the 3.5-inch mark on the ruler.
8. Number the paragraphs of the body of the minutes.
9. Right-align the closing lines (Respectfully submitted through Board of Directors).
10. Change the three-line heading to 14 point, Century Gothic, bold.
11. Bold each of the section headings (Attendance, Treasurer's Report, etc.) and italicize the headings for each of the committee reports.
12. Save the document as S2SATMIN.DOC.
13. Spell check, preview, then print the document.

E

14. Number the paragraphs of the body of the minutes using roman numeral format.
15. Change the amount of the hanging indent for the numbered list to 0.5 inch.
16. Save the document as S2MIN2.DOC.
17. Preview then print the document.
18. Close the document.

Case Problems

1. The Cost of Administrative Services at Tyler Fasteners

Marjorie Rominofski is the administrative services manager for Tyler Fasteners, which manufactures a variety of fasteners for the construction industry. One of her responsibilities each month is to write a memo to the department heads in the plant. In this memo she informs the department heads about the cost of administrative services charged to each department's budget. You will format Marjorie's memo.

Open P2ADMSER.DOC from your Student Disk, then complete the following:

1. Insert the title Memorandum at the top of the document, then press [Enter] twice.
2. Align the information after the memo headings (TO:, FROM:, and so on) at the 1-inch mark.
3. Change the top margin to 2 inches and the left and right margins to 1.75 inches.
4. Double space the memo headings.
5. Move the sentence beginning "These amounts . . ." and the two spaces after it to the beginning of the last paragraph ("If you have . . .").
6. Center the title Memorandum.
7. Insert a $1\frac{1}{2}$ point, double line border around Memorandum.

8. Indent the three expenditure lines (Photocopies, and so on) to the 1-inch mark.
9. Align the decimal for the amounts in the expenditure lines at the 4-inch mark.
10. Change Memorandum to 18-point Bookman Old Style, bold, and all caps.
11. Save the document as S2ADMSER.DOC.
12. Spell check, preview, then print the document.
13. Change the left and right margins to 1.25 inches and move the tab for the expenditures from the 4-inch mark to the 4.5-inch mark.

E 14. Remove the border from the title Memorandum.

E 15. Change the font to Arial for all the text except the title.
16. Save the document as S2TYLER.DOC.
17. Preview then print the document.
18. Dismiss the Borders toolbar, if necessary, and close the document.

2. Total Quality Management at English Engineering, Inc.

Janetta Coleman is the manager of the Human Resources Development Department for English Engineering, Inc., an aeronautical engineering systems firm in Huntsville, Alabama. As part of the team of contractors responsible for the life-support system on board the space shuttle, English is participating in the total quality management program mandated by the federal government of all space shuttle contractors. At a recent retreat, Janetta's staff developed its vision statement. Janetta created and edited a simple flyer that will serve as a reminder to her staff of their vision for the direction of the department. Now she needs to format and print it.

Open P2VISION.DOC from your Student Disk, then complete the following:
1. Scroll through the document. The flyer consists of three parts—the heading Vision on Ln 5, the vision statement on Ln 18 through 20, and the department identification on Ln 33 through 35.
2. Center the heading Vision and the vision statement.
3. Right-align and double space the department identification.
4. Place a 1½ point double rule approximately 1 inch above and below the vision statement.
5. Add the following character attributes to Vision:
   a. Century Gothic font
   b. 36 point
   c. bold
   d. italic
   e. all caps
   f. expanded spacing
6. Add the following character attributes to the vision statement:
   a. Century Gothic font
   b. 24 point
   c. bold
   d. italic
7. Add the following character attributes to the department identification:
   a. Century Gothic font
   b. 18 point
   c. bold
8. Save the document as S2VISION.DOC.
9. Preview then print the document.

E 10. Insert the Wingdings character set symbol A (you will find it on the seventh row) at the beginning of the line, Human Resources Development Department.
11. Increase the amount of space between each character in the heading Vision to 3 point.
12. Save the document as S2HRD2.DOC.
13. Preview then print the document.
14. Dismiss the Borders toolbar then close the document.

3. Safety Measures at University General Hospital

Raul Fernandez is the director of the Environmental and Physical Safety Department of University General Hospital. He has decided to prepare a memo motivating employees to be aware of the potential safety hazards in their work environment and informing them whom to call for information or help.

Complete the following:

1. Create the document as shown in Figure 2-38. Type the memo headings, body of the memo, and telephone information without making any formatting decisions. When typing the memo headings (TO:, FROM:, and so on), insert one tab between the heading and the information that follows. When typing the personnel information, insert a tab between the title (for example, Director) and the name (Raul Fernandez).

Memorandum

TO: Hospital Staff
FROM: Raul Fernandez
RE: Safe and healthful work environments
DATE: September 2, 1995

Whether you work in a laboratory, hospital ward, or an office, it is important for you to be aware of the hazards and safety procedures for your work area. Attend safety meetings, learn about fire extinguishers, evacuation plans, personal protective equipment, and techniques for handling and storing potentially harmful materials.

The Environmental and Physical Safety Department maintains programs in chemical safety, radiation safety, biosafety, asbestos control, hazardous waste management, fire safety, hazard communication, and general safety. On the next page is a list of the individuals responsible for these programs. Please keep this sheet readily available, and contact the appropriate person whenever you have a question or concern about safety issues. Thank you!

Whom to Call

749-4271

Director   Raul Fernandez
Manager, Fire and Physical Safety   Bob Lane
Manager, Hazardous Materials   Janet Hunter
Manager, Radiation Safety   Le Chiu
Office Manager   Ann Schuler

Figure 2-38

2. Save the document as S2SAFETY.DOC.
3. Double space the memo headings and the personnel information.
4. Center the title Memorandum.
5. Justify the body of the memo.
6. Indent the body of the memo to the 1-inch mark.
7. Align the colons in the memo headings by inserting a right-aligned tab stop at the 0.75-inch mark, then inserting a tab in front of each heading.
8. Insert a hard page break before Whom to Call.
9. Insert a $^3/_4$ point single rule below Whom to Call.
10. Center the telephone number.
11. Indent the personnel information from both margins 1 inch.
12. Set a right-aligned, dot leader tab for the personnel information at the 5-inch mark.
13. Bold the title Memorandum.
14. Change the font for all the text on page 2 to Arial Rounded MT Bold.
15. Change the telephone number to 24 point.
16. Save the document.
17. Spell check, preview, then print the document.
18. Insert the Wingdings special character set symbol for the telephone above the telephone number.
19. Center the telephone.
20. Change the telephone special character to 36 point.
21. Save the document as S2UGH2.DOC.
22. Preview then print the document.
23. Dismiss the Borders toolbar and close the document.

Creating a Multiple-Page Document with Tables

Developing a Travel Expense Policy Report

 Powell International Petroleum Services, Inc. Barbara Svoboda is a recent business school graduate with a specialty in human resources management. For the last two years, she has been working for Powell International Petroleum Services, Inc. (PIPSI) at its corporate headquarters in Baton Rouge, Louisiana. PIPSI specializes in retrofitting older refineries and pipelines with the latest production technologies. Most recently, PIPSI has started numerous projects in the Commonwealth of Independent States; as a result, employee travel expenses have increased.

PIPSI's executive management has asked Barbara's manager, Nancy McDermott, to develop a new travel expense policy that will control domestic and foreign travel expenses. Nancy has almost finished the policy statement but has been called out of town. She gives Barbara the disk containing the report and tells her to finish the report, then edit and format it before submitting it to management.

Barbara decides to use the productivity strategy to complete her task. She will finish creating the travel expense policy, then edit the document for any changes or corrections she needs to make. Next, she will format the policy statement following the format used for other policy statements in the company's policy manual. Barbara will then print the completed travel expense policy.

To start Word and open the document that Nancy created:

❶ Start Word, if necessary, and conduct the screen check as described in Tutorial 1.

❷ Insert your Student Disk in the disk drive, then open the file C3PERDM.DOC from your Student Disk. After C3PERDM.DOC is open, scroll through the document to become familiar with it. Compare your document to Figure 3-1 on the following page. Notice that the document is two pages long and divided into four major sections—Standard Per Diem Allowance, Domestic Travel, Foreign Travel, and Exceptions. Eventually, the Domestic Travel and Foreign Travel sections will contain basically the same information arranged in the same order.

❸ Click **File** then click **Save As...** and save the document as S3PERDM.DOC to your Student Disk.

❹ Click **OK** or press **[Enter]**. The title bar changes to reflect the new document name.

Barbara begins by looking over the printed copy of the unfinished travel expense policy that Nancy left (Figure 3-1). She decides to begin her work in the document by adding the following: explanations for the components of the per diem allowance (Insert A), a table of information about the domestic travel per diem (Insert B), and a table of information about foreign travel per diem (Insert C). Depending on the printer selected, your document might break between pages one and two at a point different from that shown in Figure 3-1.

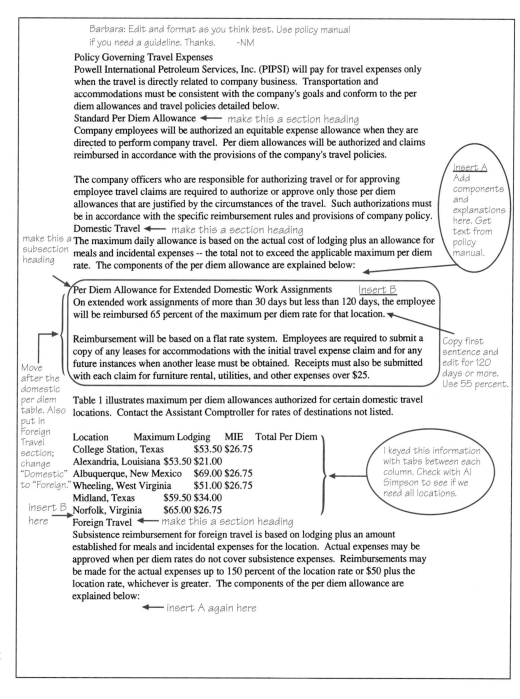

Barbara: Edit and format as you think best. Use policy manual if you need a guideline. Thanks.   -NM

Policy Governing Travel Expenses

Powell International Petroleum Services, Inc. (PIPSI) will pay for travel expenses only when the travel is directly related to company business. Transportation and accommodations must be consistent with the company's goals and conform to the per diem allowances and travel policies detailed below.

Standard Per Diem Allowance ← *make this a section heading*

Company employees will be authorized an equitable expense allowance when they are directed to perform company travel. Per diem allowances will be authorized and claims reimbursed in accordance with the provisions of the company's travel policies.

Insert A — Add components and explanations here. Get text from policy manual.

The company officers who are responsible for authorizing travel or for approving employee travel claims are required to authorize or approve only those per diem allowances that are justified by the circumstances of the travel. Such authorizations must be in accordance with the specific reimbursement rules and provisions of company policy.

Domestic Travel ← *make this a section heading*

make this a subsection heading The maximum daily allowance is based on the actual cost of lodging plus an allowance for meals and incidental expenses -- the total not to exceed the applicable maximum per diem rate. The components of the per diem allowance are explained below:

Per Diem Allowance for Extended Domestic Work Assignments   *Insert B*
On extended work assignments of more than 30 days but less than 120 days, the employee will be reimbursed 65 percent of the maximum per diem rate for that location.

Copy first sentence and edit for 120 days or more. Use 55 percent.

Reimbursement will be based on a flat rate system. Employees are required to submit a copy of any leases for accommodations with the initial travel expense claim and for any future instances when another lease must be obtained. Receipts must also be submitted with each claim for furniture rental, utilities, and other expenses over $25.

Move after the domestic per diem table. Also put in Foreign Travel section; change "Domestic" to "Foreign."

Table 1 illustrates maximum per diem allowances authorized for certain domestic travel locations. Contact the Assistant Comptroller for rates of destinations not listed.

Location	Maximum Lodging	MIE	Total Per Diem
College Station, Texas	$53.50	$26.75	
Alexandria, Louisiana	$53.50	$21.00	
Albuquerque, New Mexico	$69.00	$26.75	
Wheeling, West Virginia	$51.00	$26.75	
Midland, Texas	$59.50	$34.00	
Norfolk, Virginia	$65.00	$26.75	

I keyed this information with tabs between each column. Check with Al Simpson to see if we need all locations.

insert B here

Foreign Travel ← *make this a section heading*

Subsistence reimbursement for foreign travel is based on lodging plus an amount established for meals and incidental expenses for the location. Actual expenses may be approved when per diem rates do not cover subsistence expenses. Reimbursements may be made for the actual expenses up to 150 percent of the location rate or $50 plus the location rate, whichever is greater. The components of the per diem allowance are explained below:

← *insert A again here*

Figure 3-1
Nancy's edited document
(page 1 of 2)

Table 2 illustrates maximum per diem allowances authorized for certain foreign travel locations. Contact the Assistant Comptroller for rates of destinations not listed. ←— insert C here

←— insert B here

Exceptions ←— make this a section heading

Any exceptions to the standard per diem allowance must be in writing to the Assistant Comptroller's office.

Here's the information for the Foreign Travel Per Diem table. Check with Al to see if there are other locations.

Location	Maximum Lodging	MIE	Maximum Per Diem	
Usinsk, Komi	$23	$8	$31	
Baku, Azerbaijan	$35	$12	$47	
Lisitschansk, Ukraine	$40	$12	$52	Insert C

Figure 3-1
Nancy's edited document
(page 2 of 2)

Creating a Table

Tables are an important means of communicating information in business documents, because they allow the reader to analyze complex data quickly. A **table** is simply information organized horizontally in rows and vertically in columns. The intersection of a row and column is called a **cell**.

In Tutorial 2 you learned to align text vertically by using tabs. That procedure works well for information in two or three columns, with each item in the table containing only one row of information. But if the information is more complex, or if you want a more professional-looking table, using tabs to create tables becomes awkward and tedious.

Word's table feature relieves the tedium of setting up data in columns and rows. It also enables you to lay out other types of information, such as text and graphics, side by side in a more readable format. The elements of a Word table are illustrated in Figure 3-2. Like text typed in a paragraph, text entered in a cell wraps automatically within that cell.

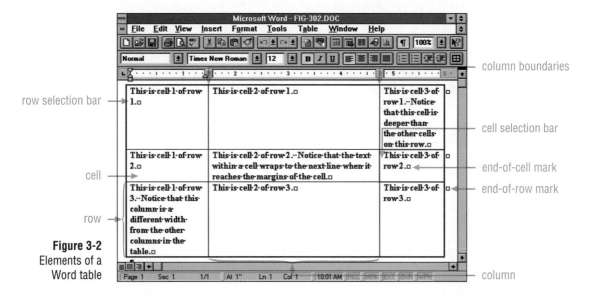

Figure 3-2
Elements of a
Word table

Word's table feature allows you to create a blank table, then insert information in it, or to convert existing text to a table. Whichever method you choose, Word makes it easy for you to create the **structure**—the number of rows and columns—of a table.

To see the outline of the table structure in your document, the Gridlines option on the Table menu must be activated, which it is by default. To check whether the Gridlines option is activated, open the Table menu and look for a checkmark in front of the Gridlines option. The gridlines that are used to display the blank table structure do not print, however. If you want a border around any part of a table, you must specifically format the table or individual cells with borders.

Creating a Table Using the Table Button

In addition to arranging data in rows and columns, Word's table feature allows you to create side-by-side text paragraphs, such as when you need to define words or include explanations of catalog items. One method to create a blank table structure is to use the Insert Table button on the Standard toolbar to specify the number of rows and columns you need in your table. Word then inserts a blank table structure with the specified number of rows and columns at the insertion point.

As she noted on page 1 of her draft, Nancy wants Barbara to insert explanations of the two components of the per diem allowance: "Maximum lodging expense allowance" and "Meals and incidental expense allowance." Barbara will use the table feature to create side-by-side text paragraphs, with the per diem component name on the left side and the explanation of the component on the right side. Barbara needs to create a table that has two rows and two columns. She decides to use the Insert Table button to specify the table structure.

To create a blank table structure using the Insert Table button:

❶ Scroll through the document until you see the Domestic Travel heading.

❷ Place the insertion point in front of the heading, Per Diem Allowance for Extended Domestic Work Assignments (Page 1, Ln 20).

    TROUBLE? Your choice of printer might affect the location of the insertion point shown in your status bar. Use the line reference given in the tutorial as a guide, but continue to refer to the figures.

❸ Click the **Insert Table button** 🔲 on the Standard toolbar. The Insert Table button grid, a miniature table, appears. See Figure 3-3.

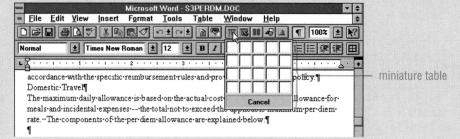

Figure 3-3
Insert Table
button grid

❹ Place the pointer in the upper-left cell of the miniature table, then click and drag it across the grid so that two rows and two columns are highlighted. As you highlight cells, Word indicates the size of the table at the bottom of the grid (rows x columns).

❺ Release the mouse button. An empty 2 x 2 table grid structure appears in the document, and the insertion point is in cell 1 of row 1. See Figure 3-4.

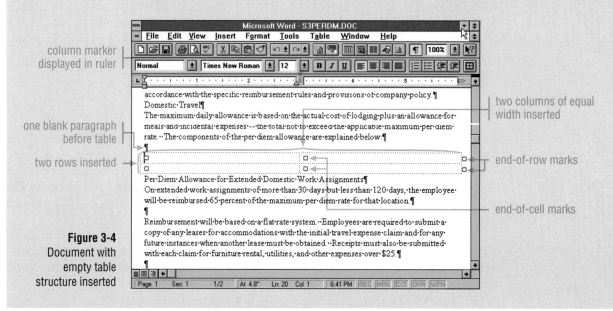

Figure 3-4
Document with
empty table
structure inserted

Notice that, by default, Word automatically creates two columns of equal width between the margins of the document. Each cell contains an end-of-cell mark, and each row contains an end-of-row mark. Also notice the change in the ruler: each column is indicated by column markers on the ruler, the indent markers for the active cell are displayed, and between column spacing has been inserted.

TROUBLE? If you are not satisfied with the table you created, immediately click the Undo button 🔲 on the Standard toolbar (or click Edit then click Undo Insert Table), then repeat Steps 2 through 5.

TROUBLE? If you do not see the end-of-cell and end-of-row marks, you need to click the Show/Hide ¶ button 🔲 on the Standard toolbar.

❻ Click the **Save button** 🔲 on the Standard toolbar (or click **File** then click **Save**) to save your changes.

Now that Barbara has created the structure for her table, she is ready to enter text in it.

Entering Text in a Table and Using AutoCorrect

You enter text in tables just as you do in the rest of your document—simply start typing. If the text in a cell takes up more than one line, Word automatically wraps the text to the next line and increases the height of the cell. To move to a new cell, either click in that cell to move the insertion point or press [Tab]. Press [Shift][Tab] to move the insertion point to the previous cell. If a cell that you are moving to contains text or data, using [Tab] or [Shift][Tab] will highlight the contents of the cell. Figure 3-5 lists other keyboard techniques for moving within a table.

To move the insertion point:	Press:
One cell to the right or to the first cell in the next row	[Tab]
One cell to the left	[Shift][Tab]
The first cell in the current row	[Alt][Home]
The last cell in the current row	[Alt][End]
The top cell in the current column	[Alt][PgUp]
The bottom cell in the current column	[Alt][PgDn]

Figure 3-5
Keyboard techniques for moving within a table

When entering text in a table, you can correct errors just as you correct errors when typing text in the main document. In addition, the Spelling command will find spelling errors in the text of a table.

Word's AutoCorrect feature corrects some of the more common typing mistakes you might make when entering text anywhere in a document, including a table. For instance, if you mistakenly type *teh* for *the* or *adn* for *and*, AutoCorrect automatically corrects the error after you press the Spacebar. Figure 3-6 shows the AutoCorrect dialog box, which you display by choosing the AutoCorrect command from the Tools menu.

default options

entries to correct
common typing
errors

Figure 3-6
AutoCorrect
dialog box

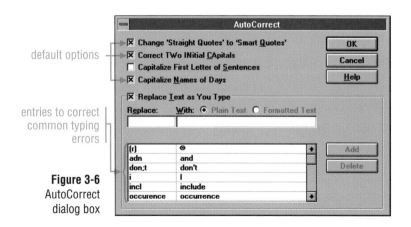

Word provides AutoCorrect entries for many common typing errors, and you can also add your own entries for the typing errors you make most often. In addition, the dialog box provides default options that automatically change straight quotes to smart (curly) quotes; correct words typed with two initial capital letters; and capitalize the days of the week as you type.

Now that Barbara has created the table structure, she is ready to insert the components of the per diem allowance ("Maximum lodging expense allowance" and "Meals and incidental expense allowance") and their explanations in the table, as specified in Figure 3-1, Insert A. When she does, she'll make some intentional typing errors to see how AutoCorrect fixes them.

To enter the text in the table:

❶ Place the insertion point in the first cell in row 1, if it is not already there.

❷ Type **Maximum lodging expense allowance**. The end-of-cell mark moves to the right as you type within the cell.

❸ Press **[Tab]**. The insertion point moves to cell 2 in row 1.

   TROUBLE? If you accidentally press [Enter] instead of [Tab], you will create a new paragraph within a cell rather than move the insertion point to another cell. Simply delete the paragraph mark or click the Undo button 🔄 (or click Edit then click Undo Typing). Then press [Tab] to move to the next cell.

To see how AutoCorrect works, you'll make a typing error.

❹ Type **Teh** then press **[Spacebar]**. Notice how Word automatically corrects your typing mistake.

   TROUBLE? If the error is not corrected after you press [Spacebar], the AutoCorrect feature has been deactivated. Correct the error then type the remaining text for the explanation as shown in Figure 3-7, then skip to Step 7.

❺ Type **per diem rates authorized under this category**. When you reach the end of the first line in the cell, Word automatically wraps the insertion point to the next line, which increases the height of the cells across the entire row. By increasing the height of the cells, you can keep the explanation of the component next to the name of the per diem component.

The AutoCorrect feature also expands abbreviations you might substitute for text when typing. In the next step, you'll see how this works.

❻ Press **[Spacebar]**, type **incl** then press **[Spacebar]**. Notice how Word automatically expands the abbreviation "incl" to the complete word "include." Type the remaining explanation of the first term as shown in Figure 3-7.

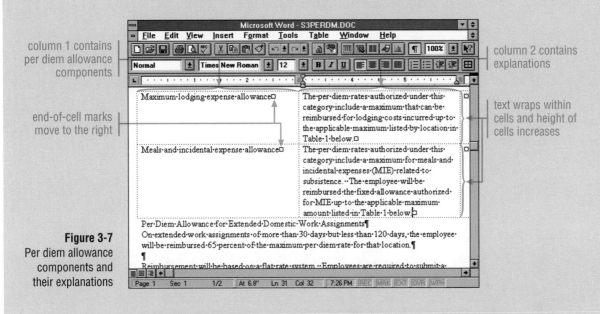

column 1 contains per diem allowance components

column 2 contains explanations

end-of-cell marks move to the right

text wraps within cells and height of cells increases

Figure 3-7
Per diem allowance components and their explanations

TROUBLE? Don't worry about correcting other errors now; you will edit the text later.

❼ Press **[Tab]**. The insertion point moves to cell 1 in row 2.
❽ Type **Meals and incidental expense allowance**, press **[Tab]**, then type its explanation as shown in Figure 3-7. This explanation also aligns next to its component name.
❾ Save the changes you have made.

Barbara next decides to create a table for the foreign travel per diem data that Nancy wants her to insert at the end of the Foreign Travel section (Figure 3-1, Insert C). Barbara thinks she needs a table structure that is four rows by four columns; she knows that if this is not the right size, she can easily change the table structure. She decides to use the Insert Table command to create this table.

Creating a Table Using the Insert Table Command

The Insert Table command on the Table menu displays the Insert Table dialog box. In this dialog box, you can specify additional features for your table that are not available with the Insert Table button, such as the exact width for each column or a predefined format for the table with the Table AutoFormat option. You can also have Word take you step by step through the creation of a table with the Table Wizard option.

Barbara will use the Insert Table command to create the table containing the foreign travel per diem data.

To insert the table using the Insert Table command:

❶ Scroll to the end of the document until you see the Exceptions heading, then place the insertion point in front of the "E" in Exceptions (Pg 2, Ln 17).

❷ Click **Table** then click **Insert Table….** The Insert Table dialog box appears.

❸ Click the **Number of Columns up arrow** until it reaches 4.

❹ Click the **Number of Rows up arrow** until it reaches 4. See Figure 3-8. Barbara decides to create evenly spaced columns so she leaves the Column Width setting at Auto.

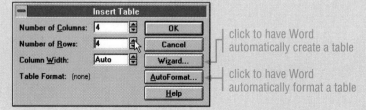

Figure 3-8
Insert Table
dialog box

click to have Word automatically create a table

click to have Word automatically format a table

❺ Click **OK** or press **[Enter]**. A blank 4 x 4 table appears on the screen, and the insertion point is placed in cell 1 of row 1. Notice that the columns are of equal width.

❻ Type the information for the table as shown in Figure 3-9. Remember to press [Tab] to move to the next cell; to move to a previous cell, press [Shift][Tab]. Leave the cells below the last column heading, Total Per Diem, blank for now.

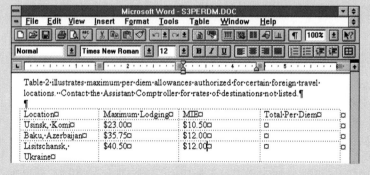

Figure 3-9
Completed Foreign
Travel Per Diem table

❼ Save the changes you have made.

Word provides several ways to insert an empty table structure in a document. Moreover, Word can convert existing text to a table so that you can lay out the information more easily.

Converting Existing Text to a Table

You can convert existing text that is consistently separated by paragraph marks, tabs, or commas to a table. Word uses these three types of characters to separate the selected text into cells.

REFERENCE WINDOW

Converting Text to a Table

- Select the text to be converted to a table.
- Click the Insert Table button on the Standard toolbar (or click Table then click Convert Text to Table...). If the selected text contains a variety of possible separator characters, such as paragraph marks, tabs, or commas, then the Convert Text to Table dialog box appears.
- Choose the appropriate option to convert the text to a table according to either the paragraph marks, tabs, or commas in the text.
- Click OK or press [Enter].

Barbara needs to convert to a table the data about the domestic travel per diem rates that Nancy originally typed. This text will be easy to convert because Nancy separated each piece of data with a tab and put a paragraph mark at the end of each line.

To convert the text to a table:

❶ Scroll through the document until you see the data for the domestic per diem rates (Pg 1, Ln 45). Notice that each piece of information in a row is separated by a tab character and that each row ends with a paragraph mark.

❷ Use the selection bar to select the rows from "Location..." through "Norfolk, Virginia..."

❸ Click the **Insert Table button** 🔳 on the Standard toolbar (or click **Table** then click **Insert Table...**). Because the text was originally separated by tabs, Word creates a table with four columns of equal width, replacing the tabs with column boundaries. Eventually Barbara will calculate the total per diem amounts to complete the last column of the table.

❹ Deselect the table. Notice that the table splits across the page break between pages 1 and 2. See Figure 3-10. By default, Word inserts the page break *within* a row if the entire row won't fit at the bottom of the page. Word does not move the entire row to the next page.

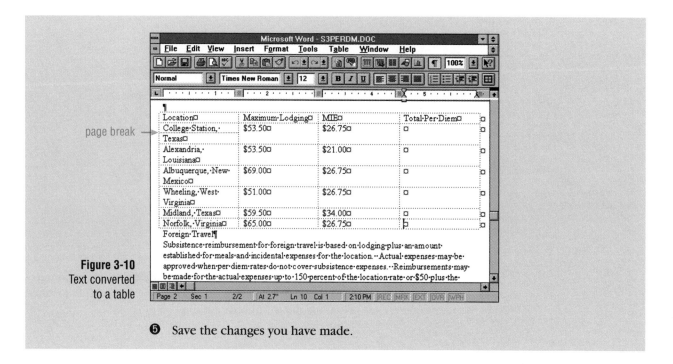

page break →

Figure 3-10
Text converted
to a table

❺   Save the changes you have made.

If you want to take a break and resume the tutorial at a later time, you can close the current document, then exit Word by double-clicking the Control menu box in the upper-left corner of the screen. When you want to resume the tutorial, start Word, place your Student Disk in the disk drive, then complete the screen check procedure described in Tutorial 1. Open the document S3PERDM.DOC, make sure the Gridlines option is activated on the Table menu, press [Shift][F5] to return to your last point in the document, then continue with the tutorial.

■   ■   ■

Barbara has several tasks to complete during the editing phase of the productivity strategy, some of which will be done more easily with the use of the Clipboard.

Using the Clipboard

The **Clipboard**, a standard feature in Windows applications, provides a temporary storage area for information that you need to copy or move from one location to another. To **copy** information means that the original text stays in its current location and a duplicate is created in a new location; to **move** information means that the original text is removed from its current location and placed in a new location. You would use the Clipboard when you need to copy or move information more than once or when you need to copy or move information between Word documents or between Word and other applications, such as spreadsheets. Clipboard operations using the Cut, Copy, and Paste commands from Word's Edit menu operate as they do in Windows. Word also provides Cut, Copy, and Paste buttons on the Standard toolbar.

Once you place information on the Clipboard by cutting or copying, you can paste the contents of the Clipboard as many times as you need. The contents of the Clipboard are overwritten, however, with any new text that you subsequently cut or copy.

Copying and Pasting Text

The Copy command is helpful when you need to use similarly worded text throughout a document. By using the Copy command, you eliminate possible keyboarding errors and you save time.

Barbara needs to add a second sentence to the end of the first paragraph after the heading, Per Diem Allowance for Extended Domestic Work Assignments, concerning work assignments of 120 days or more. The wording of the new sentence is similar to the first sentence with only a few corrections, so Barbara decides to copy the first sentence and paste it at the end of the paragraph; then she will edit the pasted sentence appropriately.

To copy and paste the sentence about per diem allowances:

❶ Place the insertion point in the first sentence of the first paragraph below the heading, Per Diem Allowance for Extended Domestic Work Assignments (Pg 1, Ln 34).

❷ Press **[Ctrl]** and click to select the entire sentence, including the period. Note that the ending paragraph mark is *not* selected. See Figure 3-11.

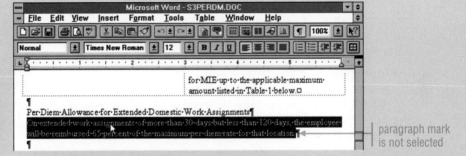

Figure 3-11
Selected sentence
to be copied

paragraph mark
is not selected

❸ Click the **Copy button** on the Standard toolbar (or click **Edit** then click **Copy**). The selected text is copied to the Clipboard and remains highlighted.

TROUBLE? If the selected text disappeared, you chose Cut instead of Copy. Click the Undo button on the Standard toolbar (or click Edit then click Undo Cut). Then repeat Steps 2 and 3.

❹ Place the insertion point after the period at the end of the selected sentence. The text is deselected.

❺ Click the **Paste button** on the Standard toolbar (or click **Edit** then click **Paste**). The copied selection appears at the insertion point, with one space between the two sentences. Adding spaces to pasted text is part of Word's Smart Cut and Paste feature.

Barbara wants two spaces between sentences, and she needs to edit the pasted sentence.

❻ Place the insertion point between the two sentences, press **[Spacebar]**, then edit the pasted sentence to read "On extended work assignments of *120 days or more*, the employee will be reimbursed *55* percent of the maximum per diem rate for that location." See Figure 3-12. Do not type the quotation marks or use italics.

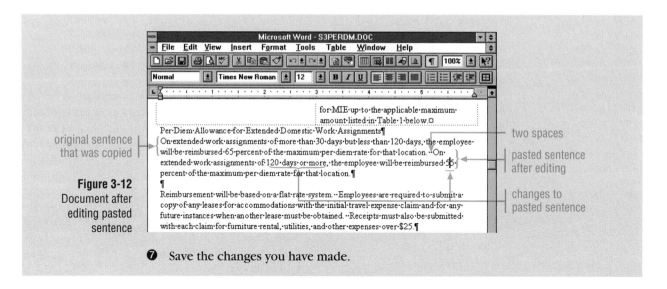

original sentence that was copied

Figure 3-12
Document after editing pasted sentence

two spaces

pasted sentence after editing

changes to pasted sentence

❼   Save the changes you have made.

Barbara checks Nancy's draft of the policy statement and sees that she needs to move the heading, Per Diem Allowance for Extended Domestic Work Assignments, and the two following paragraphs just before the Foreign Travel section.

Cutting and Pasting Text

In Tutorial 2 you used the drag-and-drop feature and the Move command to move text short distances within a document. These commands, however, do not place the selected text on the Clipboard. Using the Cut command places the selected text on the Clipboard so that you can paste the text as many times as you need.

Barbara will use the Cut and Paste buttons to move the heading about extended domestic work assignments and the two following paragraphs.

To cut and paste the heading and the two following paragraphs:

❶   Use the selection bar to select from the heading, Per Diem Allowance for Extended Domestic Work Assignments (Pg 1, Ln 33) through "...expenses over $25." Do not include the blank paragraph after the second paragraph. See Figure 3-13.

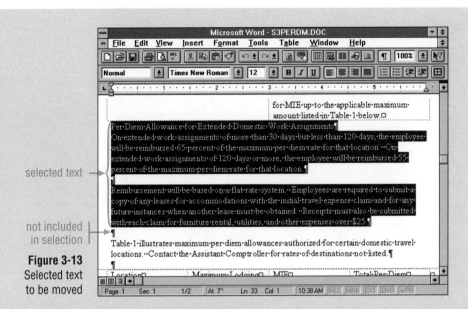

selected text ⟶

not included
in selection

Figure 3-13
Selected text
to be moved

❷ Click the **Cut button** 🔲 on the Standard toolbar (or click **Edit** then click **Cut**). The selected text disappears. The Clipboard now contains the cut text instead of the previously copied text.

Barbara wants to move the text to the end of the Domestic Travel section.

❸ Place the insertion point directly before the "F" in the Foreign Travel heading (Pg 2, Ln 2).

❹ Click the **Paste button** 🔲 on the Standard toolbar (or click **Edit** then click **Paste**). The cut text appears at the insertion point.

TROUBLE? If you moved the text to the wrong location, click the Undo button 🔲 on the Standard toolbar (or click Edit then click Undo Paste). The pasted text is removed from the document, but it still remains on the Clipboard. Place the insertion point in the correct location, then paste again.

❺ Scroll through the document to see that the cut text has been pasted to the correct location. See Figure 3-14.

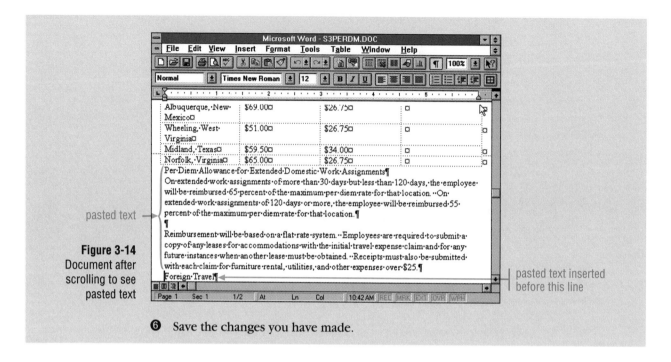

Figure 3-14
Document after
scrolling to see
pasted text

❻ Save the changes you have made.

Next, Barbara needs to put the same information at the end of the Foreign Travel section just before the Exceptions heading. Rather than retype it, she can paste that information again from the Clipboard, then edit the title appropriately.

To paste the heading and the two following paragraphs again:
❶ Place the insertion point in front of the "E" in the Exceptions heading at the end of the document (Pg 2, Ln 28).
❷ Click the **Paste button** 🗎 on the Standard toolbar (or click **Edit** then click **Paste**). The previously pasted text is pasted again in the new location.
❸ Scroll through the document to verify that the text has been pasted at the proper location.
❹ Select the word **Domestic** in the second occurrence of the pasted text and change it to **Foreign**.
❺ Save the changes you have made.

Barbara now sees some editorial changes she wants to make to Nancy's draft. She wants to replace references to "the company" or "company" with the acronym of the company's name—PIPSI—to make the travel expense policy sound less formal.

Finding and Replacing Text

In editing long documents, you often need to change every occurrence of a word or string of characters within the document. Word makes this process easy with the Replace command on the Edit menu. This command allows you to find specified text or formatting, then replace it with different text or formatting. Word can also find and replace special characters such as tabs, paragraph marks, and hyphens within your document. Word starts the process from the current location of the insertion point.

With the Replace command, you specify the text, formatting, or special characters that you want Word to search for and the text, formatting, or special characters that you want to substitute for the search text. Word searches for all instances of the text you have specified, even if it is part of another word. For instance, if you search for the word "win," Word would stop at Window, window, winter, or swindle as well as win.

Barbara wants to replace the phrase "the company" with PIPSI, and she wants PIPSI bolded. She can do both tasks at the same time.

To specify the text and formatting options for the search and replace operation:
❶ Place the insertion point at the beginning of the document.
❷ Click **Edit** then click **Replace....** The Replace dialog box appears.
❸ Type **the company** in the Find What text box.
❹ Press **[Tab]** to place the insertion point in the Replace With text box.
❺ Type **pipsi** in the Replace With text box.
❻ Click **Format** in the Replace section, then click **Font....** The Replace Font dialog box appears.
❼ Click **Bold** in the Font Style list box, then click the **All Caps check box** in the Effects section.
❽ Click **OK** or press **[Enter]**. The completed Replace dialog box appears with the formatting options to be applied to the replacement text specified. See Figure 3-15.

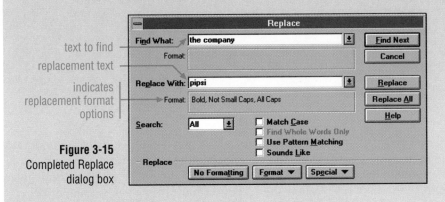

Figure 3-15
Completed Replace
dialog box

text to find
replacement text
indicates
replacement format
options

Now that the Find What and Replace With options are specified, Barbara is ready to start the replace process. Because Barbara wants to check each instance of "the company" to determine whether she wants to replace it with **PIPSI**, she'll use the Replace button instead of the Replace All button.

To replace the specified text:
❶ In the Replace dialog box, click **Find Next** or press **[Enter]** to start the replace process. Word begins the search and stops at "... with *the company*'s goals..." Remember, Word searches for all matches of the characters specified, not just whole words, unless the Find Whole Words Only option is selected in the Replace dialog box. Barbara decides to replace this instance of the search text with **PIPSI**.

TROUBLE? If the Replace dialog box obscures the highlighted text, drag the dialog box out of the way.

❷ Click **Replace**. Word resumes the search and stops at "... provisions of *the company*'s travel..." Barbara decides to replace this instance also.

❸ Click **Replace** or press [**Enter**]. Word resumes the search and stops at "*The company* officers..." The Match Case option was not specified, so Word ignores differences in capitalization. Barbara wants this instance replaced also.

❹ Click **Replace** or press [**Enter**]. The following message appears: Word has finished searching the document.

❺ Click **OK** or press [**Enter**].

❻ Click **Close** in the Replace dialog box.

❼ Scroll through your document to verify that the replacements were done correctly. See Figure 3-16.

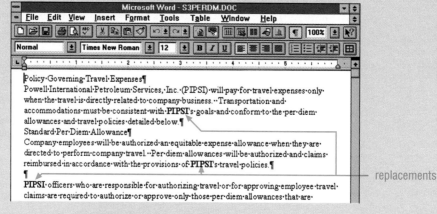

Figure 3-16
Document after replacing text

replacements

❽ Save the changes you have made.

Barbara next must edit the tables in the policy statement. She sees from Nancy's draft that the table she created in the Domestic Travel section, which contains the components of the per diem allowance and their explanations, must also be included in the Foreign Travel section. Also, some information she received from Al Simpson has shown her that she needs to add one location to the Foreign Travel Per Diem table and delete one location from the Domestic Travel Per Diem table. Barbara also decides that both the tables would be easier to read if the locations were arranged alphabetically. She also needs to calculate the total amounts in Tables 1 and 2, and finally, she wants to add captions to both tables.

Selecting Within a Table

To make all these editing changes in the tables, Barbara must select different parts of the table. You select text *within* cells just as you select text within a document. However, Word provides you with special techniques for selecting an *entire* cell, row, column, and the entire table. Once an area within a table is selected, you can follow the "select, then do" principle to modify it.

You are already familiar with using the selection bar to the left of your document to select text. Each element of a table—cell, row, column—also has its own selection bar. The selection bar for an individual cell is located at the left edge of the cell. The pointer changes to ⬁ when it moves into the cell selection bar, and it changes to ↓ when it moves into the column selection bar. Figure 3-17 describes different selection techniques for various elements of a table.

To:	Do this:	Or:	Or:
Select a cell	Click in the cell selection bar	Drag across the contents of a cell, including the end-of-cell mark	Press [Tab] to select the contents of the next cell
Select a row	Click in the row selection bar next to the row to be selected	Place the insertion point in the row to be selected, click Table, then click Select Row	Double-click in the cell selection bar of any cell in the row to be selected
Select a column	Click in the column selection bar above the column to be selected	Place the insertion point in the column to be selected, click Table, then click Select Column	
Select a table	Place the insertion point anywhere within the table to be selected, click Table, then click Select Table	Press [Alt][5] (on the numeric keypad) with Num Lock turned off	

Figure 3-17
Table selection
techniques

Barbara needs to add the components of the standard per diem and their explanations to the Foreign Travel section. She decides to copy that information from the Domestic Travel section and paste it. First she needs to select the table before copying it.

To select the table:
❶ Place the insertion point anywhere within the table created for the explanations of the per diem allowance components in the Domestic Travel section (beginning on Pg 1, Ln 20).
❷ Click **Table** then click **Select Table**. The entire table is selected.

TROUBLE? If the Select Table command is dimmed, you did not have the insertion point within the table before you chose Select Table from the Table menu. Repeat Steps 1 and 2.

Now Barbara is ready to copy the selected table, then paste it after the first paragraph of the Foreign Travel section.

To copy and paste the selected table:

❶ Click the **Copy button** 📋 on the Standard toolbar (or click **Edit** then click **Copy**). The selected table is copied to the Clipboard.

❷ Deselect the table.

❸ Place the insertion point in the blank line between the first and second paragraphs in the Foreign Travel section (Pg 2, Ln 19), then press **[Enter]** once. This inserts a blank line above the table.

❹ Click the **Paste button** 📋 on the Standard toolbar (or click **Edit** then click **Paste**). The copied table is pasted in its new location.

❺ Scroll through the document to verify that the table has been pasted correctly.

Barbara notices that she must change the pasted text to read Table 2 instead of Table 1.

❻ Change the two instances of Table 1 to Table 2 in the pasted table. See Figure 3-18.

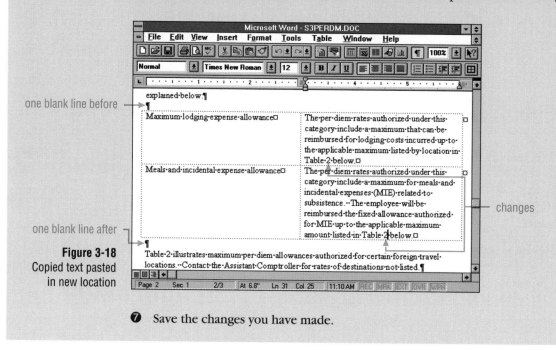

Figure 3-18
Copied text pasted
in new location

❼ Save the changes you have made.

Next, based on the information from Al Simpson, Barbara needs to add the other location to Table 2.

Modifying a Table Structure

When you originally create the structure for a table, you often do not know how many rows or columns you will actually need. However, you can easily modify or change a table's structure after creating it. Figure 3-19 describes the various ways to insert or delete rows or columns in a table.

To:	Within a table:	At the end of a table:
Insert a row	Select the entire row below the one you want to add, click Table, then click Insert Rows	Place the insertion point in the last cell of the last row, then press [Tab]
Insert a column	Select the entire column to the left of the one you want to add, click Table, then click Insert Columns	Select the end-of-row markers, click Table, then click Insert Columns
Delete a row	Select the entire row or rows you want to delete, click Table, then click Delete Rows	
Delete a column	Select the entire column or columns you want to delete, click Table, then click Delete Columns	

Figure 3-19
Techniques for inserting and deleting rows and columns

Barbara decides to insert the new location at the bottom of Table 2. To do so she must insert a row.

To insert a blank row at the bottom of Table 2 and add the information about the new location:

❶ Place the insertion point in the last cell of the last row in Table 2 (Pg 2, Ln 40). This cell is currently empty.

❷ Press **[Tab]**. A blank row is added to the bottom of the table with the same characteristics as the row above it.

   TROUBLE? If a blank row is not added to the bottom of the table, perhaps you did not have the insertion point in the last cell of the last row. Repeat Steps 1 and 2.

❸ Type **Radusny, Western Siberia** then press **[Tab]**; type **$23.00** then press **[Tab]**; type **$10.50**. See Figure 3-20.

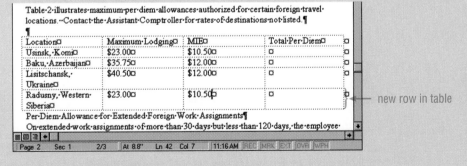

Figure 3-20
Table 2 after inserting row at bottom

❹ Save the changes you have made.

Barbara now needs to delete the row containing information about Wheeling, West Virginia, from Table 1 per instructions from Al Simpson.

With Word, you can delete either the *contents* of the cells in a selected row or the *entire row* from a table. To delete the contents of the cells in a selected row, just press the

Delete key. However, to delete the selected row entirely from the table structure, including the contents of the cells, you must choose the Delete Rows command from the Table menu.

According to Al Simpson, Barbara needs to remove the information about Wheeling, West Virginia, from Table 1 because PIPSI has completed work at the location and no longer sends employees there. Barbara decides to use the Shortcut Table menu, which contains the most often used commands for working with tables, to delete the row.

To delete the row for Wheeling, West Virginia, using the Shortcut Table menu:

❶ Place the insertion point in the Wheeling, West Virginia, row of Table 1 (Pg 1, Ln 44).

❷ Click **Table** then click **Select Row** (or double-click in the cell selection bar of any cell in the row).

To display the Shortcut Table menu, you simply place the insertion point within a table, then click the right mouse button.

❸ With the mouse pointer over the selected text, click the **right mouse button**. The Shortcut Table menu appears. See Figure 3-21.

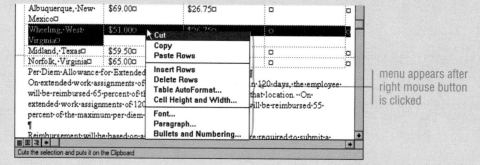

Figure 3-21
Shortcut Table menu

menu appears after right mouse button is clicked

❹ Click **Delete Rows**. The selected row is deleted from the table structure.

❺ Save the changes you have made.

Barbara has finished changing the table structure of the tables in her document by inserting and deleting rows.

The next editing change Barbara needs to make is to arrange the travel locations alphabetically in Tables 1 and 2.

Sorting Rows in a Table

Word allows you to sort information in alphabetical, numerical, or date order quickly and easily. The most common use for sorting is to rearrange rows in a table, but you can use the sorting feature to sort any list of information. You can sort a table by up to three columns within a table. Word recognizes whether or not your table contains a header row, that is, whether the first row of the table contains column headings.

Barbara decides to arrange the locations in Table 1 in alphabetical order.

To sort the information in Table 1:

❶ Place the insertion point anywhere within Table 1, if necessary.

❷ Click **Table** then click **Sort...**. The entire table is selected, and the Sort dialog box appears. See Figure 3-22.

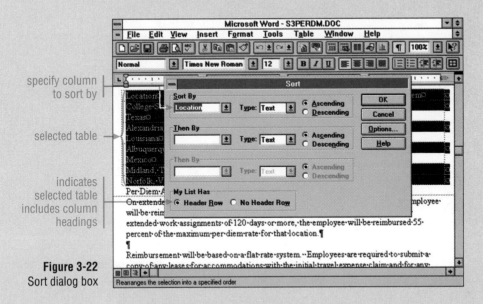

specify column to sort by

selected table

indicates selected table includes column headings

Figure 3-22
Sort dialog box

Barbara can sort by any column in the table, but she wants to sort by the Location column in *ascending* alphabetical order—that is, from A to Z—rather than in *descending* alphabetical order (from Z to A), so she doesn't need to change any of the settings in the dialog box. "Location" appears in the Sort By list box automatically because it is the first column heading in the table. Also, Word recognizes that the first row of the table contains the column headings; therefore, the Header Row option is selected in the My List Has section. This means that the contents of the first row will not be sorted. If you wanted to include the first row in the sort, you would click the No Header Row button.

❸ Click **OK** or press **[Enter]** then deselect the highlighted rows. Rows 2 through 6 of Table 1 are arranged alphabetically by the first word in the Location column. See Figure 3-23.

rows sorted alphabetically by first word in first column

Figure 3-23
Table 1 after sorting

TROUBLE? If the sort was unsuccessful, immediately click the Undo button ↺ on the Standard toolbar (or click Edit then click Undo Sort). Then repeat Steps 1 through 3.

Now Barbara needs to sort the locations in Table 2.

❹ Repeat Steps 1 through 3 to sort by location in Table 2. Deselect the table. See Figure 3-24.

rows sorted alphabetically by first word in first column

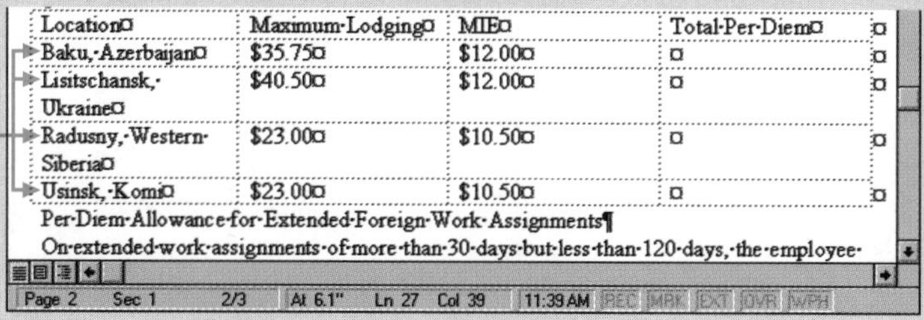

Figure 3-24
Table 2 after sorting

Location☐	Maximum·Lodging☐	MIE☐	Total·Per·Diem☐	☐
Baku,·Azerbaijan☐	$35.75☐	$12.00☐	☐	☐
Lisitschansk,·Ukraine☐	$40.50☐	$12.00☐	☐	☐
Radusny,·Western·Siberia☐	$23.00☐	$10.50☐	☐	☐
Usinsk,·Komi☐	$23.00☐	$10.50☐	☐	☐

Per·Diem·Allowance·for·Extended·Foreign·Work·Assignments¶
On·extended·work·assignments·of·more·than·30·days·but·less·than·120·days,·the·employee·

Page 2   Sec 1   2/3   At 6.1"   Ln 27   Col 39   11:39 AM REC MRK EXT OVR WPH

❺ Save the changes you have made.

Next, Barbara needs to calculate the total per diem allowed for each of the domestic and foreign locations.

Performing Mathematical Calculations in Tables

A popular use of tables is to display data, perhaps showing the results of a mathematical calculation like a sum of numbers. Word's Table Formula command allows you to perform simple calculations, such as adding, subtracting, multiplying, dividing, and calculating percentages, averages, and minimum and maximum values. For involved calculations, you would use a spreadsheet application like Microsoft Excel, then link or embed the spreadsheet in your Word document.

Barbara needs to calculate the total per diem values for the domestic and foreign locations. Because these are simple calculations, she decides to use Word's Table Formula command.

To calculate the total per diem values in Table 1 and Table 2:

❶ Place the insertion point in the last cell of the second row in Table 1(Pg 1, Ln 38).

❷ Click **Table** then click **Formula...**. The Formula dialog box appears. Word analyzes the table, then displays a formula based on the data in the table, in this case one that will sum all numbers in the cells to the left of the insertion point. This is the correct formula. See Figure 3-25.

indicates that numbers to the left of the insertion point will be summed

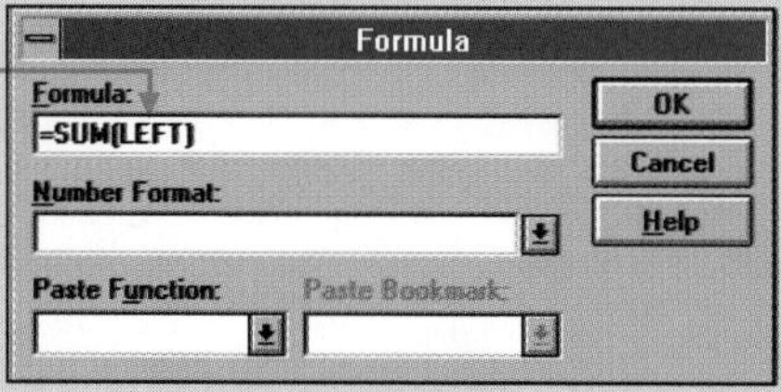

Figure 3-25
Formula dialog box

Formula	
Formula:	OK
=SUM(LEFT)	Cancel
Number Format:	Help
	±	
Paste Function:	Paste Bookmark:
±	±

❸ Click **OK** or press **[Enter]**. The sum of the two numbers ($95.75) appears, properly formatted as currency.

Barbara needs to repeat this procedure for each total needed in this table, as well as those in Table 2. She decides to use Word's Repeat command [F4], which repeats the last change made to a document.

❹ Place the insertion point in the next empty cell below, then press **[F4]**. The sum for that set of numbers appears.

❺ Repeat Step 4 for each of the remaining rows in Table 1, scroll to Table 2 (Pg 2, Ln 36), then repeat Step 4 for each row in it also. Pressing [F4] will not repeat the scrolling; it will still repeat the last command, which sums the row of numbers.

❻ Save the changes you have made.

If a value used in a calculation subsequently changes, the new result will not be automatically updated. You must delete the current answer, then choose the Table Formula command again.

Next, Barbara wants to insert captions identifying the tables because the document refers to them as Table 1 and Table 2.

Inserting a Caption

A **caption** is a number or title that identifies tables or figures in a document. The Insert Caption command allows you to add automatically numbered captions easily to tables and figures.

Barbara decides to insert table captions containing both a number and a title so that employees reading the travel expense policy can better identify the tables' contents.

To insert captions for Table 1 and Table 2:

❶ Select all the rows in Table 1, click **Insert**, then click **Caption....** The Caption dialog box appears with the text Table 1 inserted in the Caption text box. Word analyzes the selected text and inserts an appropriate label, in this instance Table. You can, however, change the caption label if you want.

❷ Type **.** (a period), press **[Spacebar]** twice, then type **Domestic Travel Per Diem**.

Barbara wants the captions to appear below the tables, so she needs to change the Position setting.

❸ If necessary, click the **Position list box down arrow**, then click **Below Selected Item**. See Figure 3-26.

caption for table ──

determines
placement of caption ──

Figure 3-26
Completed Caption
dialog box

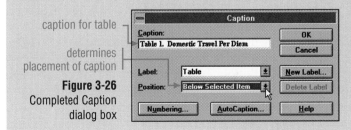

❹ Click **OK** or press **[Enter]**. The specified caption is inserted below Table 1. See Figure 3-27. Notice that Word applied a predefined set of formats, also called a style, to the caption, which you can change if you want. You will learn more about styles later in this tutorial.

Location¤	Maximum·Lodging¤	MIE¤	Total·Per·Diem¤	¤
College·Station,·Texas¤	$53.50¤	$26.75¤	$80.25¤	¤
Alexandria,·Louisiana¤	$53.50¤	$21.00¤	$74.50¤	¤
Albuquerque,·New·Mexico¤	$69.00¤	$26.75¤	$95.75¤	¤
Midland,·Texas¤	$59.50¤	$34.00¤	$93.50¤	¤
Norfolk,·Virginia¤	$65.00¤	$26.75¤	$91.75¤	¤

caption → **Table·1.··Domestic·Travel·Per·Diem**¶

Per·Diem·Allowance·for·Extended·Domestic·Work·Assignments¶
On·extended·work·assignments·of·more·than·30·days·but·less·than·120·days,·the·employee·

| Page 1 | Sec 1 | 1/2 | At 7" | Ln 32 | Col 88 | 1:40 PM | REC | MRK | EXT | OVR | WPH |

Figure 3-27
Caption below
Table 1

❺ Select all the rows in Table 2, then repeat Steps 1 through 4 to insert the following caption: **Table 2. Foreign Travel Per Diem**.
❻ Save the changes you have made.

If you delete a table with a numbered caption, Word will automatically renumber the captions for the remaining tables.

If you want to take a break and resume the tutorial at a later time, you can close the current document, then exit Word by double-clicking the Control menu box in the upper-left corner of the screen. When you want to resume the tutorial, start Word, place your Student Disk in the disk drive, then complete the screen check procedure described in Tutorial 1. Open the document S3PERDM.DOC, make sure the Gridlines option is activated on the Table menu, press [Shift][F5] to return to your last point in the document, then continue with the tutorial.

To follow the format used in the company policy manual, Barbara needs to insert page numbers at the top of her document on all pages but the first, and insert the title of the document and the revision date at the bottom of all pages.

Using Headers and Footers

As you learned in Tutorial 2, you should format a document starting with the page-level decisions, then proceed to the paragraph- and font-level decisions. One of Word's more popular page-level formatting features is the use of headers and footers.

A **header** is information that is repeated at the top of each page of a document. A **footer** is information that is repeated at the bottom of each page. In addition to including text in a header or footer, you can also insert page numbers, the date, and the time. You can format the contents of a header or footer just as you format text in the document, including inserting borders, rules, or graphics.

When you insert headers or footers in a document, Word changes to page layout view and the insertion point moves to the point in the document where the header will print. To speed the process of inserting headers or footers, Word provides you with a Header and Footer toolbar.

Inserting a Header

Barbara wants to insert the page number at the top right margin of all pages of her document except the first. It is a standard practice to omit the page number from the first page of a document.

To insert a header containing the page number:

❶ Press **[Ctrl][Home]** to move the insertion point to page 1, click **View**, then click **Header and Footer**. The Header and Footer toolbar appears, the insertion point is placed in the Header text area at the top of page 1 surrounded by a dashed line, the main text of the document becomes dimmed, and the screen changes to page layout view. See Figure 3-28.

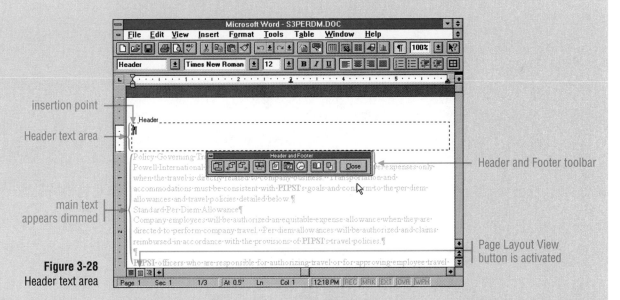

Figure 3-28
Header text area

TROUBLE? If the Header and Footer toolbar obscures the Header text area, drag the toolbar out of the way.

TROUBLE? Depending on the type of monitor you're using, the main text of the document might not appear on the screen; just continue with the tutorial.

Barbara does not want the header to appear on the first page.

❷ Click the **Page Setup button** 🖳 on the Header and Footer toolbar (or click **File** then click **Page Setup...**). The Layout tab of the Page Setup dialog box appears.

❸ Click the **Different First Page check box** in the Headers and Footers section. See Figure 3-29.

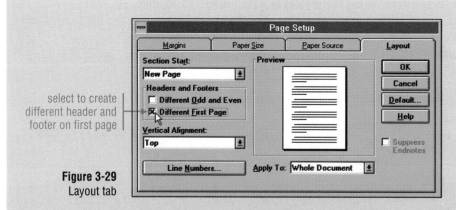

select to create different header and footer on first page

Figure 3-29
Layout tab

❹ Click **OK** or press **[Enter]**. You return to the document, but now the Header text area is labeled First Page Header. Any text typed here would print only on the first page.

Barbara does not want any text to appear in the header on the first page of the document so she can move to the Header text area on page 2.

❺ Click the **Show Next button** 🔲 on the Header and Footer toolbar. Notice that the insertion point moves to page 2. Now the Header text area is labeled "Header"; any text typed here would print on this and all subsequent pages. Notice also that the ruler in effect for the header is different from the ruler for the rest of the document: it contains a centered tab at the 3-inch mark and a right-aligned tab at the 6-inch mark, even with the right margin. Because header and footer text typically appears at the left margin, center, or right margin, Word provides formats for these text areas.

Barbara wants the page number of the document to appear at the right margin.

❻ Press **[Tab]** twice to move the insertion point to the right-aligned tab stop at the right margin of the Header text area.

❼ Click the **Page Numbers button** 🔲 on the Header and Footer toolbar. A page number appears at the right-aligned tab. Word also automatically places the correct page number on all subsequent pages of the document. See Figure 3-30.

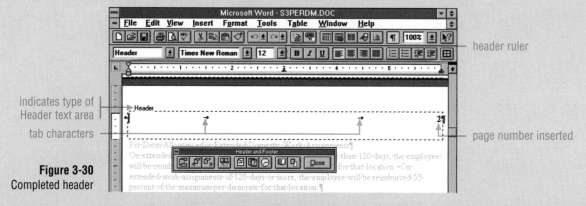

indicates type of Header text area

tab characters

header ruler

page number inserted

Figure 3-30
Completed header

❽ Click the **Close button** on the Header and Footer toolbar. You return to the document. Normal view does not display headers and footers; you need to switch to print preview (or page layout view) to see the header you just inserted.

⑨ Click the **Print Preview button** 🔍 on the Standard toolbar (or click **File** then click **Print Preview**). Notice that the header does not appear on page 1 but that it does appear on pages 2 and 3.

    TROUBLE? If you cannot see all three pages at one time in print preview, click the Multiple Pages button ▦ on the Print Preview toolbar, then drag across the grid to select three pages.

⑩ Click the **Close button** on the Print Preview toolbar. You return to the document in normal view.

Next Barbara wants to add a footer containing the text, Policy Governing Travel Expenses, and the current date.

Inserting a Footer

Even though Barbara wants the same footer information to appear on all pages, including the first, she must insert it twice—in both the First Page Footer text area and the Footer text area—because the Different First Page check box is selected in the Page Setup dialog box. This setting affects both headers and footers. She also wants the footer text to appear in 10-point bold type.

To insert the footer:

❶ Click **View** then click **Header and Footer**. The insertion point appears in the First Page Header text area of the document.

Barbara needs to switch to the First Page Footer text area.

❷ Click the **Switch Between Header and Footer button** 🔲 on the Header and Footer toolbar. The insertion point is placed in the First Page Footer text area.

Barbara wants the text "Policy Governing Travel Expenses" to appear at the left margin of the footer and the date to appear at the right.

❸ Type **Policy Governing Travel Expenses** then press **[Tab]** twice.

❹ Click the **Date button** 📅 on the Header and Footer toolbar. The current date appears. The date will be updated automatically each time the document is printed.

    TROUBLE? If you chose the wrong button from the Header and Footer toolbar, you must select the incorrect text, then press [Del] before inserting the correct text.

Barbara wants to format the footer text in 10-point bold type.

❺ Click in the selection bar to select the entire footer, then use the Formatting toolbar to change the font format to 10 point and bold. Deselect the text. See Figure 3-31. Note that the date shown on your screen will be different from the one shown in the figure.

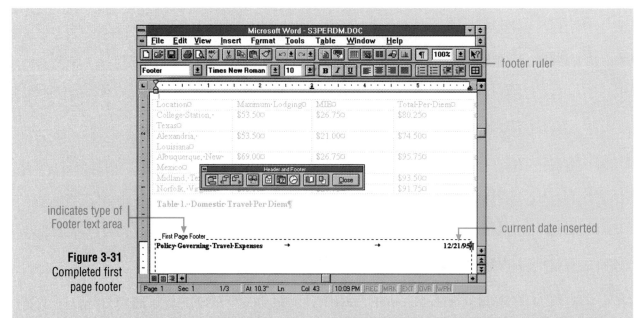

indicates type of
Footer text area

current date inserted

Figure 3-31
Completed first
page footer

Barbara decides to use the Copy and Paste buttons to copy the footer information from the First Page Footer text area to the Footer text area. Copying and pasting the footer eliminates the need to type and format the text again, and ensures that the same text appears in the footer on all pages.

❻ Click in the selection bar to select the entire footer, then click the **Copy button** 📋 on the Standard toolbar (or click **Edit** then click **Copy**).

❼ Click the **Show Next button** 🔲 on the Header and Footer toolbar to move the insertion point to the Footer text area.

❽ Click the **Paste button** 📋 on the Standard toolbar (or click **Edit** then click **Paste**) to paste the copied text in the Footer text area. You need to insert the footer on page 2 only, and it will appear on all remaining pages.

❾ Click the **Close button** on the Header and Footer toolbar to return to your document.

Barbara wants to view the document in print preview to make sure she entered the footer information correctly.

To view the footer information in print preview:

❶ Click the **Print Preview button** 🔍 on the Standard toolbar (or click **File** then click **Print Preview**). Notice that the footer appears on all pages of the document.

TROUBLE? If you cannot see all three pages at one time in print preview, click the Multiple Pages button 🔲 on the Print Preview toolbar, then drag across the grid to select three pages.

❷ Click the **Close button** on the Print Preview toolbar to return to the document in normal view.

❸ Save the changes you have made.

Barbara wants the different parts of her document to be attractively formatted with a variety of paragraph and font formats. She doesn't, however, want to take the time to select each of the different parts and then directly apply formats one at a time. She decides to use Word's Style feature to speed up the formatting process.

Using Styles

In Tutorial 2 you used direct formatting to change the appearance of text within your document. Another method for changing the formatting of a document is to use Word's style feature. A **character style** is a collection of font formatting options that you save and reuse. A **paragraph style** is a collection of font and paragraph formatting options that you save and reuse. A paragraph style can include any and all of the following formatting options: tab settings, font, point size, type style, line spacing, borders, and indents. Rather than apply each formatting option individually, you apply a style that contains all the formatting options you want. A **style sheet** is a listing, which you can print, that describes the formatting characteristics of each style used in a document.

Each Word document comes with a set of standard paragraph styles: Normal (the default paragraph style for a Word document), Heading 1, Heading 2, and Heading 3. Word also contains a default character style called Default Paragraph Font. The current style is shown in the Style list box on the Formatting toolbar, and all styles available in a document are listed in the Style list, which you display by clicking the down arrow next to the Style list box. You can also use the Format Style command to view the paragraph and font attributes of each style in use. When certain other features, such as headers, footers, and captions, are used in a document, their styles are automatically added to the list.

You can define your own styles for use in documents, or you can use the predefined styles in Word's templates. A **document template** is a pattern, or model, on which a document is built. All documents based on a template take on the features defined for that template. In addition to its styles, a template's features can include boilerplate, or standard, text and specialized menu bars, toolbars, or keyboard shortcuts. These defined features help to automate the production of a document.

The NORMAL template is Word's default template, but Word contains many templates for other types of typical business communications. Figure 3-32 lists the names of the predefined templates available in Word. The file extension for a Word template is "DOT."

BROCHURE1	DIRECTR1	FAXCOVR1	FAXCOVR2
INVOICE	LETTER1	LETTER2	LETTER3
MANUAL1	MANUSCR1	MANUSCR3	MEMO1
MEMO2	MEMO3	NORMAL	PRESENT1
PRESREL1	PRESREL2	PRESREL3	PURCHORD
REPORT1	REPORT2	REPORT3	RESUME1
RESUME2A	RESUME4	THESIS1	WEEKTIME

Figure 3-32
Word's templates

To use the styles in one of the predefined templates, you can choose a template other than NORMAL when you first create a document, or you can *attach* a template to a document you've already created using the NORMAL template.

REFERENCE WINDOW

Attaching a Template to the Current Document

- Click File then click Templates…. The Templates and Add-ins dialog box appears.
- Click the Automatically Update Document Styles check box.
- Click Attach…. The Attach Template dialog box appears with all of Word's predefined templates listed.
- Click the template to be attached, then click OK or press [Enter] to close the Attach Template dialog box.
- Click OK or press [Enter] to close the Templates and Add-ins dialog box.

If you want to preview the predefined styles of a template before attaching it to the current document, you can use Word's Style Gallery feature. You can preview the styles of any template or document by using this feature.

Barbara's document contains several levels of headings, and she wants to differentiate among them with different paragraph styles. She decides to use the predefined styles of the MANUAL1 template. It has been a while since she used this template, so she decides to review its styles using Word's Style Gallery feature.

To use the Style Gallery to preview the MANUAL1 template styles:

❶ Click the **Style list box down arrow**. The list of styles assigned to the NORMAL template appears. The paragraph styles are bolded, and the character styles are shown in lighter type. Press **[Esc]** to close the list without selecting any styles.

❷ Click **Format** then click **Style Gallery…**. The Style Gallery dialog box appears with the current document displayed in the Preview section.

Barbara wants to review each style assigned to the MANUAL1 template.

❸ Click **Manual1** then click the **Style Samples radio button**. Each style defined for this template is displayed with the specific paragraph and font formatting characteristics applied to sample text. See Figure 3-33.

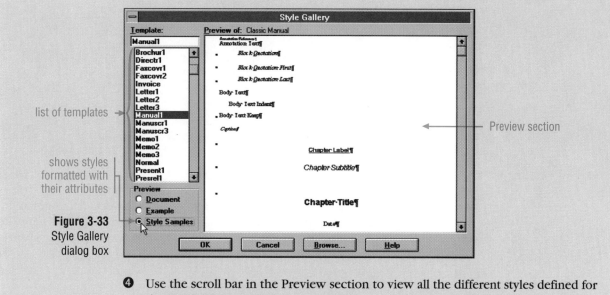

list of templates →

shows styles
formatted with
their attributes

Figure 3-33
Style Gallery
dialog box

Preview section ←

❹ Use the scroll bar in the Preview section to view all the different styles defined for the MANUAL1 template.

❺ Click **Cancel** to return to the document.

Barbara wants to attach the MANUAL1 template to her current document so she can use the styles provided in the template. Note that any existing style in Barbara's document having the same name as a style in the new template she attaches will be overwritten by the new style.

To attach the MANUAL1 template to the document:

❶ Click **File** then click **Templates....** The Templates and Add-ins dialog box appears with "normal" in the Document Template text box.

❷ Click **Attach....** The Attach Template dialog box appears. Only the template files are listed in the File Name list box. See Figure 3-34.

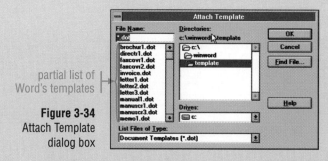

partial list of
Word's templates

Figure 3-34
Attach Template
dialog box

❸ Click **manual1.dot**, then click **OK** or press [Enter]. You return to the Templates and Add-ins dialog box; the name and file location of the new template now appear in the Document Template text box.

❹ Click the **Automatically Update Document Styles check box** to update your document with the new styles.

⑤ Click **OK** or press **[Enter]** to return to the document. Notice that the font size in your document has changed to 10 point, which is the default font size for the MANUAL1 template.

Barbara must change the font size for the entire document to 12 point.

⑥ Click **Edit**, click **Select All**, then change the font size to 12 point.

⑦ Click the **Style list box down arrow**. Scroll through the list to see that all the styles of the MANUAL1 template have been copied to the document.

⑧ Press **[Esc]** to close the list without making any choices.

⑨ Save the changes you have made.

Barbara's document contains several levels of headings, and she decides to differentiate among them by using different paragraph styles. She attached the MANUAL1 template to her document so she could use its predefined styles. Now she needs to apply those styles.

Applying Styles

Once you determine which styles you want to use—either Word's default styles or styles that you define—you must apply them to the text in your document to format it. The easiest way to apply a style to selected text is to use the Style list box.

Barbara is ready to apply paragraph styles to her document.

To apply paragraph styles to selected text using the Style list box:

① Click anywhere within the document title, **Policy Governing Travel Expenses**.

② Click the **Style list box down arrow** on the Formatting toolbar to open the Style list. Scroll through the list, then click **Title**. The combination of paragraph and font formatting attributes assigned to the Title style is applied to the selected paragraph. See Figure 3-35. Note that a small black box appears in the margin indicating that the text was formatted with one of Word's predefined styles. This box does not appear for text formatted with user-defined styles.

font format attributes applied

current style

indicates text formatted with predefined style

text formatted with Title style

Figure 3-35
Title style applied

While she can see from the Formatting toolbar that the font format has changed, Barbara wants to review the exact attributes assigned to the Title style.

Using Reveal Formats

The Reveal Formats feature allows you to display information about the formatting that has been applied to paragraphs or characters either directly (as you learned in Tutorial 2) or through the use of styles. To use the Reveal Formats feature, click the Help button on the Standard toolbar, then click the Help pointer on the character or paragraph you want information about. Word displays an information box describing the formatting applied to the selected text. To dismiss the information box, press [Esc] or click the Help button.

To check the formats applied to the title:

❶ Click the **Help button** on the Standard toolbar, then click anywhere in the title, **Policy Governing Travel Expenses**. The Reveal Formats box appears. See Figure 3-36. The description indicates that the font used in the Title style has the following font formatting: Arial, 20 pt, bold; and the following paragraph formatting: a blank line equal to 18 pt inserted above the paragraph and a blank line equal to 8 pt inserted below the paragraph. Notice that no direct formatting has been applied to this text.

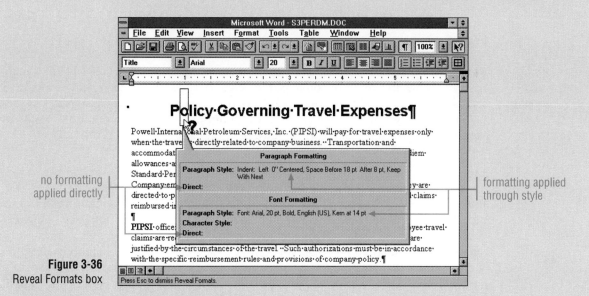

Figure 3-36
Reveal Formats box

❷ Press **[Esc]** or click to close the Reveal Formats box.

Barbara continues to apply styles to the rest of the document.

❸ Click anywhere within the **Standard Per Diem Allowance** heading (Pg 1, Ln 6) to select it.

❹ Click the **Style list box down arrow** on the Formatting toolbar, then click **Heading 1**. The formatting attributes for the Heading 1 style are applied to the selected text. Use the Reveal Formats feature to determine the attributes applied to the selected heading.

❺ Click anywhere in the **Domestic Travel** heading (Pg 1, Ln 15), click the **Style list box down arrow**, then click **Heading 1**. The formatting attributes of the Heading 1 style are applied to the selected paragraph.

❻ Click anywhere in the heading, **Per Diem Allowance for Extended Domestic Work Assignments** (Pg 2, Ln 8), click the **Style list box down arrow**, then click **Heading 2**. The Heading 2 style is applied to the selected text.

Barbara also notices that the Caption style has been applied to the table caption, which is now in italics and a smaller point size. Recall that when you attach a new template to a document, any style in the document having the same name as a style in the new template is overwritten by the new style. Use the Reveal Formats feature to determine the attributes applied to the selected heading.

❼ Repeat Steps 5 and 6 for those similar headings in the Foreign Travel section.

❽ Click anywhere in the **Exceptions** heading, click the **Style list box down arrow**, then click **Heading 1**.

❾ Save the changes you have made.

Barbara is now ready to format the tables in her document.

Formatting Tables

Word provides a variety of features to enhance the appearance of tables in documents. You can change the width of columns, the height of rows, or the alignment of text within cells; and you can place borders around cells, parts of a table, or the entire table.

First, Barbara wants to decrease the width of the first column in the side-by-side text paragraphs so that this table takes up fewer lines.

Changing Column Width

You sometimes need to adjust the width of the columns in a table to improve its appearance. If you need the column to be a precise measurement, use the Table Cell Height and Width command so that you can specify the exact width of the column. Otherwise you can drag either the right column marker on the ruler or the right column boundary (gridline) of the column you want to change to the desired position. All other columns to the right are resized proportionally, but the overall width of the table does not change. For more information about other options for adjusting the width of a column, see the *Microsoft Word User's Guide*.

Barbara wants to decrease the width of the first column in the side-by-side text paragraphs to 1.5 inches. She decides to do so by dragging the column boundary, using the ruler as a guide.

To change the width of the first column by dragging the column boundary:

❶ Place the insertion point anywhere in the table containing the side-by-side text paragraphs in the Domestic Travel section (beginning Pg 1, Ln 20). Make sure that you do not have any cells selected.

❷ Move the mouse pointer over the boundary between columns 1 and 2. The mouse pointer changes to ↔.

❸ Click and drag the pointer to the 1.5" mark on the ruler, then release the mouse button. Notice that as the first column decreases in width, the second column increases, but the overall width of the table does not change.

Barbara wants to make two other formatting changes to the table: she wants to increase the space between the two rows and bold the text in the first column.

To finish making formatting changes to the table:
❶ Place the insertion point in row 1 of the table, click the **right mouse button** to display the Table Shortcut menu, then click **Paragraph....** The Paragraph dialog box appears.
❷ Increase the Spacing After box to **12 pt**, then click **OK** or press **[Enter]**.
❸ Select the first column of text, then click the **Bold button** **B** on the Formatting toolbar. Deselect the selected cells. See Figure 3-37.

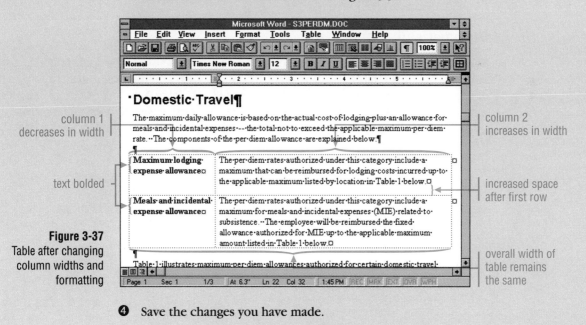

column 1 decreases in width

column 2 increases in width

text bolded

increased space after first row

Figure 3-37
Table after changing column widths and formatting

overall width of table remains the same

❹ Save the changes you have made.

Next Barbara needs to make the same formatting changes to the same table in the Foreign Travel section of the document. This time she'll use the column marker instead of the column boundary to change the column width.

To format the table in the Foreign Travel section:
❶ Place the insertion point in the table containing side-by-side text paragraphs in the Foreign Travel section of the document (beginning Pg 2, Ln 21).
❷ Move the mouse pointer over the column marker in the ruler between columns 1 and 2. The mouse pointer changes to ↔.

❸ Click and drag the column marker to the 1.5" mark on the ruler, then release the mouse button.

❹ Place the insertion point in row 1 of the table, click the **right mouse button** to display the Table Shortcut menu, then click **Paragraph...** The Paragraph dialog box appears.

❺ Increase the Spacing After box to **12 pt**, then click **OK** or press **[Enter]**.

❻ Select the first column of text, then click the **Bold button** B on the Formatting toolbar. Deselect the selected cells.

❼ Save the changes you have made.

Word also allows you to change the width of selected individual cells or groups of cells within a table. You would follow the same procedures to change their widths as you do for changing entire columns.

Next, Barbara decides to use the Table AutoFormat command on the Table menu to add borders and shading to Tables 1 and 2.

Automatically Formatting Tables

You can add borders, rules, and shading to tables just as you do for text: first select the table or part of the table that you want to outline with a border, then make appropriate option choices from the Borders toolbar. However, the Table AutoFormat command makes it much easier to create professionally formatted tables using a predefined table format.

Barbara will use Table AutoFormat to add borders and shading to Tables 1 and 2 automatically.

To add borders and shading to the tables using the Table AutoFormat command:

❶ Place the insertion point in Table 1, click **Table**, then click **Table AutoFormat...** The Table AutoFormat dialog box appears.

Barbara is not sure which format she wants to use so she decides to explore her options.

❷ Click several different table format options in the Formats list to view the various formats available.

Barbara decides that the Classic 2 format is the one that suits her data the best.

❸ Click **Classic 2**. See Figure 3-38. Barbara wants Word to adjust the width of the column so that each column is only as wide as the longest item in the column, so she leaves the AutoFit option in the Formats to Apply section activated.

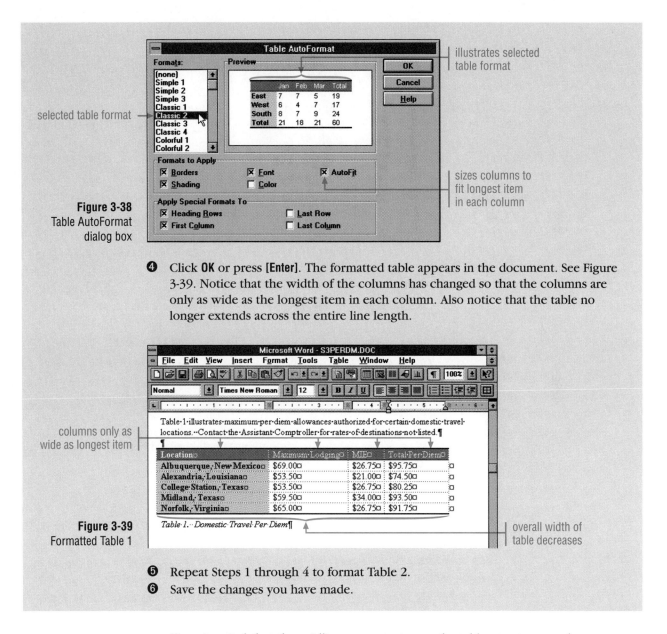

illustrates selected
table format

selected table format ———

sizes columns to
fit longest item
in each column

Figure 3-38
Table AutoFormat
dialog box

❹ Click **OK** or press **[Enter]**. The formatted table appears in the document. See Figure 3-39. Notice that the width of the columns has changed so that the columns are only as wide as the longest item in each column. Also notice that the table no longer extends across the entire line length.

columns only as
wide as longest item

Figure 3-39
Formatted Table 1

overall width of
table decreases

❺ Repeat Steps 1 through 4 to format Table 2.
❻ Save the changes you have made.

Keep in mind that the gridlines you use to see the table structure on the screen are not the same as the borders that you apply using the Borders toolbar or the Table AutoFormat command; gridlines do not print.

Next Barbara decides to center the table across the page, center the dollar amounts within the cells, and center the caption below the table.

Centering a Table

If a table does not take up the entire width of a line, you might want to center it between the left and right margins. If you use the Center button on the Formatting toolbar to center a selected table, the *text* within the cells is centered between each cell boundary; the table is not centered across the page. To center a table, you must use the Table Cell Height and Width command.

Barbara begins by centering Table 1.

To center Table 1 across the page, then center the column headings:
1. Place the insertion point anywhere within Table 1, click **Table**, then click **Cell Height and Width....** The Cell Height and Width dialog box appears.
2. Click the **Row tab**, if necessary. The Row tab appears.
3. Click the **Center radio button** in the Alignment section. See Figure 3-40.

centers table
across the page

Figure 3-40
Row tab

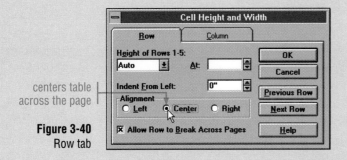

4. Click **OK** or press **[Enter]**. Table 1 is adjusted so that it is centered across the page.

Next Barbara wants to center the column headings for Table 1. She must first select the row containing the column headings.
5. Select the first row, then click the **Center button** ≣ on the Formatting toolbar.

Barbara wants to center the dollar amounts within Table 1. She must first select only the cells in the table that contain dollar amounts.

To center the text in the cells containing dollar amounts in Table 1:
1. Click in the cell selection bar of the first dollar amount, $69.00 (Maximum Lodging amount for Albuquerque, New Mexico). The entire cell is selected.
2. Press the mouse button, drag through $91.75 (Maximum Per Diem amount for Norfolk, Virginia), then release the mouse button.

TROUBLE? Just the dollar amounts within the table should be highlighted. If not, click the Undo button ↶ (or click Edit then click Undo), then start again.

3. Click the **Center button** ≣ on the Formatting toolbar. Just the highlighted dollar amounts are centered. Deselect the text.
4. Save the changes you have made.

Next Barbara wants the caption centered across the page below Table 1.

To center the caption for Table 1:
1. Click anywhere within the caption for Table 1.
2. Click the **Center button** ≣ on the Formatting toolbar. See Figure 3-41.

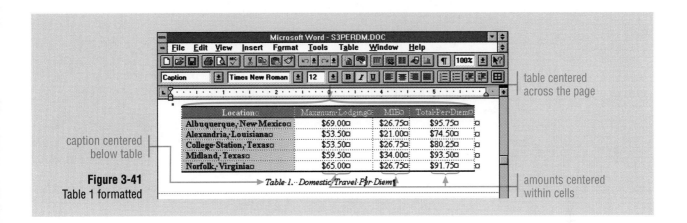

caption centered
below table

Figure 3-41
Table 1 formatted

table centered
across the page

amounts centered
within cells

Barbara has applied formatting changes to Table 1. She now needs to make the same format changes to Table 2 (Pg 2, Ln 31). Use what you have learned in the preceding steps to help you make the changes to this table.

To apply format changes to Table 2:
❶ Center the table across the page, then center the column headings.
❷ Center the dollar amounts.
❸ Center the caption under Table 2. See Figure 3-42.

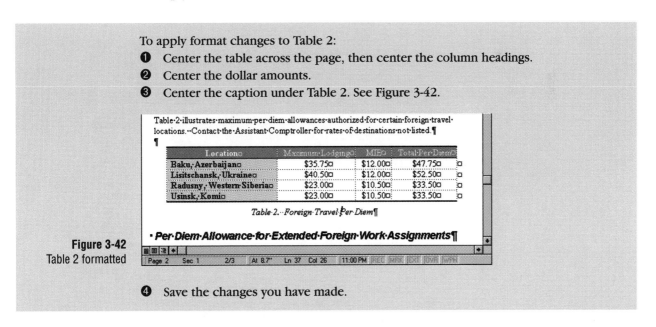

Figure 3-42
Table 2 formatted

❹ Save the changes you have made.

Barbara has finished formatting her document and now is ready to spell check, preview, then print it.

To spell check, preview, then print the document:
❶ Click the **Spelling button** 📝 on the Standard toolbar (or click **Tools** then click **Spelling...**). Complete the spell check following the procedures you learned in Tutorial 1, then save your changes as necessary.
❷ Click the **Print Preview button** 🔍 on the Standard toolbar (or click **File** then click **Print Preview**).

❸ If necessary, click the **Multiple Pages button** 🔳 on the Print Preview toolbar, then select three pages to display all pages of the document.
❹ Click the **Print button** 🖨 on the Print Preview toolbar to print the document.
❺ Click the **Close button** on the Print Preview toolbar. You return to the document.
❻ Close the document then exit Word.

Barbara's completed document appears in Figure 3-43 on this page and the following two pages.

Policy Governing Travel Expenses

Powell International Petroleum Services, Inc. (PIPSI) will pay for travel expenses only when the travel is directly related to company business. Transportation and accommodations must be consistent with **PIPSI**'s goals and conform to the per diem allowances and travel policies detailed below.

Standard Per Diem Allowance

Company employees will be authorized an equitable expense allowance when they are directed to perform company travel. Per diem allowances will be authorized and claims reimbursed in accordance with the provisions of **PIPSI**'s travel policies.

PIPSI officers who are responsible for authorizing travel or for approving employee travel claims are required to authorize or approve only those per diem allowances that are justified by the circumstances of the travel. Such authorizations must be in accordance with the specific reimbursement rules and provisions of company policy.

Domestic Travel

The maximum daily allowance is based on the actual cost of lodging plus an allowance for meals and incidental expenses -- the total not to exceed the applicable maximum per diem rate. The components of the per diem allowance are explained below:

Maximum lodging expense allowance   The per diem rates authorized under this category include a maximum that can be reimbursed for lodging costs incurred up to the applicable maximum listed by location in Table 1 below.

Meals and incidental expense allowance   The per diem rates authorized under this category include a maximum for meals and incidental expenses (MIE) related to subsistence. The employee will be reimbursed the fixed allowance authorized for MIE up to the applicable maximum amount listed in Table 1 below.

Table 1 illustrates maximum per diem allowances authorized for certain domestic travel locations. Contact the Assistant Comptroller for rates of destinations not listed.

Location	Maximum Lodging	MIE	Total Per Diem
Albuquerque, New Mexico	$69.00	$26.75	$95.75
Alexandria, Louisiana	$53.50	$21.00	$74.50
College Station, Texas	$53.50	$26.75	$80.25
Midland, Texas	$59.50	$34.00	$93.50
Norfolk, Virginia	$65.00	$26.75	$91.75

Table 1. Domestic Travel Per Diem

Policy Governing Travel Expenses   12/21/95

Figure 3-43
Completed document
(page 1 of 3)

2

Per Diem Allowance for Extended Domestic Work Assignments

On extended work assignments of more than 30 days but less than 120 days, the employee will be reimbursed 65 percent of the maximum per diem rate for that location. On extended work assignments of 120 days or more, the employee will be reimbursed 55 percent of the maximum per diem rate for that location.

Reimbursement will be based on a flat rate system. Employees are required to submit a copy of any leases for accommodations with the initial travel expense claim and for any future instances when another lease must be obtained. Receipts must also be submitted with each claim for furniture rental, utilities, and other expenses over $25.

Foreign Travel

Subsistence reimbursement for foreign travel is based on lodging plus an amount established for meals and incidental expenses for the location. Actual expenses may be approved when per diem rates do not cover subsistence expenses. Reimbursements may be made for the actual expenses up to 150 percent of the location rate or $50 plus the location rate, whichever is greater. The components of the per diem allowance are explained below:

Maximum lodging expense allowance	The per diem rates authorized under this category include a maximum that can be reimbursed for lodging costs incurred up to the applicable maximum listed by location in Table 2 below.
Meals and incidental expense allowance	The per diem rates authorized under this category include a maximum for meals and incidental expenses (MIE) related to subsistence. The employee will be reimbursed the fixed allowance authorized for MIE up to the applicable maximum amount listed in Table 2 below.

Table 2 illustrates maximum per diem allowances authorized for certain foreign travel locations. Contact the Assistant Comptroller for rates of destinations not listed.

Location	Maximum Lodging	MIE	Total Per Diem
Baku, Azerbaijan	$35.75	$12.00	$47.75
Lisitschansk, Ukraine	$40.50	$12.00	$52.50
Radusny, Western Siberia	$23.00	$10.50	$33.50
Usinsk, Komi	$23.00	$10.50	$33.50

Table 2. Foreign Travel Per Diem

Per Diem Allowance for Extended Foreign Work Assignments

On extended work assignments of more than 30 days but less than 120 days, the employee will be reimbursed 65 percent of the maximum per diem rate for that location. On

Figure 3-43
Completed document
(page 2 of 3)

3

extended work assignments of 120 days or more, the employee will be reimbursed 55 percent of the maximum per diem rate for that location.

Reimbursement will be based on a flat rate system. Employees are required to submit a copy of any leases for accommodations with the initial travel expense claim and for any future instances when another lease must be obtained. Receipts must also be submitted with each claim for furniture rental, utilities, and other expenses over $25.

Exceptions

Any exceptions to the standard per diem allowance must be submitted in writing to the Assistant Comptroller's office.

Policy Governing Travel Expenses   **12/21/95**

Figure 3-43
Completed document
(page 3 of 3)

Barbara faxes Nancy a copy of the finished travel expense policy. Nancy is pleased with the document's appearance and gives Barbara her approval to submit it to management.

Questions

1. Describe three methods for creating tables.
2. Describe the elements of a table.
3. Explain the purpose of the AutoCorrect feature.
4. Explain the difference between the Cut and Paste procedure and the Copy and Paste procedure.
5. Explain the purpose of the Replace command on the Edit menu.
6. Explain the process for inserting a row:
   a. Between existing rows of a table
   b. At the bottom of a table
7. Explain the procedure for inserting a column:
   a. Between existing columns of a table
   b. At the end of a table
8. Explain the procedure for sorting information within a table.
9. What is the function key that repeats the last change to a document?
10. Explain the procedure for adding a caption to a table.
11. Explain the difference between a header and a footer.
12. Briefly define each of the following terms:
    a. template
    b. paragraph style
    c. character style
    d. style sheet
13. Describe the procedure for attaching a template other than the NORMAL template to the current document.
14. Describe the procedure for using the Style Gallery to preview a template's styles.
15. Describe the different methods for changing column widths.
16. Describe the procedure for using the Table AutoFormat command to apply formatting to a table.

Use Word Help to answer Questions 17 through 23.

E 17. What is a Table Wizard?

E 18. How do you copy and paste or cut and paste from one Word document to another Word document?

E 19. How do you print the style sheet for a document?

E 20. What is the purpose of the Find command on the Edit menu?

E 21. What is the procedure to merge cells within a table?

E 22. How do you change the numbering format used in a caption?

E 23. How do you print a range of pages within a document?

Tutorial Assignments

Start Word, if necessary, and conduct a screen check. Open the file T3PIPSI1.DOC from your Student Disk, then complete the following:

1. Save the document as S3PIPSI1.DOC.
2. Move the entire Domestic Travel section after the Foreign Travel section.
3. Change all occurrences of "company" to PIPSI (not bolded).

4. Change the header so that:
   a. The page number is centered rather than at the right margin.
   b. It is Arial 12 point bold.
   c. It does not print on the first page.
5. Apply the Heading 1 style to the heading Standard Per Diem Allowance.
6. Apply the Heading 2 style to the headings Domestic Travel and Foreign Travel.
7. Apply the Heading 3 style to the Per Diem Allowance for Extended Work Assignments headings in both sections.

E

8. Replace all instances of three consecutive paragraph marks with one paragraph mark.
9. Save your changes.
10. Preview, print, then close the document.

Open the file T3PIPSI2.DOC from your Student Disk, then complete the following:
11. Save the document as S3PIPSI2.DOC.
12. Decrease the width of the column containing the component names (Maximum lodging expense allowance and Meals and incidental expense allowance) to 1.25 inches without decreasing the overall width of the table.
13. Bold and center the component names, then change the font to Arial.
14. Insert a 12 point blank line after row 1 of the side-by-side text table, which explains the per diem components.
15. Insert a row at the top of the Foreign Travel Per Diem table to contain column headings: Location (in cell 1), Maximum Lodging (in cell 2), MIE (in cell 3), and Total Per Diem (in cell 4).
16. Insert the two rows of information shown in Figure 3-44 at the bottom of the Foreign Travel Per Diem table without changing the overall width of the table.

Figure 3-44

| Volgograd, Russia | $40.25 | $12.50 |
| Tbilisi, Georgia | $35.75 | $12.50 |

17. Calculate the total per diem amounts in the Foreign Travel Per Diem table.
18. Add a caption above the Foreign Travel Per Diem table that reads: Table 1. Foreign Travel Per Diem. Center the caption across the page.
19. Sort the rows in the table in descending order based on the total per diem amounts in the last column, then alphabetically by the Location column.
20. Insert a footer to appear on all pages with your name at the left margin, the current date at the right margin, and a 1½ point single rule across the top of the line space.
21. Use the Style Gallery to view the styles in the MANUSCR1 template, then attach the template to the document.
22. Apply the Part Title style to the heading Policy Governing Travel Expenses.
23. Apply the Heading 1 style to the headings Standard Per Diem Allowance and Exceptions.
24. Apply the Heading 2 style to the heading Foreign Travel.
25. Apply the Heading 3 style to the heading Per Diem Allowance for Extended Foreign Work Assignments.
26. Apply the Body Text style to all the text paragraphs in the document, but not to the tables.
27. Format the Foreign Travel Per Diem table using the predefined Columns 5 table format. Deselect the shading option in the Formats section, and select the Last Column option in the Special Formats to Apply section.
28. Save your changes.
29. Preview then print the document.

E

30. Insert a tab at the beginning of each text paragraph. (*Hint:* Each paragraph is preceded by one paragraph mark. Tab characters and paragraph marks are special characters.)

31. Save the document as S3PIPSI3.DOC.
32. Preview then print the document.
33. Close all documents.

Case Problems

1. Hiring Practices at Teisch Manufacturing, Inc.

Jerome Ellis is the assistant director of Personnel Services for Teisch Manufacturing, Inc., of St. Louis, Missouri. His manager, Felicia Santana, has asked him to write a memo covering the company's hiring practices during the past year. Jerome is to report on how many males and females were hired so that Felicia can determine whether Teisch has complied with Equal Employment Opportunity Commission (EEOC) guidelines.

Open the file P3TEISCH.DOC then complete the following:
1. Save the document as S3TEISCH.DOC.
2. Insert a memo heading at the top of the document, including the title Memorandum and heading information: TO: Executive Committee; FROM: Jerome Ellis; RE: New Hire Mix; DATE: February 26, 1995.
3. Insert a hard page break at the end of the document.
4. Create a table on page 2 for the data shown in Figure 3-45.

Position	Female	Male	Total
Equipment Operator	17	10	
Plant Supervisor	1	4	
Administrative Assistant	2	4	
Salesperson	11	10	
Total			

Figure 3-45

5. Add a caption below the table that reads: Table 1. Gender Mix Among 1994 New Hires.
6. Save your changes.
7. Replace all instances of "the corporation" in the body of the memo with "Teisch."
8. Insert a first-page footer that includes the page number centered. Insert a header for subsequent pages that includes the text "Executive Committee" at the left margin, the page number at the center, and the memo date at the right margin. Add bolding to Executive Committee.
9. Apply the Document Label paragraph style to the title Memorandum.
10. Apply the Message Header First paragraph style to the memo heading TO:; apply the Message Header paragraph style to the memo headings FROM: and RE:; apply the Message Header Last paragraph style to the memo heading DATE; apply the Message Header Label character style to just the memo headings.
11. Apply the Body Text style to the body of the memo.
12. Format the table using the Columns 3 predefined table format. Select the Last Row option in the Apply Special Formats section.
13. Center the table across the page, and center the caption below the table.
14. Center the numbers of new hires within the cells.
15. Save your changes.
16. Preview then print the document.
17. Delete the caption below the table.
18. Insert one row at the top of the table.
19. Merge the cells in the inserted row.
20. Type "Gender Mix for 1994 New Hires" in the cell.

E

21. Apply the Heading 2 style to the cell, then center the text across the cell.
22. Save the document as S3MIX.DOC.

E   23. Preview then print just page 2 of the document.
24. Close the document.

2. AMICI Training Schedule

Cecilia Vance is the coordinator of staff development programs for AMICI Exploration and Production's headquarters in Houston. She asked Murry Kyle, the manager of the Information Support Services division, to provide her with a schedule of dates in June and July when the staff of the Help Desk Department could offer several training classes requested by the Headquarters' employees. Cecilia received the file today from Murry and wants to send out a flyer for distribution to all personnel.

   Open P3MSPSCH.DOC then complete the following:

1. Save the document as S3MSPSCH.DOC.
2. Select all of the lines of text in the file, then convert them to a table.
3. Insert a row at the top of the table.
4. Type the following column headings in the cells of the new row: Course Name, Dates, Prerequisite.
5. Sort the table alphabetically by course name. Specify that the table contains a header row.
6. Insert the following three-line title above the table: Microsoft Products, Training Schedule, Summer Session.
7. Type the text shown in Figure 3-46 below the table.

Figure 3-46

> Class size is limited to ten students. Please call Cecilia Vance at 4-4091 or send an e-mail message to reserve your place. Observe the suggested prerequisites.

8. Change the top margin to 2.0".
9. Format the three-line title with the following attributes:
    a. Center alignment
    b. Matura MT Script Capitals (If this font is not available, choose another script font.)
    c. 24 point
10. Insert a 12 point blank line below the last line in the title and above the last paragraph ("Class size is …").
11. Format the table using the Grid 8 predefined table format.
12. Center the table across the page and the column headings within their cells.
13. Save the document.
14. Preview then print the document.

E   15. Use Word Help to learn about moving columns in a table, then move the Prerequisite column between the Course Name and the Dates columns.

E   16. Use Word Help to learn about changing the row height in tables, then select all rows in the table. Change the row height to Exactly 24 point.
17. Save the document as S3MOVCOL.DOC.
18. Preview, print, then close the document.

3. Creating Your Own Résumé

Complete the following:
1. Create a new document.
2. Type your name, address, and telephone number on separate lines.
3. Press [Enter] twice.
4. Create a five-row by two-column table. (Note: If your résumé extends beyond one page, you will need to adjust the table structure and formatting accordingly.)

5. Decrease the width of column 1 to 1.5 inches, but do not change the overall size of the table.

6. Type the following section headings in the cells in the first column: Career Objective (in row 1), Education (in row 2), Employment (in row 3), Extracurricular Activities and Honors (in row 4), and References (in row 5).

7. In cell 2 of row 1 (next to Career Objective), type your career objective. Use the Paragraph command to insert a 12 point blank line at the bottom of the cell.

8. In cell 2 of row 2 (next to Education), list your college, its location, degree earned or expected to be earned, major, and date of graduation. Press [Enter] twice then list all the courses you have completed in your major. Use the Paragraph command to insert a 12 point blank line after the last line in the cell.

9. In cell 2 of row 3 (next to Employment), list the position title, company, location, and dates of employment for each position you have held. Start with your most recent position. On the next line, give a brief description of your duties. Skip a line between each job. Use the Paragraph command to insert a blank line after the last entry in the cell.

10. In cell 2 of row 4 (next to Extracurricular Activities and Honors), list any organizations you participate in and any awards you have received. Use the Paragraph command to insert a blank line after the last entry in the cell.

11. In cell 2 of row 5 (next to References), type "Available upon request."

12. Center your name, address, and telephone number. Change the font to 14 point Arial, then bold your name, address, and telephone number.

13. Change the section headings in column 1 of the table to bold and all capitals.

14. Insert bullets in front of each course in your major.

15. Bold each title of the positions you have held.

16. Spell check the document.

17. Save the document as S3RESUME.DOC.

18. Preview, print, then close the document.

T U T O R I A L   4

Merging Documents

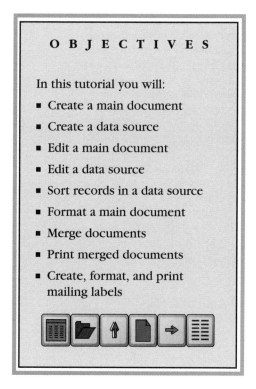

OBJECTIVES

In this tutorial you will:
- Create a main document
- Create a data source
- Edit a main document
- Edit a data source
- Sort records in a data source
- Format a main document
- Merge documents
- Print merged documents
- Create, format, and print mailing labels

Writing a Confirmation Form Letter

CASE **Mecklenburg County Roads and Bridges Department**   Paul Krueger is the administrative assistant to Greg Sterling, superintendent of the Roads and Bridges Department for Mecklenburg County in North Carolina. The department is responsible for building and maintaining all roads and bridges within the county that are not within any city's corporate limits.

Because of declining state revenues, the state of North Carolina established a volunteer cleanup program, called the Adopt-a-Highway program, for state highways through the State Department of Highways and Public Transportation. In conjunction with the state's program, Greg recently established the Adopt-a-County-Mile program, whereby civic and nonprofit organizations within Mecklenburg County could assist the local government with county road cleanup.

After a recent local television report on the Adopt-a-County-Mile program, several organizations contacted the Roads and Bridges Department to volunteer their services for the project. Now Greg wants Paul to write a confirmation letter that explains the details of the program to the contact person for each of these organizations (Figure 4-1).

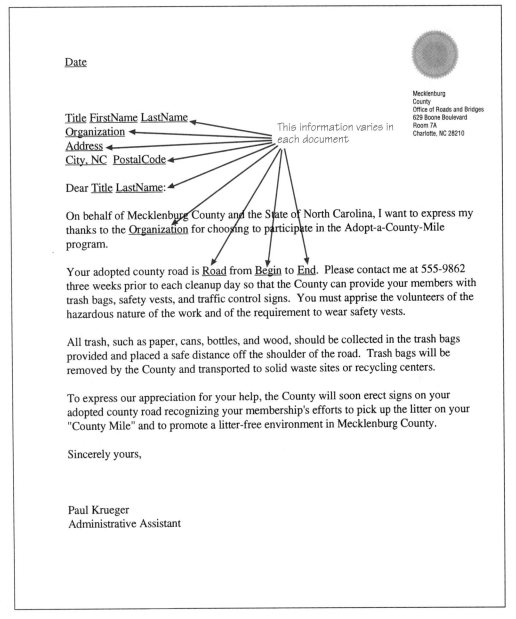

Date

Title FirstName LastName
Organization
Address
City, NC PostalCode

This information varies in
each document

Mecklenburg
County
Office of Roads and Bridges
629 Boone Boulevard
Room 7A
Charlotte, NC 28210

Dear Title LastName:

On behalf of Mecklenburg County and the State of North Carolina, I want to express my
thanks to the Organization for choosing to participate in the Adopt-a-County-Mile
program.

Your adopted county road is Road from Begin to End. Please contact me at 555-9862
three weeks prior to each cleanup day so that the County can provide your members with
trash bags, safety vests, and traffic control signs. You must apprise the volunteers of the
hazardous nature of the work and of the requirement to wear safety vests.

All trash, such as paper, cans, bottles, and wood, should be collected in the trash bags
provided and placed a safe distance off the shoulder of the road. Trash bags will be
removed by the County and transported to solid waste sites or recycling centers.

To express our appreciation for your help, the County will soon erect signs on your
adopted county road recognizing your membership's efforts to pick up the litter on your
"County Mile" and to promote a litter-free environment in Mecklenburg County.

Sincerely yours,

Paul Krueger
Administrative Assistant

Figure 4-1
Paul's confirmation
form letter

Paul's task requires him to send the same basic letter to several different people. He
needs to determine the best productivity strategy to complete this task. The letters should
be personalized for each volunteering organization, but Paul doesn't have the time to create each letter individually or to edit an existing letter several times.

Word provides a time-saving procedure to help Paul solve his problem. The Mail
Merge command on the Tools menu allows him to combine a main document—a file containing text that stays the same for every printed copy—with a data source—a file containing information that varies for every printed copy—to produce customized
documents. Paul will follow the productivity strategy by creating the main document and
the data source, then editing and formatting them. Finally, he will merge the two documents before printing.

The Merge Process

Word's Mail Merge facility is one of its most automated features. It allows you to produce multiple copies of a form document, with each copy personalized according to your instructions, in a fraction of the time it would take to create and print each copy individually. The Mail Merge feature is most often used to create customized form letters, but you can also use it to create labels, catalogs, directories, and legal documents.

As illustrated in Figure 4-2, a mail merge is a three-step process:

1. Create a main document containing the standard text that does not vary from letter to letter, as well as merge instructions to Word about where to insert the variable information from the data source.
2. Create a data source containing the information that varies from letter to letter. In Paul's case, this variable information is the organization's name, the name and address of the contact person, the name of the adopted county road, and the portion of the road that has been adopted.
3. Merge the data source with the main document. Then either view the merged documents on the screen or print them.

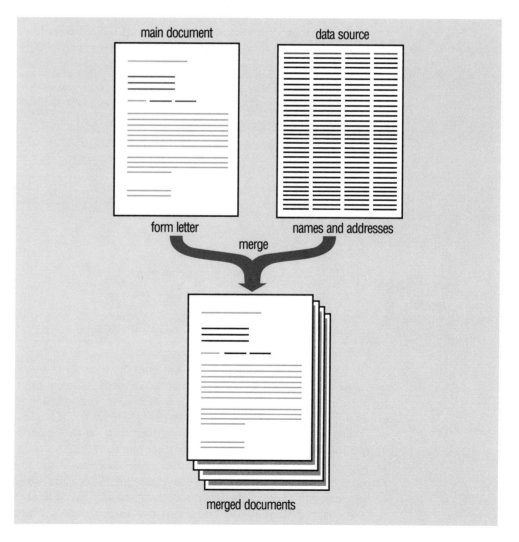

Figure 4-2
Merge process

Word gives you a variety of ways to complete the steps in the merge process. In this tutorial, you will use the most automated way to complete the merge process for situations in which you create both the main document and the data source from scratch. This tutorial will explain when and how the procedures would be different if you had previously created either the main document or the data source.

Creating a Main Document

The **main document** contains the text that stays the same in all the merged documents, as well as the instructions that tell Word where to place the information from the data source. In this first step of the merge process, you must indicate which document you intend to use as the main document. You can either create a new document or use an existing document as the main document.

Paul will create a new document—the form letter—as his main document.

To start Word and set up the main document:

❶ Start Word then conduct the screen check as described in Tutorial 1.

❷ Insert your Student Disk in the disk drive, then save the new blank document as S4ACMAIN.DOC. This will be Paul's form letter document.

   If you had already created a main document, you would open it instead. The important point to remember about Word's Mail Merge feature is to make sure that the main document is the active document when you begin the merge process; that is, when you choose the Mail Merge command from the Tools menu.

❸ Click **Tools** then click **Mail Merge....** The Mail Merge Helper dialog box appears. See Figure 4-3. It indicates the step-by-step procedure you follow to create merged documents.

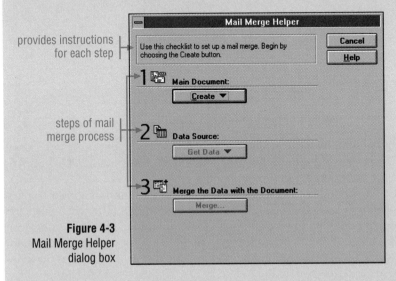

provides instructions for each step

steps of mail merge process

Figure 4-3
Mail Merge Helper dialog box

❹ Click **Create** in the Main Document section. The list of main document types appears.

❺ Click **Form Letters....** A message box appears with choices for which document to use as the main document. You'll use the document in the active window as the main document.

❻ Click **Active Window**. You return to the Mail Merge Helper dialog box. Notice that the type of merge and the name of the main document are specified in the Main Document section. You have now established the active document— S4ACMAIN.DOC—as the main document.

Paul will type the text of the letter and add the merge instructions to the main document after he creates the data source, which is the next step in the Mail Merge process.

Creating a Data Source

The **data source** is a document that contains all the variable information used to personalize the main document. As shown in Figure 4-4, the data source is basically a Word table made up of three components: data records, data fields, and a header row. Each row, except the first, is a **data record** that contains all the information necessary to customize one merged document. Each column is a **data field** that contains a single type of information; for instance, the last name of the contact person for each volunteering organization.

The **header row**, the first row of the data source, contains the **data field names**, or descriptions, of the different types of information in each of the columns. Each data field name in the header row must be unique, can contain up to 40 characters (including numbers, letters, and underscores), cannot contain spaces, and must start with a letter.

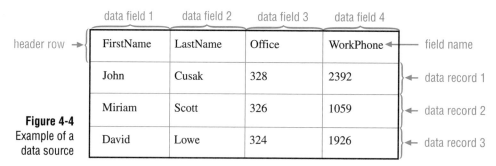

Figure 4-4
Example of a
data source

In the mail merge process when you specify the name of the data source document, you *attach* that document to the main document. Word then knows which file contains the variable information to be placed in the main document.

Paul has not created a document that contains the data source information so he must do that now. He begins by identifying the types of variable information he will be using in his letter. He lists descriptions of this information; then, following the conventions for naming data fields, he assigns names to the different categories of variable information for use in the header row of the data source. Figure 4-5 lists the data field names for the information Paul will use in his letter. Notice the field name "City_NC." Because all the organizations are located within North Carolina, Paul includes "NC" in the field name. Otherwise, he would have had a separate field for "State."

Category of Information	Data Field Name
Name of volunteer organization	Organization
Title of contact person	Title
First name of contact person	FirstName
Last name of contact person	LastName
Street address of contact person	Address
City location of contact person	City_NC
Zip code for location of contact person	PostalCode
Name of adopted county road	Road
Beginning point of county mile	Begin
Ending point of county mile	End

Figure 4-5
Data field names for
Paul's data source

First, Paul begins by attaching the data source to the main document.

Attaching the Data Source

Word must know which document contains the variable information that is to be inserted into the main document during the merge process. You can either open an existing document that was set up as a data source, or you can create a new data source document. Paul needs to create a new data source document.

To attach the data source to the main document:
❶ Click **Get Data** in the Data Source section of the Mail Merge Helper dialog box. The Data Source menu appears.

Paul has not created the data source information yet. He will start by creating the header row of the data source.

Creating the Header Row

Paul has established the data fields for each of the categories of variable information, and he is ready to create the header row for his data source.

To create the data field names for the header row in the data source:
❶ Click **Create Data Source**.... The Create Data Source dialog box appears. See Figure 4-6. The Field Names in Header Row list box provides commonly used data field names for a header row in a data source.

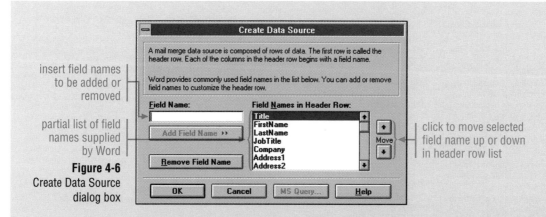

insert field names
to be added or
removed

partial list of field
names supplied
by Word

Figure 4-6
Create Data Source
dialog box

Paul wants to see if he can use any of the data field names that Word has supplied.

❷ Scroll through the list of data field names.

Paul can use some of the field names—Title, FirstName, LastName, Address1 (for Address), and PostalCode—but he will need to add other field names for Organization, City_NC, Road, Begin, and End.

❸ Type **Organization** in the Field Name text box, then click **Add Field Name** or press **[Enter]**. "Organization" is added to the end of the Field Names in Header Row list.

❹ Repeat Step 3 to add the following four data field names to the list: **City_NC**, **Road**, **Begin**, **End**.

Next Paul needs to remove the unnecessary field names.

❺ Scroll to the top of the field name list, click **JobTitle**, then click **Remove Field Name**.

❻ Repeat Step 5 for each of the following unnecessary field names: **Company**, **Address2**, **City**, **State**, **Country**, **HomePhone**, **WorkPhone**.

To make it quicker to add the specific information he has received for each data record, Paul needs to rearrange the order of the data field names.

❼ Click **Organization** then click the **Move up arrow button** until Organization is moved to the top of the field name list, directly above Title.

TROUBLE? The field names in the list scroll continuously. Make sure you move Organization immediately above Title.

❽ Click **City_NC** then click the **Move up arrow button** until City_NC is between Address1 and PostalCode.

❾ Click **OK**. The Save Data Source dialog box appears.

❿ Type **s4acmdat** in the File Name text box. Make sure the drive for your Student Disk is selected, then click **OK** or press **[Enter]**. The data source document, S4ACMDAT.DOC, is now attached to the main document, S4ACMAIN.DOC.

A message box appears with choices for either entering the variable information into the data source or editing the main document. Paul wants to complete the data source by inserting the variable information for each organization. To do so he'll use the data form.

Using the Data Form

You can either enter the data directly in the data source, just as you would enter information in a table, or you can use the on-line data form that Word provides to make the process easier.

Paul decides to use the data form to enter the information about the volunteering organizations in the data source.

To enter information in the data source using the data form:

❶ In the message box, click **Edit Data Source** or press **[Enter]**. The Data Form dialog box appears with the data field names for the header row listed next to blank text boxes, which you complete with the necessary variable information. See Figure 4-7.

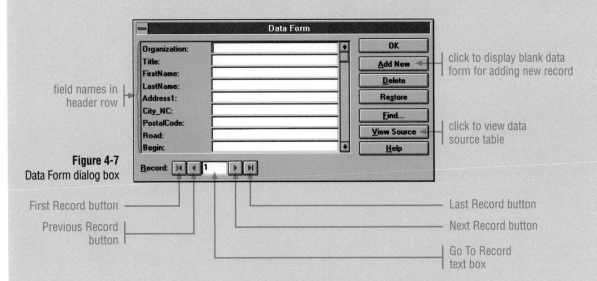

Figure 4-7
Data Form dialog box

To move to the next blank text box, press [Tab] or [Enter]; to move to the previous text box, press [Shift][Tab]. Do not enter any trailing spaces at the end of a text box—you will add the necessary spacing around the merge instructions in the main document rather than in the data records.

Figure 4-8 lists the information Paul has gathered about each organization that has volunteered for the Adopt-a-County-Mile program. To help him complete the data form, he has marked off the different pieces of data that he must enter for each field.

/Noon Kiwanis Club/
/Ms./Leola/Williams/
/1887 Goldston Lane/
/Charlotte, NC/ 28078/
/Grier Road/from/W. T. Harris Blvd./to/John Russell Road/

/Mint Museum Employees/
/Mr./John/Diaz/
/13523 Primwood Street/
/Pineville, NC /28134/
/Lebanon Road/from/Margaret Wallace Road/to/Lawyers Road/

/Charlotte Association of Retired Persons/
/Mr./Brian/Anderson/
/10038 Wrentree Drive/
/Charlotte, NC / 28211/
/W. T. Harris Blvd./from/Mallard Creek Blvd./to/Research Drive/

/Huntersville Chamber of Commerce/
/Mrs./Oma/Cristini/
/Rt. 4, Box 51/
/Huntersville, NC /28210/
/Huntersville Road/from/Alexandria Road/to/Hambright Road/

Figure 4-8
Organization
information for
Paul's data source

❷ Type **Noon Kiwanis Club** then press **[Enter]** or **[Tab]** to enter the data for the first field and move to the next field.

❸ Type **Ms.** (make sure to include the period) then press **[Enter]** or **[Tab]**.

❹ Type **Leola** then press **[Enter]** or **[Tab]**.

❺ Type **Williams** then press **[Enter]** or **[Tab]**.

❻ Type **1887 Goldston Lane** then press **[Enter]** or **[Tab]**.

❼ Type **Charlotte, NC** then press **[Enter]** or **[Tab]**.

❽ Type **28078** then press **[Enter]** or **[Tab]**.

❾ Type **Grier Road** then press **[Enter]** or **[Tab]**.

❿ Type **W. T. Harris Blvd.**, press **[Enter]** or **[Tab]**, then type **John Russell Road** to complete the form. See Figure 4-9.

Figure 4-9
First data record in
Paul's data source

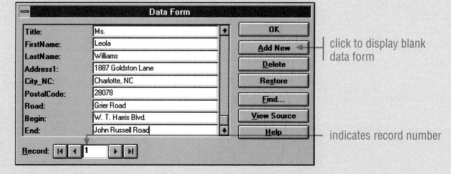

Paul has entered all the information for the first record in the data source. Now he is ready to enter the information for the remaining three records shown in Figure 4-8.

To enter the remaining information in the data source:
❶ Click **Add New** to display a blank data form. Notice that the text box at the bottom of the data form now shows record 2.
❷ Enter the information for the second and third data records shown in Figure 4-8.
❸ Enter the information for the fourth data record shown in Figure 4-8, but *do not click Add New* when you are finished. Clicking Add New would add a blank record as the fifth record.

TROUBLE? If you accidentally insert a blank fifth record, click Delete.

Paul wants to proofread each data record to make sure he typed the information correctly. He wants to move to the beginning of the data source using the data record access buttons at the bottom of the dialog box.

To move to records within the data source:
❶ Click the **First Record button** at the bottom of the form. The data record number changes to 1, and the information for the first data record you entered is displayed in the form.
❷ Proofread the data, making corrections if necessary, then click the **Next Record button** at the bottom of the form. The data record number changes to 2, and the information for the second data record is displayed in the form.
❸ Repeat Step 2 until you have viewed all four records, making corrections where necessary.

Now that Paul has proofread the records using the data form, he needs to save the data source document. He cannot save the document while the data form is displayed; he must first view the data source.

To save the data source:
❶ Click **View Source**. The inserted data in the form of a table is displayed. Note that the Database toolbar also appears. This is the toolbar you use for working with the data source.

Paul wants to be able to see the full width of the data source table on the screen.
❷ Click the **Zoom Control list box down arrow** on the Standard toolbar, then click **Page Width**. The entire table is displayed across the screen. Notice that the contents wrap within the cells. You do not need to worry about the appearance of the text in the table because you will not print the table. See Figure 4-10.

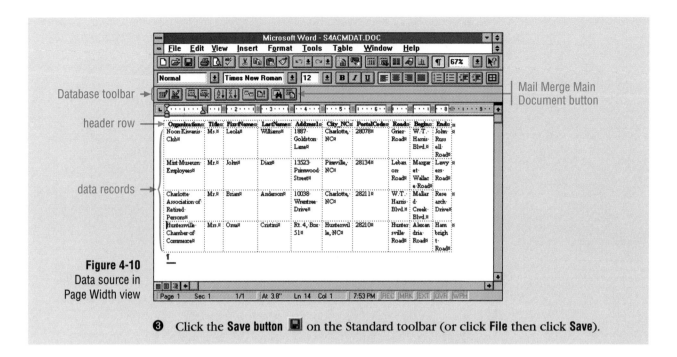

Database toolbar →

Mail Merge Main
Document button

header row →

data records →

Figure 4-10
Data source in
Page Width view

❸   Click the **Save button** 🖫 on the Standard toolbar (or click **File** then click **Save**).

Although Paul's data source eventually will contain many more volunteering organizations, it contains enough records now to demonstrate Word's Mail Merge feature. He is ready to type the text of his confirmation form letter and insert merge instructions in the main document.

Editing a Main Document

You created the main document earlier, but you did not enter any text or merge instructions yet. You are now ready to edit the main document.

Paul knows he needs to begin his letter with a date, but he also knows that if he types the current date he will have to modify the main document each time he sends this letter to a new volunteering organization. He decides to insert a **date field code** that will automatically insert the current date each time the document is printed.

To insert the date field code:

❶   Click the **Mail Merge Main Document button** 🖺 on the Database toolbar. You return to the blank main document—S4ACMAIN.DOC. Notice that the main document contains the Mail Merge toolbar, which appears between the Formatting toolbar and the ruler. See Figure 4-11.

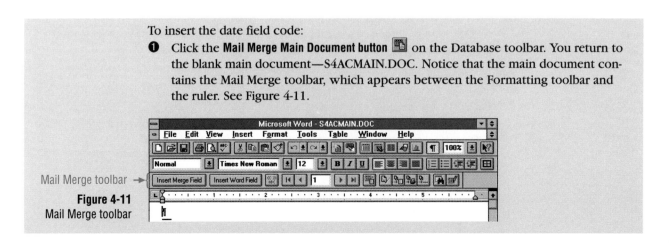

Mail Merge toolbar →

Figure 4-11
Mail Merge toolbar

❷ Click **Insert** on the menu bar, then click **Date and Time....** The Date and Time dialog box appears.

❸ Click the fourth date format from the top of the list of available formats (Month xx, 19xx). See Figure 4-12.

choose this date format

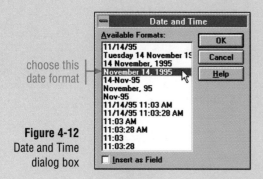

Figure 4-12
Date and Time
dialog box

❹ Click **OK** or press **[Enter]**. The current date appears in the document. In the future, whenever Paul prints the merged document letters for new volunteering organizations, the current date will appear.

TROUBLE? If you see text surrounded by curly brackets {} instead of the date, click Tools, click Options..., then deselect the Field Codes option in the Show section on the View tab.

Inserting Merge Field Codes

The main document contains the text that stays the same in all the merged documents, as well as the instructions that tell Word where to place the information from the data file. These instructions in the main document are called **merge field codes.**

Paul has entered the date and now is ready to enter the merge field codes for the inside address. Recall from Figure 4-1 that the variable information for the inside address includes the title, first name, last name, organization name, and address of the contact person for each organization. As you enter these merge field codes, be sure to insert the proper spacing and punctuation around the codes so that the personalized documents will print correctly.

To insert the merge field codes:

❶ Press **[Enter]** four times to leave three blank lines between the date and the first line of the inside address.

❷ Click the **Insert Merge Field button** on the Mail Merge toolbar. A list appears containing all the field names that you previously created for the header row in the attached data source.

❸ Click **Title** in the data fields list. The data field name, Title, appears in the main document, surrounded by chevrons (« »). The chevrons distinguish merge field codes from the rest of the text in the main document.

❹ Press **[Spacebar]** to insert a space after the Title merge field code, click the **Insert Merge Field button**, then click **FirstName** in the list. The FirstName merge field code appears.

⑤ Press **[Spacebar]** to insert a space after the FirstName merge field code, click the **Insert Merge Field button,** then click **LastName** in the list. The LastName merge field code appears.

⑥ Press **[Enter]** to move the insertion point to the next line, click the **Insert Merge Field button**, then click **Organization** in the list. The Organization merge field code appears.

⑦ Press **[Enter]** to move the insertion point to the next line. Continue inserting the appropriate merge field codes to complete the inside address and the salutation (Dear «Title» «LastName»:) until your document looks like Figure 4-13.

TROUBLE? If you make a mistake inserting merge field codes, you must select the entire field code, including the chevrons, then press [Del]. You can then continue to insert the correct merge field code.

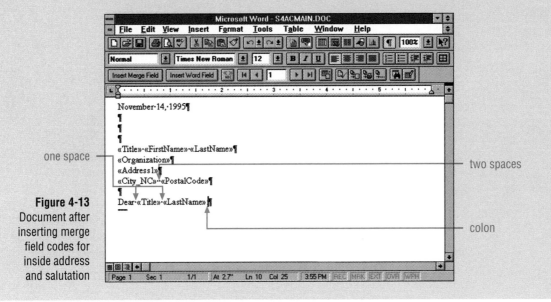

Figure 4-13
Document after inserting merge field codes for inside address and salutation

Now Paul can continue typing the body of the letter and the remaining merge fields.

To finish entering the main document:

❶ Press **[Enter]** twice after the salutation to insert a blank line between the salutation and the body of the letter.

Paul wants to further personalize the letter by including the name of the organization, the adopted county road, and the beginning and ending points on the road.

❷ Continue typing the body of the letter, including the appropriate merge field codes, as illustrated in Figure 4-14.

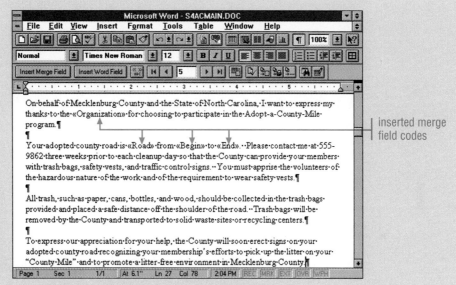

inserted merge
field codes

Figure 4-14
Document with
merge field codes
inserted in body
of letter

You are now ready to type the closing lines.

❸ Press **[Enter]** twice, type **Sincerely yours**, press **[Enter]** four times, type **Paul Krueger**, press **[Enter]**, then type **Administrative Assistant**. Your completed document should look like Figure 4-15. You will need to scroll up and down to see the entire document.

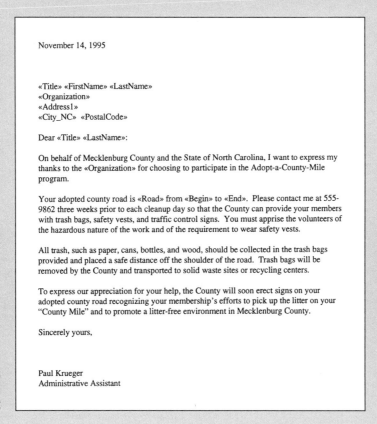

Figure 4-15
Completed main
document

Paul is satisfied with the content and wording of the confirmation letter, and now he wants to spell check the main document.

To spell check and save the main document:
❶ Spell check the main document, making any necessary corrections.
❷ Click the **Save button** 🖫 on the Standard toolbar (or click **File** then click **Save**).

Paul already proofread the data source, but he now notices that the title for the Huntersville Chamber of Commerce contact person should be "Dr." instead of "Mrs." He needs to correct the error in the data source.

Editing the Data Source

To edit the records in the data source document, you use the Edit Data Source button on the Mail Merge toolbar. Paul needs to make one correction to a record in his data source.

To edit the data source:
❶ Click the **Edit Data Source button** 🖼 on the Mail Merge toolbar, then click **View Source**.
❷ Use the cell selection bar to select the contents of cell 2 of row 5, then type **Dr.** (be sure to include the period).
❸ Save your changes.

Sorting Records

In his job Paul is accustomed to mailing large numbers of letters and brochures. Whenever he does this, he needs to bundle together letters going to the same postal code, as required by the U.S. Post Office, to speed processing. He saves himself time by printing the letters in postal code order. To print the letters in postal code order, he must first organize the data source in postal code order by sorting it. He decides to do this by using the Database toolbar.

To sort the data source records by postal code:
❶ Place the insertion point anywhere in the PostalCode column.
❷ Click the **Sort Ascending button** 🖳 on the Database toolbar. The records are sorted from the lowest to the highest postal code, and the column is selected. Deselect the column. See Figure 4-16.

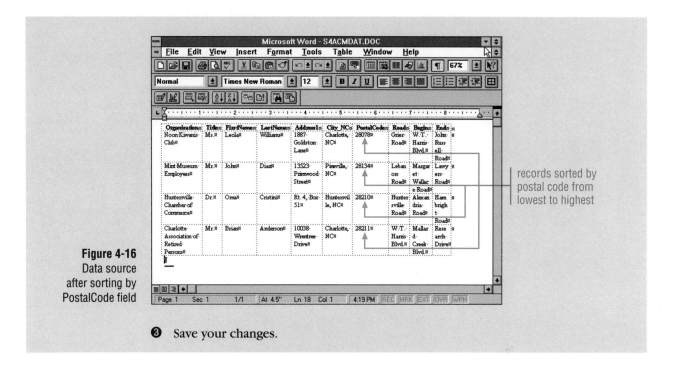

Figure 4-16
Data source
after sorting by
PostalCode field

❸ Save your changes.

Paul is now finished editing both the main document and the data source. He needs to make a few slight formatting changes to the main document before he is ready to merge the two documents.

Formatting a Main Document

Paul has some minor formatting changes to make to the main document. He does not plan to print the data source by itself, so he doesn't need to format it.

Paul must switch to the main document to make his formatting changes. Let's do that now.

To switch to the main document:
❶ Click the **Mail Merge Main Document button** 🖻 on the Database toolbar to return to the main document. The main document becomes the active document. The data source is still open but not visible.

Paul wants to change the top margin of the main document to 1.5 inches. He also wants to bold the volunteering organization's name in the first paragraph, as well as the words "three weeks prior" in the second paragraph. To apply format options such as bolding to a merge field code, you must select the entire field code, including the surrounding chevrons.

To format the main document:

❶ Change the top margin to 1.5". Refer to Tutorial 2 if you need to review how to change margins.

❷ Place the insertion point in the merge field code «Organization» in the first paragraph of the body of the letter. Notice that the entire field code becomes shaded. This is Word's way of helping to distinguish field codes from regular text in a document. The field code is *not selected*.

❸ Select the merge field code «**Organization**» in the first paragraph; the entire field code becomes highlighted with a darker shade of gray than before. Make sure you include the chevrons on either side of "Organization" when selecting.

❹ Click the **Bold button** 🅱 on the Formatting toolbar.

❺ Select **three weeks prior** in the second paragraph of the body of the letter, then click 🅱 on the Formatting toolbar. Deselect the text.

❻ Save your changes.

Paul has completed formatting his document and now moves to the final stage of the productivity strategy: printing.

Merging Documents

Paul has created his main document and has attached the completed data source to it. He has also made all the necessary editing and formatting changes. Now he is ready to merge the two documents to produce the customized letters. Paul has only four letters to print now, but he doesn't want to waste time and resources printing letters that contain mistakes. He decides to view the document as it will appear when merged.

To view the merged document as it will appear when printed:

❶ Click the **View Merged Data button** 🔲 on the Mail Merge toolbar. Word inserts the information for the first data record into the text of the main document. The beginning of the first letter (to Leola Williams) appears in the document window.

❷ Scroll through the letter to see that you have inserted the merge field codes and the spacing around them correctly. If you see errors, it is best to correct them here in the main document, then save the changes; do not merge the letters then correct each individual merged document.

Paul is satisfied that the merge will work properly and is ready to merge and print the documents.

❸ Click 🔲 again to return to the usual display of the main document.

❹ Click the **Merge to Printer button** 🔲 on the Mail Merge toolbar.

❺ Click **OK** or press [Enter] in the Print dialog box. During the merge process, Word inserts the appropriate variable information for each data record in the data source document wherever a merge field code appears in the main document. All four merged documents print. The complete merged document to Leola Williams appears in Figure 4-17.

❻ Save your changes.

November 14, 1995

Ms. Leola Williams
Noon Kiwanis Club
1887 Goldston Lane
Charlotte, NC 28078

Dear Ms. Williams:

On behalf of Mecklenburg County and the State of North Carolina, I want to express my
thanks to the **Noon Kiwanis Club** for choosing to participate in the Adopt-a-County-Mile
program.

Your adopted county road is Grier Road from W. T. Harris Blvd. to John Russell Road.
Please contact me at 555-9862 **three weeks prior** to each cleanup day so that the County
can provide your members with trash bags, safety vests, and traffic control signs. You
must apprise the volunteers of the hazardous nature of the work and of the requirement to
wear safety vests.

All trash, such as paper, cans, bottles, and wood, should be collected in the trash bags
provided and placed a safe distance off the shoulder of the road. Trash bags will be
removed by the County and transported to solid waste sites or recycling centers.

To express our appreciation for your help, the County will soon erect signs on your
adopted county road recognizing your membership's efforts to pick up the litter on your
"County Mile" and to promote a litter-free environment in Mecklenburg County.

Sincerely yours,

Paul Krueger
Administrative Assistant

Figure 4-17
Merged document
to Leola Williams

If you want to take a break and resume the tutorial at a later time, you can close both the main document and the data source document, then exit Word by double-clicking the Control menu box in the upper-left corner of the screen. When you want to resume the tutorial, start Word, place your Student Disk in the disk drive, then complete the screen check procedure described in Tutorial 1. Open the main document, S4ACMAIN.DOC, then continue with the tutorial.

As Paul looks over the last merged document, he receives a telephone call from Molly Suen of the Student Political Action Committee at the University of North Carolina, Charlotte campus. Her organization wants to adopt a county mile, too. Paul takes down the information he needs so he can get her letter in the mail along with the others.

Selecting a Data Record to Merge

Paul needs to add the information for the Student Political Action Committee to the data source. Because he has already printed the merged documents for the other data records in the data source, he needs to merge only the variable information for the new organization with the main document.

First, Paul needs to add the information for the new volunteer organization to the data source. This time he'll enter the new record directly in the data source.

To add the new record to the data source:

❶ Click the **Edit Data Source button** 🖉 on the Mail Merge toolbar of the main document to switch to the data source form.

❷ Click **View Source** to switch to the data source table. Now you can enter the new record, then save this change to the data source.

❸ Click the **Add New Record button** 🗒 on the Database toolbar. A blank row is added to the bottom of the table.

Paul can now add the data for the new organization just as he would enter information into any table.

❹ Type **Student Political Action Committee** in cell 1 of the new row.

❺ Using Figure 4-18, continue typing the remaining information for the new volunteer organization into the data source table.

/Student Political Action Committee/
/Ms./Molly/Suen/
/2911 Lakeview Drive/
/Charlotte, NC/28211/
/Rocky River Road West/from/University City Blvd./to/Old Concord Road/

Figure 4-18
Information for
new data record

❻ Proofread the new data record carefully, correcting errors if necessary.

❼ Save your changes.

Now that Paul has entered the information for the new organization, he is ready to print that record. He can specify that Word merge only the new record and the main document, then print just that letter.

To find the new record:

❶ Click the **Mail Merge Main Document button** 🗒 on the Database toolbar to switch to the main document. Notice that the Go To Record text box on the Mail Merge toolbar indicates data record 1.

Paul wants to print just the letter to Molly Suen, but first he must move to that data record.

❷ Click the **Find Record button** 🗚 on the Mail Merge toolbar. The Find in Field dialog box appears. See Figure 4-19.

type text to
search for

click to see field
names in header row

Figure 4-19
Find in Field
dialog box

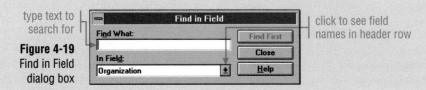

❸ Type **Suen** in the Find What text box.

❹ Click the **In Field list box down arrow**, then click **LastName**.

❺ Click **Find First** or press **[Enter]**. Now the Go To Record text box indicates record number 5.

❻ Click **Close** to close the Find in Field dialog box.

Paul wants to print just the merged document to Molly Suen, data record 5.

To print the merged document to Molly Suen:

❶ Click the **Mail Merge button** 🗐 on the Mail Merge toolbar. The Merge dialog box appears. See Figure 4-20.

click to specify
merge to printer

specify range of
records to merge

Figure 4-20
Merge dialog box

❷ Click the **Merge To list box down arrow**, then click **Printer**.

Now Paul must specify the number of the data record that he wants to print, in this case, 5.

❸ Click the **From radio button** in the Records to Be Merged section, type **5**, press **[Tab]**, then type **5** in the To text box.

❹ Click **Merge**. The Print dialog box appears.

❺ Click **OK** or press **[Enter]**. The merged document to Molly Suen prints.

❻ Save both S4ACMAIN.DOC and S4ACMDAT.DOC, then close both documents.

Paul has completed the personalized letters to those organizations that volunteered to participate in the Adopt-a-County-Mile program. He can now use the merging process to help him quickly create a mailing label for each merged document.

Creating Mailing Labels

Paul uses transparent address labels for the laser printer that are each 1 inch x 2⅚ inches. They come on sheets that look like Figure 4-21. Word uses the product numbers of a popular manufacturer of labels, Avery, to specify the various formats for labels it can produce. You must know the product number or the Avery equivalent of the specific label type you will be using. The Avery product number for the labels that Paul uses is 5660.

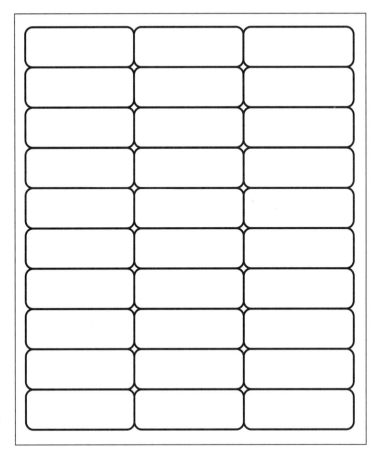

Figure 4-21
Layout of sheet of
mailing labels

Paul already has a data source that contains the names and addresses of the contacts for each of the volunteering organizations (S4ACMDAT.DOC), but he needs to create the main document that will contain the merge field codes arranged as they would appear on a mailing label. Then he can merge the mailing label main document with the data source document.

To create the mailing label main document:

❶ Click the **New button** 🗋 on the Standard toolbar. A new blank document appears.

❷ Click **Tools** then click **Mail Merge...**. The Mail Merge Helper dialog box appears.

❸ Click **Create** in the Main Document section, then click **Mailing Labels...**. A message box appears.

❹ Click **Active Window** in the message box. You return to the Mail Merge Helper dialog box.

Paul will use the addressee information in the data source document he just created—S4ACMDAT.DOC.

❺ Click **Get Data** in the Data Source section, then click **Open Data Source...**.

❻ Select S4ACMDAT.DOC from your Student Disk. A message box appears for setting up the main document.

❼ Click **Set Up Main Document**. The Label Options dialog box appears.

❽ Make sure the Laser radio button is selected in the Printer Information section, then click **5660 - Address** in the Product Number list box. See Figure 4-22.

select product
number of labels
to be used

Figure 4-22
Completed
Label Options
dialog box

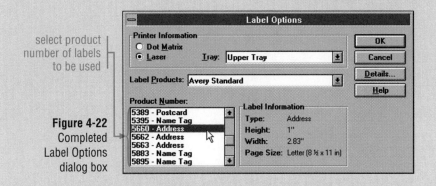

TROUBLE? If you are using a dot matrix printer, your document will not print exactly as shown.

❾ Click **OK** or press **[Enter]**. The Create Labels dialog box appears.

Now Paul must build the contents of the mailing label. He wants the mailing label to look like the inside address of the letter. Paul creates the label by selecting the merge fields he wants to appear on the label from the Insert Merge Field list, then inserting any necessary spacing, just as he did when he inserted the inside address into the confirmation form letter.

Now let's place merge field codes into the mailing label document.

To insert merge field codes into the mailing label document:

❶ Click **Insert Merge Field**, click **Title** in the list, then press **[Spacebar]**. The selected merge field appears in the Sample Label box.

TROUBLE? If you make a mistake after you add an item, you can edit the text directly in the Sample Label box.

The first name of the contact person is the next item to be added to the mailing label.

❷ Click **Insert Merge Field**, click **FirstName**, then press **[Spacebar]**.

Next you need to enter the last name of the contact person, then return the insertion point to the beginning of the next line.

❸ Click **Insert Merge Field**, click **LastName**, then press **[Enter]**. The LastName field code is added to the mailing label, and the insertion point moves to the beginning of the next line.

Now that you have entered the first line of the label, you can enter the remaining three lines.

❹ Set up the remaining lines of the mailing label address as shown in Figure 4-23. Remember to press **[Enter]** at the end of each line to return the insertion point to the beginning of the next line.

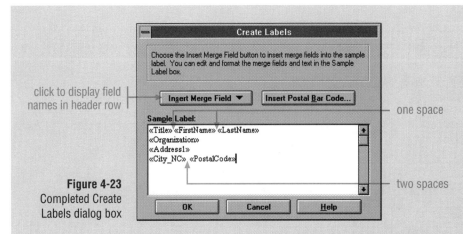

click to display field
names in header row

one space

two spaces

Figure 4-23
Completed Create
Labels dialog box

❺   Click **OK** when you are finished building the address for the label. You return to the Mail Merge Helper dialog box.

Before Paul merges the label main document with the data source, he wants to make sure that the main document is set up properly.

❻   Click **Edit** in the Main Document section of the Mail Merge Helper dialog box. The name of the current label main document appears.

❼   Click **Mailing Label: Document2**. Notice that the label main document is a table, with each cell being the equivalent of one label on a sheet of mailing labels. The label you built is copied to each cell of the label main document you created.

TROUBLE? The document name of your mailing label main document might be different; click the name of your label main document, then continue with the tutorial.

Paul can't see the entire last column of the mailing label main document on the screen.

❽   Click the **Zoom Control list box down arrow**, then click **Page Width**.

Paul decides to save the label main document so he doesn't have to create it each time he has a mailing to send out.

❾   Click the **Save button** 🖫 on the Standard toolbar (or click **File** then click **Save As...**). Save the label document to your Student Disk as S4ACMLAB.DOC.

Paul sees that he needs to format the label main document so that the necessary information will fit on the label.

Formatting Labels

You can format the mailing label main document the same way you format other Word documents. Paul decides to change the font of the label main document to Arial to make the labels more readable and to reduce the size of the font to 10 point so that the text will fit better on the label. Let's do that now.

To change the format of the mailing label main document:

❶ Place the insertion point anywhere inside the table, click **Table**, then click **Select Table**. The entire table is selected.

❷ Click the **Font list box down arrow** on the Formatting toolbar, then click **Arial**.

❸ Click the **Font Size list box down arrow** on the Formatting toolbar, then click **10**. The font and the font size for the label document have been changed. Deselect the mailing label main document.

❹ Save your changes.

Paul wants to see what the formatted labels will look like after they are merged.

❺ Click the **View Merged Data button** 🔳 on the Mail Merge toolbar.

Paul is satisfied that the text will fit properly on the labels.

❻ Click 🔳 again to return to the usual view of the label main document.

Printing Labels

Now that Paul has formatted the label main document, he inserts a sheet of labels in the printer and prints the merged documents. You will simply print the labels on a sheet of paper.

To print the mailing labels:

❶ Click the **Merge to Printer button** 🔳 on the Mail Merge toolbar. The Print dialog box appears.

❷ Click **OK** or press **[Enter]**. Word merges the label main document with the data source and sends the resulting merged document directly to the printer. See Figure 4-24.

❸ Save the changes you have made to S4ACMLAB.DOC.

❹ Close the label main document then exit Word.

Figure 4-24
Printed mailing label
merged document

Ms. Leola Williams Noon Kiwanis Club 1887 Goldston Lane Charlotte, NC 28078	Mr. John Diaz Mint Museum Employees 13523 Primwood Street Pineville, NC 28134	Dr. Oma Cristini Huntersville Chamber of Commerce Rt. 4, Box 51 Huntersville, NC 28210
Mr. Brian Anderson Charlotte Association of Retired Persons 10038 Wrentree Drive Charlotte, NC 28211	Ms. Molly Suen Student Political Action Committee 2911 Lakeview Drive Charlotte, NC 28211	

Paul now has the confirmation letters and the accompanying labels. He attaches the labels to the envelopes, inserts the letters in the envelopes, and mails them.

Questions

1. Describe the merge process.
2. Define each of the following terms:
   a. main document
   b. data source
   c. header row
   d. data record
   e. data field
   f. field name
   g. merge field code
   h. date field code
3. How do you establish the document you need to use as the main document?
4. Which of the following names are legal field names:
   a. ProductInventoryNumber
   b. 1995_Sales
   c. Employee_ID
5. What are two methods for entering data into a data source?
6. Describe the purpose of the Page Width option provided by the Zoom Control feature.
7. When formatting a merge field code in a main document, what must you remember to do?
8. Describe the process you would follow to merge then print one specific data record only.
9. Describe the process for creating and printing mailing labels if you have a data source already created.

Use Word Help to answer Questions 10 through 12:

E   10. How do you add a field to an existing data source?

E   11. What is the purpose of the Query button in the Mail Merge Helper dialog box?

E   12. How do you return a main document to a regular Word document?

Tutorial Assignments

Start Word, if necessary, then conduct a screen check. Complete the following:

1. Open a new document then create a form letter main document. Save it as S4ACMAGR.DOC.
2. Attach T4MECDAT.DOC from your Student Disk as the data source.
3. Scroll through the data records. Notice the two new data fields—Date_1 and Date_2.
4. Save the data source as S4MECDAT.DOC.
5. Switch to the main document.
6. Create the main document shown in Figure 4-25, inserting merge field codes as indicated.

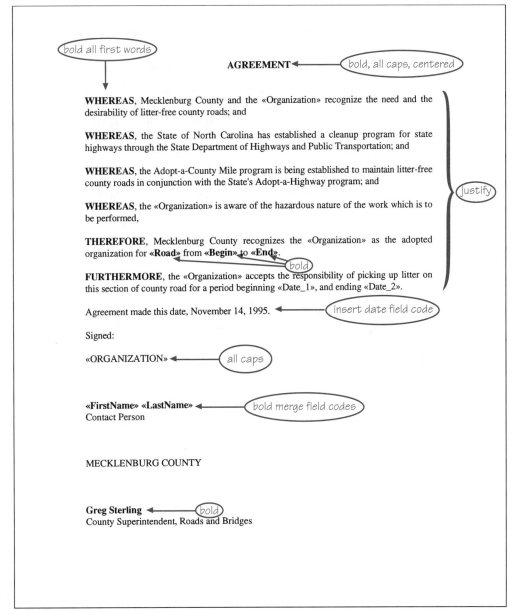

bold all first words

AGREEMENT ← bold, all caps, centered

WHEREAS, Mecklenburg County and the «Organization» recognize the need and the desirability of litter-free county roads; and

WHEREAS, the State of North Carolina has established a cleanup program for state highways through the State Department of Highways and Public Transportation; and

WHEREAS, the Adopt-a-County Mile program is being established to maintain litter-free county roads in conjunction with the State's Adopt-a-Highway program; and

WHEREAS, the «Organization» is aware of the hazardous nature of the work which is to be performed,

THEREFORE, Mecklenburg County recognizes the «Organization» as the adopted organization for **«Road»** from **«Begin»** to **«End»**.

justify

bold

FURTHERMORE, the «Organization» accepts the responsibility of picking up litter on this section of county road for a period beginning «Date_1», and ending «Date_2».

Agreement made this date, November 14, 1995. ← insert date field code

Signed:

«ORGANIZATION» ← all caps

«FirstName» «LastName» ← bold merge field codes
Contact Person

MECKLENBURG COUNTY

Greg Sterling ← bold
County Superintendent, Roads and Bridges

Figure 4-25

7. Spell check the document.
8. Format the document as indicated in Figure 4-25.
9. Save the changes to the main document.
10. View the document as it will appear when merged, and check for any mistakes.
11. Merge and print records 3 and 4.
12. Close all documents.

Case Problems

1. Writing a Form Memo to Employees at Associated Credit Services

Tommy Hiebert is the assistant director of the Telecommunications Department for Associated Credit Services of Boston, Massachusetts. One of his responsibilities is to publish the company employee directory. Because of the recent installation of a new telephone system, he wants to update the directory. He decides to send a memo asking employees to confirm the accuracy of their information before he publishes the final version of the directory.

Complete the following:

1. Open a new document then create a form letter main document. Save the document as S4DRMAIN.DOC
2. Create a data source, S4DIRDAT.DOC, with the following field names in the header row: FirstName, Middle, LastName, Department, Phone, Office.
3. Insert the information shown in Figure 4-26 into a data source.

Figure 4-26

Linda F. McCown	Accounting	3-9035	409
Charles A. Abbate	Online Services	3-9276	312
Richard L. Swartz	Online Services	3-9279	310
Ronnie D. Gajeske	Accounting	3-9052	411
Leroy L. Keese	Support Services	3-9167	493
Joel Y. Aldape	Telecommunications	3-9641	385
Hillary Abramson	Accounting	3-9038	407
Leah T. Abbate	Online Services	3-9274	308

4. Sort the data records by office number in descending order.
5. Switch to the main document.
6. Create a standard memo heading:
   a. After TO: insert the merge field codes FirstName, Middle, LastName, and Department with appropriate spacing between each code.
   b. After FROM: insert Tommy Hiebert.
   c. After RE: insert Directory Listing.
   d. After DATE: insert the date field code, using the date format you prefer.
7. Type the message shown in Figure 4-27, substituting the appropriate merge field codes for the blank lines.

Figure 4-27

We are in the process of updating the employee directory to reflect the latest telephone number changes. According to our records, your current telephone number is _____ and your office number is _____. Is this information correct? Please respond immediately.

8. Spell check the memo.
9. Change the top margin to 2 inches and the side margins to 1.5 inches.
10. Bold the memo headings and the phone and office merge field codes in the message.
11. Save the changes to the main document.
12. View the document as it will appear when merged, and check for any mistakes.
13. Merge and print documents for records 5 and 6 only.
14. Close all documents.

2. Creating Mailing Labels for the NAPT Newsletter

Marilyn Taff is chair of the Communications Committee for the National Association of Performance Technologists (NAPT). She has just completed the quarterly issue of the NAPT newsletter and is ready to mail it to the members, but she still needs to prepare mailing labels. Marilyn purchased a box of Avery number 5160 address labels for a laser printer. She already has a disk copy of the membership data source.

Open a new document then complete the following:

1. Create a mailing label main document, making appropriate choices for Laser 5160 address labels.
2. Use the data source P4NAPT.DOC from your Student Disk.
3. Add your name and appropriate information to the data source.
4. Build the layout of the mailing label as shown in Figure 4-28.

Figure 4-28

```
<FirstName> <Middle> <LastName>
<Company>
<Address1>
<City>, <State> <PostalCode>
```

5. View the document as it will appear when merged, and check for any mistakes.
6. Format the label merged document with Arial 8 point font.
7. Merge the labels.
8. Save the merged label document as S4NAPTLB.DOC.

E

9. Marilyn needs the mailing labels in postal code order, alphabetically by last name, then by first name. Use Word Help to find out how the Query option on the Mail Merge Helper dialog box can help you solve this problem. Then create and print the mailing labels for the data records in P4NAPT.DOC in the correct order.
10. Close all documents.

3. A Cover Letter for Your Résumé

Complete the following:

1. Gather application information for three job openings in which you are interested.
2. Open a new document to serve as the main document, then save it as S4COVLET.DOC.
3. Attach a data source with the following field names in its header row and others you feel are appropriate: Title, FirstName, LastName, JobTitle, Company, Address1, City, State, and PostalCode.
4. Save the data source as S4JOBDAT.DOC.
5. Insert the data you collected for your jobs into the appropriate field, one job to a record.
6. Switch to the main document.
7. Enter the date field code.
8. Insert three blank lines.
9. Enter the appropriate merge field codes for the inside address and salutation.
10. Write a short, three-paragraph cover letter describing your qualifications for the job. In the first paragraph mention the reason you are applying and the job for which you are applying. In the second paragraph point out that you have enclosed your résumé, and mention a few pertinent details about your qualifications or experience. In the final paragraph, express your enthusiasm for the job or the company and your willingness to come in for an interview.
11. Spell check the letter.
12. Format the letter as appropriate, taking into consideration placement on the page.
13. Save the changes to the main document.
14. Check the main document for merging errors.
15. Merge the document to the screen.
16. Correct the main document, if necessary.
17. Print the three merged documents.
18. Close all documents.

Creating Reports

Writing a Report with a Table of Contents

CASE

Connolly/Bayle and Associates   Jessica Pangiana is a research assistant with Connolly/Bayle and Associates of San Francisco, a marketing research and analysis firm specializing in investigating economic development opportunities for municipalities. One of the firm's current clients, the Research Division of the Greater San Juan Economic Development Foundation, has contracted with Connolly/Bayle to develop a demographic and industrial profile of the greater San Juan area. The foundation will use the information to apply for grants from the federal and state governments for job training programs and to attract new businesses to the San Juan area.

Henry Santiago is Jessica's manager. He has asked her to create a preliminary report of the demographic and industrial staffing patterns in the San Juan area based on the data she has gathered. He will then use the information in this preliminary report to create a more extensive final report, which will go to the client.

Jessica will follow the productivity strategy to complete her task. In her report document, she has already created a title page, a page for the table of contents, and a third page with the body of her report—unedited and unformatted (Figure 5-1). She separated the three pages with hard page breaks. The body of the report contains three major sections: Methodology, Summary of Major Findings, and Conclusion. Both the Methodology and Summary of Major Findings sections are divided into smaller sections to help the reader digest the information. Jessica has printed the first draft of her report and indicated the changes to be made.

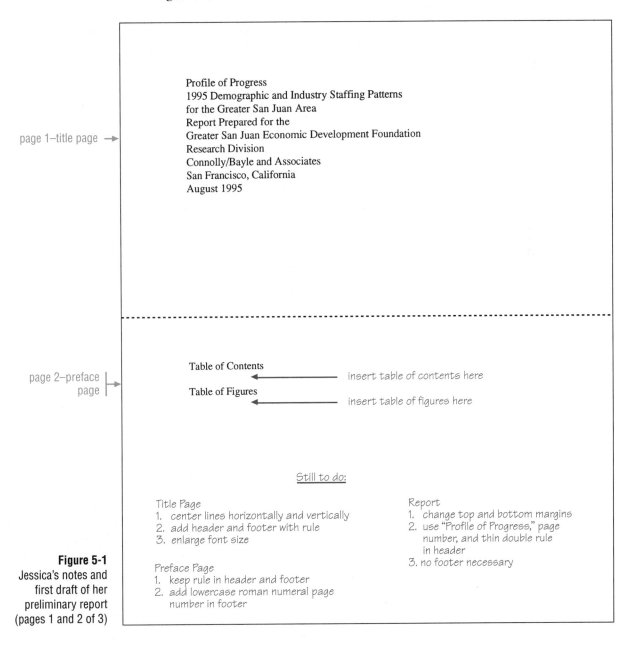

page 1–title page →

Profile of Progress
1995 Demographic and Industry Staffing Patterns
for the Greater San Juan Area
Report Prepared for the
Greater San Juan Economic Development Foundation
Research Division
Connolly/Bayle and Associates
San Francisco, California
August 1995

page 2–preface page ⊢→

Table of Contents
← insert table of contents here

Table of Figures
← insert table of figures here

Still to do:

Title Page
1. center lines horizontally and vertically
2. add header and footer with rule
3. enlarge font size

Preface Page
1. keep rule in header and footer
2. add lowercase roman numeral page number in footer

Report
1. change top and bottom margins
2. use "Profile of Progress," page number, and thin double rule in header
3. no footer necessary

Figure 5-1
Jessica's notes and first draft of her preliminary report (pages 1 and 2 of 3)

Introduction
The Profile of Progress is a compilation of industrial data designed to give the reader an overview of the population, job base, and job growth trends of the Greater San Juan area. The region, which encompasses San Juan, Bellville, Santa Maria, and Williston, continues to lead the way in California's recovery from the economic slump during the early '90s. The following report discusses both the data collection methodology and a summary of the findings.
Methodology
The Sample
The sample for this study was selected from the first quarter 1995 Employment and Wages report submitted to the California Department of Labor by the region's employers. The universe was stratified by standard industrial classification codes. Procedures involved all certainty cases.
Collection Procedures
The majority of the data was colected by mail. Each selected establishment received a structured schedule for there specific industry. The survey from included the following: instructions, occupational titles and definitions, business identification, and a standard industrial classification code. Survey procedures included three follow-up mailings to non-respondents. The telephone was used extensively to clarify data and to canvas critical non-respondents. The demographic statistics for the region was extracted from the 1990 census data.
Summary of Major Findings
Population
The 1995 Profile of Progress presents a growth statistic that continues to display the dynamic growth of the San Juan region. In 1990, the total population of the San Juan region was 192,457. This represents an increase of 48 percent over the 1980 figures and an increase of 150 percent increase over the 1970 figures. Greater numbers of jobs in the defense and computer industries accounted primarily for the population increases. Figure 1 depicts this dramatic growth.
Diversifying San Juan
Diversification, induced in part by natural forces, along with the ingenuity of area business leaders is largely responsible for the continued growth in the San Juan area. Figure 2 shows the makeup of the employing community.
Job Openings
According to our survey of the region's employers, on average, the occupational groups requiring the most education will also see the fastest job growth opportunities. Figure 3 lists the projected job openings during the next five years, including those due to replacement needs and those due to employment increases.
Conclusion
Current population growth trends indicate that the Greater San Juan area will provide a steady job force for the next five to ten years. The diversity of the area's industries will continue to provide 4,000 to 5,000 new jobs over the next five years if current trends continue. These jobs will be largely in the professions, administrative support, and service industries. The San Juan region is a vital area that has grown rapidly over the past two decades and will continue to grow well into the twenty-first century.

page 3–report →

insert chart 1

insert chart 2

insert chart 3

Figure 5-1
Jessica's notes and first draft of her preliminary report (page 3 of 3)

Jessica will edit the report, proofreading the document using Word's Thesaurus and Grammar tools. She will also transfer charts, which she created in another Word document using Microsoft Graph, from the chart document to her report. Next she will format the report. Then she'll create a table of contents and a table of figures before printing the document. Finally Jessica will create a customized document template from the existing document that she can use for other reports she might develop in the future.

To start Word and open the document that Jessica created:
❶ Start Word then conduct the screen check as described in Tutorial 1.

❷ Insert your Student Disk in the disk drive, then open the file C5SJPRPT.DOC from your Student Disk. Scroll through the document to become familiar with it. Compare your document to Figure 5-1. Notice that the document contains three pages.

❸ Click **File** then click **Save As...**, and save the document to your Student Disk as S5SJPRPT.DOC.

❹ Click **OK** or press **[Enter]**. The title bar changes to reflect the new document name.

Now Jessica is ready to start the editing phase of the productivity strategy. She begins by looking up an alternative meaning for a word she has used in her report.

Using Word's Thesaurus

You have used one of Word's proofreading tools, the Spelling command, to spell check a document for errors. Another proofreading tool that facilitates the editing process is the Thesaurus. Word's **Thesaurus** command provides synonyms and some antonyms for a selected word. Once you have looked up an alternative meaning for a word, you can immediately replace the selected word in the document with its synonym.

Jessica notices that she used the term "economic slump" in the first paragraph of the report text to describe the conditions of the local economy. She thinks that "slump" might be too negative, so she decides to use the Thesaurus command to find a synonym with a more positive meaning.

To look up a synonym for "slump" using the Thesaurus command:

❶ Move to page 3 then select the word "slump" (Pg 3, Ln 5).

❷ Click **Tools** then click **Thesaurus....** The Thesaurus dialog box appears with the word "slump" inserted in the Looked Up list box and three alternative choices in the Meanings list box. See Figure 5-2.

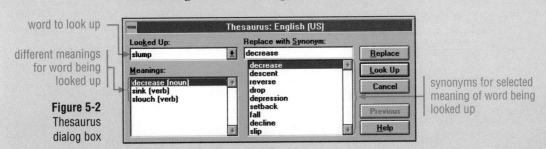

word to look up ─

different meanings for word being looked up ─

Figure 5-2
Thesaurus
dialog box

synonyms for selected meaning of word being looked up

The highlighted choice "decrease (noun)" in the Meanings list box is the appropriate meaning given the context of the word "slump" in her report, but Jessica doesn't like the choice of synonyms provided by Word. She decides to look up additional meanings for one of the listed synonyms, "depression."

❸ Click **depression** in the Replace with Synonym list box, then click **Look Up** or press **[Enter]**. The choices in the Meanings list box change to reflect options for the word "depression"; an option for antonyms also appears. The most appropriate meaning given the context in Jessica's report is "recession (noun)," not the highlighted choice "hollow (noun)."

❹ Click **recession (noun)** in the Meanings list box, then click **Look Up** or press **[Enter]**. Two meanings for recession appear in the Meanings list box, as well as an entry for Related Words.

"Economic slump (noun)" is the appropriate meaning, given the context. Jessica decides that "slowdown" is the synonym that seems most positive.

❺ Click **slowdown** in the Replace with Synonym list box, then click **Replace**. The selected word, "slowdown," replaces the original word, "slump," in the document.

❻ Save the changes you have made.

Next, Jessica will check her report for grammatical errors.

Checking Grammar

Another proofreading tool available in Word is the Grammar command. The **Grammar** command checks your document for proper grammar usage and style, in addition to checking for spelling errors.

Jessica added the Methodology section after she had checked the other sections for spelling and grammar errors, so she needs to check the grammar in just that part of her document.

To check the grammar in the Methodology section:

❶ Scroll through the document, then select the Methodology section of your document (Pg 3, Ln 8). See Figure 5-3.

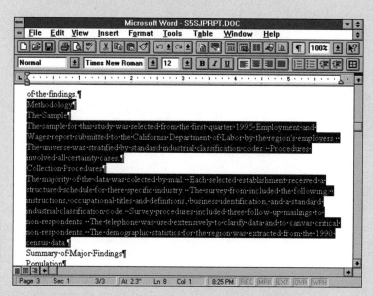

Figure 5-3
Document after selecting Methodology section

TROUBLE? Don't worry if your line endings differ from those shown here; continue with the tutorial.

❷ Click **Tools** then click **Grammar....** Word stops and highlights the sentence containing the first instance of a grammar usage or style problem. The Grammar dialog box also appears. See Figure 5-4. The sentence containing the flagged error appears in the Sentence box of the dialog box with the "problem" word or words printed in red. Word's suggestions to solve the problem appear in the Suggestions box.

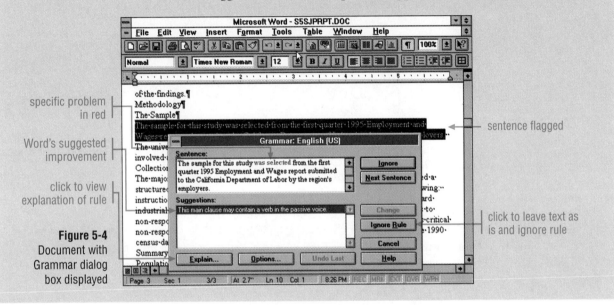

specific problem in red

Word's suggested improvement

click to view explanation of rule

Figure 5-4
Document with Grammar dialog box displayed

sentence flagged

click to leave text as is and ignore rule

Jessica needs further explanation of the problem and Word's suggested improvement.

To view the rule for the flagged grammatical error:
❶ Click **Explain....** An explanation of the grammar rule that applies to this sentence is displayed. See Figure 5-5.

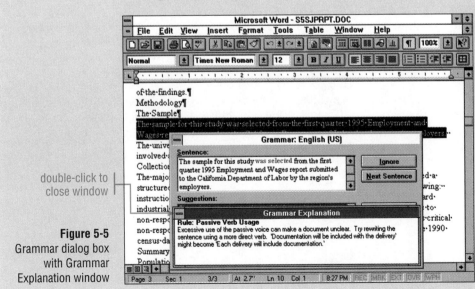

double-click to close window

Figure 5-5
Grammar dialog box with Grammar Explanation window

❷ After reading the explanation, double-click the **Control menu box** of the Grammar Explanation window to close it.

Although active voice is often preferable to passive voice, Jessica thinks that it is acceptable for a report of this nature, and she decides to ignore the rule for the flagged error.

❸ Click **Ignore Rule**. Word continues the grammar check process and stops at an incorrectly spelled word, "colected."

> **TROUBLE?** If Word did not find the misspelled word "colected," someone has deactivated the Spelling feature for the Thesaurus command. Click Cancel to close the Grammar dialog box. To activate the feature, click Tools then click Options.... In the Options dialog box, click the Grammar tab, then click the Check Spelling check box. Click OK or press [Enter], then repeat the grammar check procedure described above in this and the preceding set of steps.

As mentioned before, Word also checks for spelling errors at the same time it checks for grammatical errors.

To correct the remaining spelling and grammatical errors:

❶ Click **Change** to accept Word's spelling of "collected." Word next stops at the potential misuse of "there." Read the problem sentence and Word's suggested change.

> **TROUBLE?** If Word stops at errors other than those discussed in this section, click Ignore Rule and continue with the tutorial.

❷ Click **Change** to accept Word's suggestion. Word next stops at the potential misuse of the word "from." Read the problem sentence and Word's suggested change.

❸ Click **Change** to accept Word's suggestion. Word next stops at the potential misuse of the word "canvas." Read the problem sentence and Word's suggested change.

❹ Click **Change** to accept Word's suggestion. Word next stops at the potential misuse of the word "statistics." This time Word offers two solutions to this subject/verb agreement problem.

❺ Click the **second suggestion** in the Suggestions box (for changing the word "was" to "were"), then click **Change**.

Word finishes the grammar check of the selected block of text, and displays the following message: "Word finished checking the selection. Do you want to continue checking the remainder of the document?"

❻ Click **No** because you needed to check only the Methodology section.

Next Word calculates the readability of the selected text and displays statistics about its content in the Readability Statistics dialog box. This dialog box contains data about various counts, averages, and criteria that measure how easy your document or selected text is to read. See Figure 5-6.

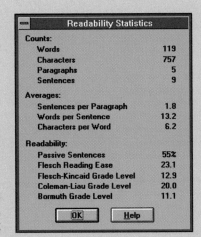

Figure 5-6
Readability Statistics
dialog box

Jessica isn't sure how to interpret the statistics so she decides to use Word Help.

❼ Click **Help** in the Readability Statistics dialog box. Read the information in the Help topic, then close the Word Help window.

❽ After looking over the readability statistics for the selected text, click **OK**, then deselect the text.

❾ Save the changes you have made.

Jessica has one more editing change to make before she moves on to the formatting phase of her task. To help her move quickly to the locations in her report where she needs to insert the three charts, she decides to mark those locations with bookmarks.

Assigning Bookmarks

You can assign a **bookmark** to mark the location of the insertion point, selected text or graphics, or other items that you need to move to quickly. You simply select the location, text, or graphics that you want to mark, then choose the Bookmark command from the Edit menu. You then give the bookmark a name. A bookmark name must begin with a letter, cannot contain more than 40 characters, and cannot contain spaces.

Jessica wants to mark the locations for the charts she must transfer to the report document (Figure 5-1).

To assign bookmarks to the three chart locations:

❶ Place the insertion point in the Population section after the sentence "Figure 1 depicts..." (Pg 3, Ln 29), then press **[Enter]**. This will be the location of Figure 1, which will show one of the charts.

❷ Click **Edit** then click **Bookmark....** The Bookmark dialog box appears.

❸ Type **figure1** in the Bookmark Name text box. See Figure 5-7.

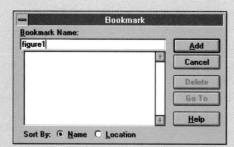

Figure 5-7
Bookmark
dialog box

❹ Click **Add** or press **[Enter]**. You return to the document.

Jessica wants to be able to view the bookmark locations in her document.

❺ Click **Tools**, click **Options...**, then click the **View tab** (if necessary).

❻ Click the **Bookmarks check box** in the Show section to select the option, then click **OK** or press **[Enter]**. The figure1 bookmark is now visible as a large I-beam. If you had marked text instead of a location, then the marked text would appear enclosed in square brackets.

TROUBLE? If the Bookmarks check box is already selected, do not clear it.

❼ Save the changes you have made.

❽ Place the insertion point in the Diversifying San Juan section after the sentence "Figure 2 shows..." (Pg 3, Ln 34), press **[Enter]**, then repeat Steps 2 through 4, naming the bookmark **figure2**. The figure2 bookmark is now visible.

❾ Place the insertion point in the Job Openings section after the sentence "Figure 3 lists..." (Pg 3, Ln 40), press **[Enter]**, then repeat Steps 2 through 4, naming the bookmark **figure3**. See Figure 5-8. Note that you might need to scroll the window to see all three bookmarks at one time.

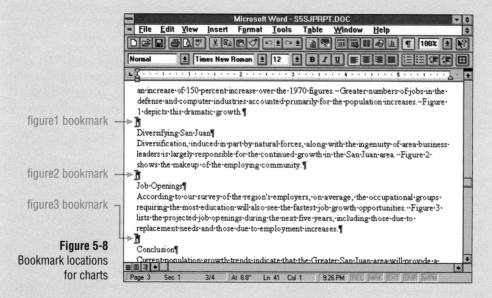

figure1 bookmark

figure2 bookmark

figure3 bookmark

Figure 5-8
Bookmark locations
for charts

❿ Save the changes you have made.

Jessica has finished the editing phase of the productivity strategy. Now she is ready to format the document.

Formatting Sections in a Document

Jessica's report poses some interesting formatting challenges. In consulting her notes (Figure 5-1), Jessica sees that she needs to align the title page vertically, change the top and bottom margins for the report pages, and create headers and footers for the title page and the table of contents that are different from the headers and footers for the report. Each of these formatting changes—adjusting vertical alignment, changing margins, and inserting different headers and footers—are page-level, or document-level, decisions. As such, they cannot be confined to specific pages as Jessica needs. In addition to these changes, she must make paragraph and font formatting changes to the title page, table of contents page, and the report.

Word's solution to situations like Jessica's is to divide a document into mini-documents called sections, each with its own page-level formatting options. A **section** is a portion of a document in which you can change page setup options, such as page orientation, margins, headers and footers, and vertical alignment. To create a section, you insert a **section break**, a division between sections in a document. When you insert a section break, a double dotted line appears across the page with the words "End of Section," and the status bar changes to reflect an increase in the number of sections in the document. You can either insert a section break using the Break command on the Insert menu, then make the necessary page-level changes, or you can use the Page Setup command on the File menu to insert section breaks as well as apply page-level formatting changes.

When Jessica created her document, she inserted a *page break* between the title page and table of contents page, and between the table of contents page and the text of the preliminary report. She wants to format the title page differently from the table of contents page and from the rest of the document, so she needs to delete the page breaks and insert *section breaks* in their place. Then Jessica can make her page-level changes to each section of the document.

Jessica's first step in making her formatting changes is to insert a section break between pages 1 and 2.

To insert a section break between pages 1 and 2:
❶ Place the insertion point at the top of page 2, directly before the "T" in Table of Contents, then press **[Backspace]** to remove the page break. The title page and table of contents page are combined temporarily. Notice that the status bar indicates that the insertion point is on page 1 of section 1. Until you insert a section break, your entire document is considered one section.
❷ Click **Insert** then click **Break....** The Break dialog box appears. See Figure 5-9.

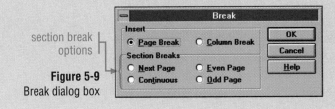

section break options

Figure 5-9
Break dialog box

Jessica wants to insert a section break, and she wants the text after the break to start on a new page.

❸ Click the **Next Page radio button** in the Section Breaks section, then click **OK** or press **[Enter]**. A double dotted line and the words "End of Section" are inserted across the page to indicate that a section break has been inserted. Notice that the status bar now indicates that the document has two sections and that the insertion point is on page 2 of section 2. See Figure 5-10.

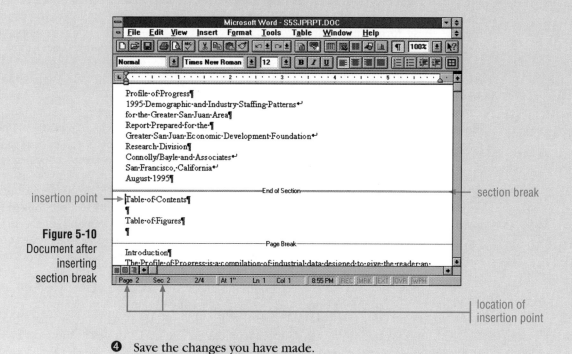

insertion point →

section break

Figure 5-10
Document after
inserting
section break

location of
insertion point

❹ Save the changes you have made.

Jessica wants to insert another section break between pages 2 and 3, and she wants the text after the break to start on a new page. She wants 0.75" top and bottom margins for just the text portion of the report.

To insert a section break between pages 2 and 3 then format the sections:

❶ Place the insertion point at the top of page 3, directly before the "I" in Introduction, then press **[Backspace]** to remove the page break.

❷ Click **File** then click **Page Setup...**. The Page Setup dialog box appears, with the Margins tab displayed.

❸ Change the top and bottom margins to 0.75", click the **Apply To list box down arrow**, then click **This Point Forward**. This option inserts a section break before the insertion point and applies the changes you just made to the margins from the section break to the end of the document. See Figure 5-11.

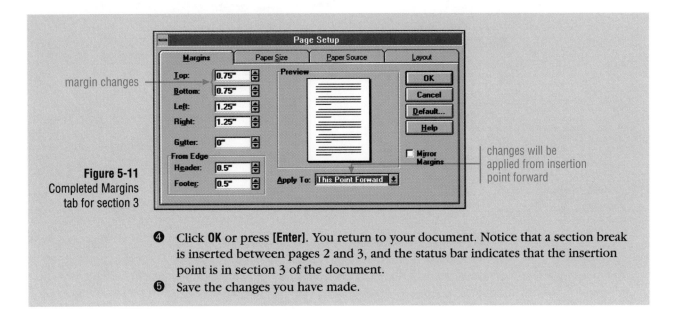

margin changes

changes will be
applied from insertion
point forward

Figure 5-11
Completed Margins
tab for section 3

❹ Click **OK** or press **[Enter]**. You return to your document. Notice that a section break
    is inserted between pages 2 and 3, and the status bar indicates that the insertion
    point is in section 3 of the document.
❺ Save the changes you have made.

Now that each part of the document—the title page, the table of contents page, and
the body of the report—is in its own section, Jessica can format each section individually.

To start, Jessica can align the title page vertically without affecting the rest of the document. When you align text vertically on a page, you align it between the top and bottom
margins.

Before changing the vertical alignment option, Jessica must first move the insertion
point into the section to be affected by the change. You can use the Go To command [F5]
to move quickly between sections.

To change the vertical alignment of the title page:
❶ Press **[F5]**. The Go To dialog box appears.
❷ Click **Section** in the Go To What list box, press **[Tab]** to move to the Enter Section
    Number text box, type **1**, then click **Go To** or press **[Enter]**. The insertion point
    moves to section 1.
❸ Click **Close** in the Go To dialog box.

Now that Jessica has moved the insertion point into section 1, she can change the
appropriate page-level options.
❹ Click **File** then click **Page Setup...**. The Page Setup dialog box appears.
❺ Click the **Layout tab**, click the **Vertical Alignment list box down arrow**, then click **Justified**.
    See Figure 5-12.

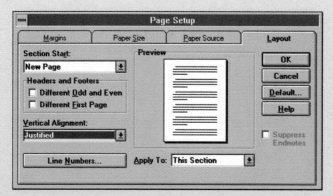

Figure 5-12
Completed Layout
tab for section 1

Notice that the Apply To list box indicates that the selected option applies only to the current section. The default Top alignment option in the Vertical Alignment list box places the contents of a page at the top margin; the Center option centers paragraphs between the top and bottom margins; and the Justified option increases the space between paragraphs on a page so that the first line is even with the top margin and the last line is even with the bottom margin.

❻   Click **OK** or press **[Enter]**.

Looking at the document in normal view, Jessica cannot tell if the title page is justified. She decides to switch to print preview.

❼   Click the **Print Preview button** 🔍 on the Standard toolbar (or click **File** then click **Print Preview**). Notice that the title page is justified between the top and bottom margins. The change in the vertical alignment of a page is a document-level option, but it affects only the section in which it is applied.

TROUBLE? If you do not see all three pages side by side in print preview, click the Multiple Pages button ▦ on the Print Preview toolbar, then drag across the grid to display three pages.

❽   Click the **Close button** on the Print Preview toolbar.

❾   Save the changes you have made.

Inserting Headers and Footers in a Multi-Section Document

Jessica indicated that she wanted to have headers and footers in all sections of her document, but, as she noted in Figure 5-1, she wants the title page and table of contents page to have both a header and a footer, and the rest of the document to have a slightly different header from the title page and no footer. Unlike other page-level formatting options applied to a section, changes to headers or footers in a section are connected to one another; that is, the header or footer in the first section becomes the default for the entire document. In addition, changes to the headers or footers in any section are reflected in all sections.

Jessica begins by inserting a header and footer in section 1.

To insert a header and footer in section 1:

❶ Place the insertion point in section 1, click **View**, then click **Header and Footer**. The Header text area, now labeled Header -Section 1, appears along with the Header and Footer toolbar.

Jessica wants the header and footer on the title page to be a ¾ point double rule across the page.

❷ Click the **Borders button** ⊞ on the Formatting toolbar, click the **Line Style list box down arrow**, then click the **¾ pt double rule**.

Jessica wants the rule to appear at the bottom of the line space in the header.

❸ Click the **Bottom Border button** ⬚ on the Borders toolbar. The double rule appears across the line space.

Next Jessica wants to place the same type of rule at the top of the line space in the footer for section 1.

❹ Click the **Switch Between Header and Footer button** ▣ on the Header and Footer toolbar. The insertion point moves into the Footer text area, which is labeled Footer -Section 1.

The ¾ pt double rule is already selected on the Borders toolbar, so Jessica must only specify its placement.

❺ Click the **Top Border button** ⬚ on the Borders toolbar to place the double rule at the top of the line space in the footer.

❻ Click the **Close button** on the Header and Footer toolbar.

Jessica wants to see how the changes to the title page appear.

❼ Click the **Print Preview button** ▣ on the Standard toolbar (or click **File** then click **Print Preview**). See Figure 5-13.

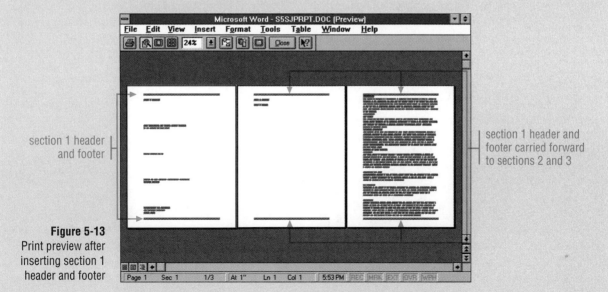

section 1 header and footer

section 1 header and footer carried forward to sections 2 and 3

Figure 5-13
Print preview after inserting section 1 header and footer

Notice that the header and the footer appear on all pages of the document, even the pages in sections 2 and 3. Header and footer changes carry forward through the next sections of a document unless they are changed.

TROUBLE? If you do not see all three pages side by side in print preview, click the Multiple Pages button ▦ on the Print Preview toolbar, then drag across the grid to display three pages.

⑧ Click the **Close button** on the Print Preview toolbar to return to your document.

⑨ Save the changes you have made.

Jessica wants the same type of rule in both the header and footer of section 2, which is the table of contents page, but she also wants the page number to appear at the center bottom of this page as a lowercase roman numeral. She must, therefore, change the format of the page number. Furthermore, she doesn't want a page number to appear in section 1.

To change the page number format:

❶ Place the insertion point in section 2, click **View**, then click **Header and Footer**. Notice that the label "Same as Previous" appears at the right of the Header text area and that the Same as Previous button ▦ on the Header and Footer toolbar is highlighted. This indicates that, unless you specify otherwise, the header for this section will be the same as the header of the previous section (in this case, section 1).

Jessica wants the double rule to appear in the section 2 header, so she can now move to the footer.

❷ Click the **Switch Between Header and Footer button** ▦ on the Header and Footer toolbar. The Footer -Section 2 text area appears with Same as Previous displayed on the right.

Jessica does *not* want the section 2 footer connected to the section 1 footer because she does not want a page number to appear in section 1.

❸ Click the **Same as Previous button** ▦ on the Header and Footer toolbar to deselect that option for this footer. The Same as Previous label disappears from the Footer -Section 2 text area.

Next Jessica wants to insert a page number at the center of the footer, and she needs to change the number format to lowercase roman numerals.

❹ Press [Tab] then click the **Page Numbers button** ▦ on the Header and Footer toolbar.

Jessica wants the page number to be a lowercase roman numeral.

❺ Select the page number, click **Insert**, then click **Page Numbers....** The Page Numbers dialog box appears.

❻ Make sure the Show Number on First Page check box is selected. This option will place the page number on the first page *of the section*.

Now Jessica needs to change the format of the page number.

❼ Click **Format....** The Page Number Format dialog box appears.

❽ Click the **Number Format list box down arrow**, then click **i, ii, iii, ...** See Figure 5-14.

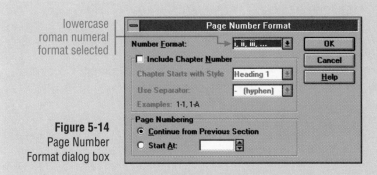

lowercase
roman numeral
format selected

Figure 5-14
Page Number
Format dialog box

⑨ Click **OK** or press **[Enter]**. You return to the Page Numbers dialog box. Click **OK** or press **[Enter]**. The page number format is changed to a lowercase roman numeral.

⑩ Close the Header and Footer toolbar, then save the changes you have made.

Jessica now needs to format the header and footer for section 3 of her document. Recall from Figure 5-1 that she wants to keep the ¾ point double rule in the section 3 header and add the name of the report and the page number. She wants to eliminate the footer altogether in section 3, because she'll include the page number in the header in this section.

To create different headers and footers in section 3 of the document:

❶ Place the insertion point in section 3, click **View**, then click **Header and Footer**. The Header -Section 3 text area opens. Notice that the Same as Previous label appears on the right and that the Same as Previous button 🖳 on the Header and Footer toolbar is highlighted, indicating that the header in this section is connected to the previous section. Also notice that the double rule doesn't appear completely because the header is too close to the text of the report.

Jessica doesn't want the header in the previous section of the document to be the same as the header in this section.

❷ Click 🖳 on the Header and Footer toolbar to deselect it. The double rule remains at the bottom of the line space, but the changes you are about to make to this header will not be reflected in the section 2 header.

❸ Type **Profile of Progress**, then press **[Tab]** twice. Type **Page**, press **[Spacebar]**, then click the **Page Numbers button** 🖼 on the Header and Footer toolbar. Select **Profile of Progress** then change its font formatting to **14 pt**, **Bold**, and **Italic**. Select **Page 3** then change its font formatting to **Bold**. Deselect the text.

Next Jessica wants to insert a blank line after the header so that it is not so close to the body of the report.

❹ Click the **right mouse button** on the header text to open the shortcut editing and formatting menu, click **Paragraph...** (or click **Format** then click **Paragraph...**), then increase the Spacing After option to **12 pt**. Click **OK** or press **[Enter]**. The additional space inserted below the double rule in the header makes the double rule completely visible now.

❺ Click the **Switch Between Header and Footer button** 🖼 on the Header and Footer toolbar. Notice that the Footer text area is labeled Footer -Section 3, that the Same as Previous label appears on the right, and that the button 🖳 is again highlighted.

Jessica wants to delete the footer in section 3 completely.

❻ Click ▦ on the Header and Footer toolbar to deselect the button, then click the **No Border button** ▦ on the Borders toolbar.

❼ Drag across the page number in the footer to select the number, then press **[Del]**.

❽ Click the **Close button** on the Header and Footer toolbar to return to your document.

Jessica wants to see how the headers and footers look.

❾ Click the **Print Preview button** � on the Standard toolbar (or click **File** then click **Print Preview**). Notice that the footer has been eliminated from section 3.

❿ Click the **Close button** on the Print Preview toolbar, then save the changes you have made.

If you want to take a break and resume the tutorial at a later time, you can close the current document then exit Word by double-clicking the Control menu box in the upper-left corner of the screen. When you want to resume the tutorial, start Word, place your Student Disk in the disk drive, then complete the screen check procedure described in Tutorial 1. Open the document S5SJPRPT.DOC, then continue with the tutorial.

▪   ▪   ▪

Jessica has finished inserting headers and footers into the different sections of her document. Now she is ready to add paragraph-level and font-level formatting, which will also enhance her report's appearance.

Defining Styles

In Tutorial 3, you learned to apply Word's predefined styles. If you do not want to use any of the styles in Word's predefined templates, you can define your own. Word provides two ways to define a new style. You can define a style by **example**—that is, by basing it on an existing paragraph that already contains the formatting options you want. You can also use the Style command on the Format menu to define a style by specifying each formatting option. Unless you indicate otherwise, user-defined styles are automatically added to the NORMAL template and, therefore, are available globally to all documents.

Jessica used the Style Gallery to preview the styles in Word's existing templates, but she did not find a template that contained the styles to fit her needs exactly. She decides to define her own styles, then save them in a customized document template, which she can use again if she needs to format a similar report.

Defining a New Style by Example

Jessica wants to apply a variety of paragraph and font formats to each line of text on the title page to improve its appearance. She wants some lines to be Arial, bold, 24 point, with centered alignment, a 72 point line space before, and a 36 point line space after. She wants other lines to be Arial, bold, 18 point, with centered alignment, and a 36 point line space before and after. Rather than apply each formatting option individually to each line, Jessica decides to define two new styles to contain the set of formats she wants to use, then apply the appropriate style to each line on the title page.

One way to define a new paragraph style is by example—that is, by using a paragraph that already has all the formats you want.

Defining a New Style by Example

- Select the example paragraph.
- Click the Style list box on the Formatting toolbar to highlight the name of the current style.
- Type a name for the new style.
- Press [Enter].

Jessica wants to define a new style for those lines on the title page that will be Arial, bold, 24 point, with centered alignment, a 72 point line space before, and a 36 point line space after the paragraph. She must first create an example paragraph with these formats, then define the style by example. Because she will be accumulating these styles eventually in a customized document template and doesn't want these new styles to be available globally, Jessica must also prevent Word from automatically saving them to the NORMAL template, thus altering the NORMAL template.

To define a new style by example:

❶ Click **Tools** then click **Options....** The Options dialog box appears.

❷ Click the **Save tab**.

Jessica wants to make sure that the styles she creates and modifies will not affect the NORMAL template.

❸ Click the **Prompt to Save Normal.dot check box**, then click **OK** or press **[Enter]**. When you select this setting, Word will display a message box asking you to confirm any changes to the NORMAL template when you exit Word. This will allow you to avoid changing the NORMAL template inadvertently.

   TROUBLE? If the check box is already activated, skip to Step 4 below.

❹ Move to page 1 then select the first line, **Profile of Progress**. Notice that the Normal style is in effect for the selected text.

❺ Change the font formatting of the selected text to **Arial, 24 pt, Bold**; then change its paragraph formatting options to a **72 pt** line space before, a **36 pt** line space after, and **Centered** alignment.

Now that you have created your "example," you will use it as the basis for your new style. The text should still be selected.

❻ Click the style named **Normal** in the Style list box on the Formatting toolbar. This highlights the Normal style.

   TROUBLE? Do not click the Style list box arrow and choose Normal from the list of styles. Simply select (highlight) the word Normal in the Style list box on the Formatting toolbar.

Next Jessica names the new style by typing a name to replace the highlighted word, Normal. A style name can be up to 253 characters in length and can contain spaces.

Style names are case sensitive so "*T*itle 1" and "*t*itle 1" can be the names given to two different styles. Make sure that names of new styles are unique and are not used by Word in its own predefined styles. Jessica wants to name this style "Title 1."

❼ Type **Title**, press **[Spacebar]**, then type **1**. "Title 1" replaces "Normal" in the Style list box.

❽ Press **[Enter]** then deselect the text.

Jessica next wants to see if the new style has been added to the Style list.

❾ Click the **Style list box down arrow** to display the Style list. The style name Title 1 is added to the Style list. The style in effect for the current location of the insertion point is highlighted. See Figure 5-15.

current style highlighted in Style box and in list

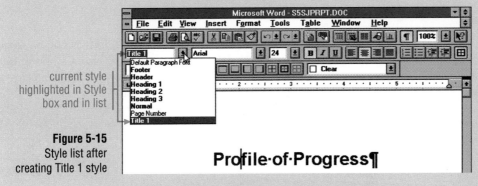

Figure 5-15
Style list after creating Title 1 style

❿ Press **[Esc]** to close the Style list.

Jessica will apply this newly defined style to other parts of the title page later, but now she needs to define another style for use on her title page.

Defining a New Style Using the Style Command

The second method for defining a new style is to use the Style command on the Format menu. Essentially you build the style from scratch by specifying all the formatting options you want the style to contain.

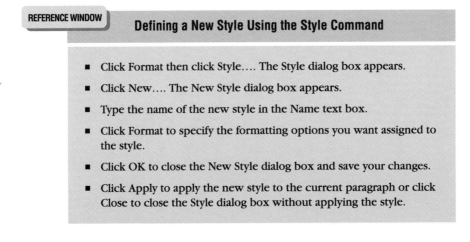

REFERENCE WINDOW

Defining a New Style Using the Style Command

- Click Format then click Style.... The Style dialog box appears.

- Click New.... The New Style dialog box appears.

- Type the name of the new style in the Name text box.

- Click Format to specify the formatting options you want assigned to the style.

- Click OK to close the New Style dialog box and save your changes.

- Click Apply to apply the new style to the current paragraph or click Close to close the Style dialog box without applying the style.

Jessica wants to name her second new style "Title 2" and to define it with the following attributes: Arial, bold, 18 point, centered alignment, and a 36 point line space before and after the paragraph. She decides to define this new style by using the Style command on the Format menu.

To define the new title style using the Style command:

❶ Select the paragraph "1995 Demographic and Industry Staffing Patterns for the Greater San Juan Area," click **Format**, then click **Style….** The Style dialog box appears with Normal highlighted and checked in the Styles list box. See Figure 5-16. The Styles list includes only those styles that have been used in the current document. The two Preview sections show the current paragraph and character styles. The Description section describes the formatting characteristics of the style applied to the selected paragraph.

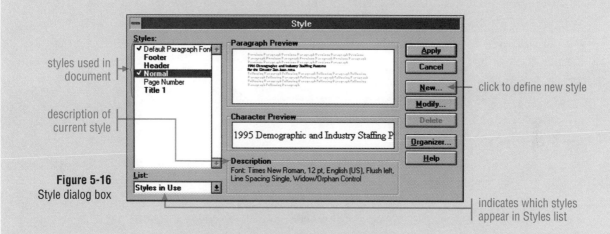

styles used in document

description of current style

Figure 5-16
Style dialog box

click to define new style

indicates which styles appear in Styles list

TROUBLE? If your Styles list includes more styles than shown in Figure 5-16, click the List box down arrow then click Styles in Use.

Jessica needs to define a new style.

❷ Click **New….** The New Style dialog box appears, with the suggested style name "Style1" highlighted in the Name text box.

Now Jessica needs to replace the style name supplied by Word with "Title 2."

❸ Type **Title 2** in the Name text box to name the new style. You can specify whether the new style is a paragraph style or a character style, which style the new style is based on, and even which style is in effect after you create a new paragraph with the new style then press [Enter]. Unless otherwise specified, new styles are based on the style applied to the paragraph currently selected.

"Normal +" appears in the Description section, signifying that the new style is based on the Normal style but could also contain additional features specifically defined for the new style. The name of the base style Normal also appears in the Based On list box.

Next Jessica specifies the formatting characteristics of the new style.

❹ Click **Format** then click **Font….** The Font dialog box appears.

❺ Change the font formatting options to **Arial, Bold, 18 pt**.

❻ Click **OK** or press **[Enter]**. The selected font options are previewed and added to the description in the New Style dialog box.

Now Jessica is ready to add the paragraph formatting options to the Title 2 style definition.

❼ Click **Format** then click **Paragraph....** The Paragraph dialog box appears.

❽ Increase the Spacing Before and Spacing After options to **36 pt**, then click **Centered** in the Alignment list box. Click **OK** or press **[Enter]**. You return to the New Style dialog box. Notice that the Description section has been updated to reflect the formatting characteristics of the new style. See Figure 5-17.

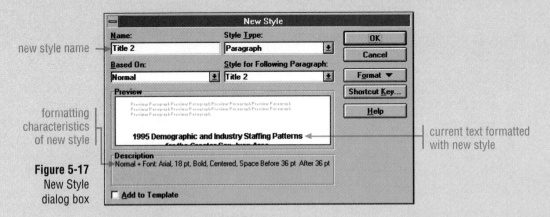

new style name

formatting
characteristics
of new style

current text formatted
with new style

Figure 5-17
New Style
dialog box

❾ Click **OK** or press **[Enter]**. You return to the Style dialog box. Title 2 has been added to the Styles list.

Jessica can now apply the new style to the selected paragraph or close the Style dialog box. Because she is not going to define any more styles for the title page, she decides to apply the style from the Style dialog box.

❿ Click **Apply** in the Style dialog box or press **[Enter]**. The new style is applied to the currently selected paragraph.

Jessica is now ready to apply the styles she has defined to the rest of the text on the title page.

Applying Styles

Word provides several methods to apply styles. As you learned in Tutorial 3, the easiest way to apply a style to selected text is to use the Style list box.

Jessica has created two new styles for her title page, and now she is ready to apply those styles to the appropriate paragraphs.

To apply styles on the title page and the table of contents page:

❶ Select the paragraph **Report Prepared for the**. The currently assigned style is Normal.

❷ Click the **Style list box down arrow** on the Formatting toolbar, then click **Title 2**. All the formatting attributes you defined for the Title 2 style are applied to the selected text.

❸ Select the paragraph **Greater San Juan Economic Development Foundation Research Division**, then apply the Title 1 style to it.

❹ Select the paragraph **Connolly/Bayle and Associates, San Francisco, California, August 1995**, then apply the Title 2 style to it.

Jessica decides to use the Repeat command ([F4]) to apply the Title 2 style to the titles on the table of contents page.

❺ Place the insertion point in the title Table of Contents on page 2, then press **[F4]**. Word repeats the steps to apply the Title 2 style to the selected paragraph.

❻ Place the insertion point in the title Table of Figures on page 2, then press **[F4]**. The Title 2 style is applied to the selected text.

Jessica wants to see how the title page and the table of contents page will appear when printed with the new styles applied.

❼ Click the **Print Preview button** 🔍 on the Standard toolbar (or click **File** then click **Print Preview**). Notice the changes to the first two pages of the document. See Figure 5-18.

new styles applied to title page

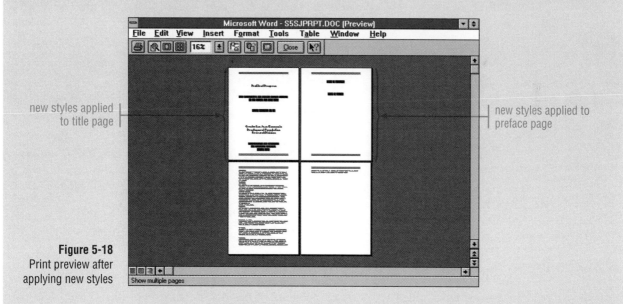

new styles applied to preface page

Figure 5-18
Print preview after applying new styles

TROUBLE? If you do not see all four pages in print preview, click the Multiple Pages button 🔳 on the Print Preview toolbar, then select four pages.

❽ Click the **Close button** on the Print Preview toolbar.

❾ Save the changes you have made.

Jessica has defined and applied styles to the title page and to the table of contents page. Now she wants to apply the predefined styles Heading 1, Heading 2, and Heading 3 to the headings in her report. Rather than using the Formatting toolbar to apply these styles, she uses the Style command on the Format menu.

To apply the heading styles using the Style command:

❶ Place the insertion point at the beginning of the heading Introduction on page 3.

❷ Click **Format** then click **Style...**. The Style dialog box appears. Notice that only the styles specifically applied to text in the current document appear in the list of styles; the predefined styles Heading 1, Heading 2, and Heading 3 are not available as they are in the Style list box on the Formatting toolbar.

Jessica wants to apply the Heading 1 style to Introduction.

❸ Click the **List box down arrow**, then click **All Styles**. All of the user-defined and prede-fined styles are listed in the Styles list box.

❹ Scroll through the list of styles, then click **Heading 1**.

❺ Click **Apply** or press **[Enter]**. The Heading 1 style is applied to the heading Introduction.

Next Jessica wants to apply the Heading 2 style to the headings Methodology, Summary of Major Findings, and Conclusion.

❻ Place the insertion point in the heading Methodology, then repeat Steps 2, 4, and 5 except click **Heading 2** in the Styles list.

Jessica uses the Repeat command to apply the Heading 2 style to the other headings.

❼ Place the insertion point in the heading Summary of Major Findings, then press **[F4]**. The Heading 2 style is applied to the selected heading.

❽ Place the insertion point in the heading Conclusion, then press **[F4]**. The Heading 2 style is applied to the selected heading.

Next Jessica wants to apply the Heading 3 style to the remaining headings.

❾ Place the insertion point in the heading The Sample, then repeat Steps 2, 4, and 5 except click **Heading 3** in the Styles list. Use the Repeat command to apply the style to the headings: Collection Procedures, Population, Diversifying San Juan, and Job Openings.

❿ Save the changes you have made.

Applying Styles Using Shortcut Keys

Jessica has applied styles to all elements of her document except to the main text para-graphs of the report. She decides to use one of Word's predefined styles, Body Text Indent, for the main text paragraphs. Because she has so many paragraphs to format with the Body Text Indent style, she decides to define a shortcut key for that style to reduce the amount of time she'll spend formatting the text.

To assign a shortcut key for applying the Body Text Indent style:

❶ Place the insertion point in the first text paragraph on page 3, click **Format**, then click **Style...**. The Style dialog box appears. Because you are going to apply the style after assigning the shortcut key, you need to place the insertion point in a para-graph to which you want to apply the style before choosing the Style command.

❷ Scroll through the Styles list, then click **Body Text Indent**. The Description section identifies the characteristics of the selected style.

❸ Click **Modify...**. The Modify Style dialog box appears. See Figure 5-19.

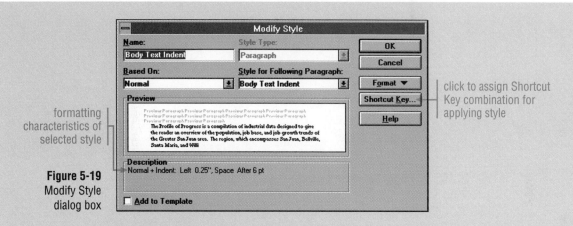

formatting characteristics of selected style

click to assign Shortcut Key combination for applying style

Figure 5-19
Modify Style dialog box

❹ Click **Shortcut Key…**. The Customize dialog box appears with the Keyboard tab displayed.

Word already has some shortcut keys assigned to options so Jessica must be certain to use a unique combination of keys. She decides to try [Alt][b] as the shortcut key combination.

❺ Press and hold **[Alt]** and press **[b]**. Release both keys. Notice that "Alt+B" appears in the Press New Shortcut Key text box, and a message appears indicating that this key combination is currently unassigned as a shortcut key combination for any other style.

❻ Click **Assign** or press **[Enter]**. The assigned shortcut key appears in the Current Keys list box. See Figure 5-20.

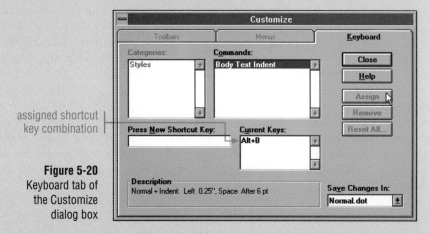

assigned shortcut key combination

Figure 5-20
Keyboard tab of the Customize dialog box

❼ Click **Close** or press **[Enter]**. You return to the Modify Style dialog box.
❽ Click **OK**. You return to the Style dialog box.
❾ Click **Apply** or press **[Enter]**. The attributes of the Body Text Indent style are applied to the selected paragraph.
❿ Save the changes you have made.

Next Jessica needs to apply this style to the remaining text paragraphs in her document.

To apply the Body Text Indent style using the shortcut key:

❶ Place the insertion point in the second text paragraph ("The sample for…").

❷ Press **[Alt][b]**. The attributes of the Body Text Indent style are applied to the selected paragraph.

❸ Continue applying the Body Text Indent style to the remaining text paragraphs using the assigned shortcut key combination.

❹ Save the changes you have made.

Jessica decides to view the document in page layout view so that she can see how it will print.

❺ Click the **Page Layout View button** 🔲 in the status bar (or click **View** then click **Page Layout**).

❻ Scroll through the document in page layout view.

❼ Click the **Normal View button** 🔲 in the status bar (or click **View** then click **Normal**) to return to normal view.

Jessica has applied styles to all elements of her document, but as she looked at the document in page layout view, she decided that she could further improve its appearance by modifying some of the styles.

Modifying Styles

You can redefine, or modify, any style, either Word's predefined styles or those that you have defined. Word automatically updates any paragraphs previously formatted with the style, thus saving you time and assuring consistent formatting throughout the document.

Jessica isn't satisfied with the appearance of the headings in her document. Rather than making manual changes to each heading in the document, she can simply redefine the formatting characteristics of the styles applied to these headings. Word then automatically updates each heading in the document based on these styles. She decides to redefine the Heading 1, Heading 2, and Heading 3 styles, and the Body Text Indent style. These changes would automatically be stored in the NORMAL template if Jessica had not first chosen the Save option to have Word confirm changes to the NORMAL template. In this way, Jessica can modify the styles for her report document only—the template will remain unchanged.

To make the heading Introduction stand out more, Jessica decides to increase the font size, change it to all uppercase letters, and increase the amount of space before and after the heading.

To modify the Heading 1 style using the Style command:

❶ Move to the top of page 3, then place the insertion point in the heading Introduction. "Heading 1" appears in the Style list box on the Formatting toolbar.

❷ Click **Format** then click **Style…**. The Style dialog box appears.

❸ Click **Modify…**. The Modify Style dialog box appears. Notice that the current definition of the Heading 1 style appears in the Description section.

❹ Click **Format**, click **Font…**, then make the following changes: **24 pt, All Caps**.

❺ Click **OK** or press **[Enter]**. You return to the Modify Style dialog box.

Next Jessica needs to change the paragraph formats for the Heading 1 style.

❻ Click **Format**, click **Paragraph...**, then make the following changes: **Spacing Before 48 pt** and **Spacing After 24 pt**.

❼ Click **OK** or press **[Enter]**. You return to the Modify Style dialog box. Notice the change in the Description section.

❽ Click **OK** or press **[Enter]**. You return to the Style dialog box.

❾ Click **Close**. Notice that the newly defined Heading 1 style is applied to Introduction. This is the only instance of a Heading 1 style in the report.

❿ Save the changes you have made.

You can also redefine a style by example using the Style list box on the Formatting toolbar.

REFERENCE WINDOW

Redefining a Style by Example

- Select a paragraph formatted with the style you want to redefine.
- Make the necessary formatting changes.
- Click the Style list box on the Formatting toolbar to select the style name in effect.
- Press [Enter]. The Reapply Style dialog box appears.
- Click the "Redefine the style using the selection as an example?" radio button, then click OK or press [Enter].

To keep the remaining headings proportional in size to the Introduction heading, Jessica also needs to redefine the predefined styles, Heading 2 and Heading 3. She used each of these styles throughout her document.

To redefine the Heading 2 style by example:

❶ Select the heading **Methodology**. The entire heading must be highlighted. The Style list box on the Formatting toolbar changes to reflect the style applied to Methodology, which is Heading 2.

Jessica wants to change several formatting options.

❷ Click the **right mouse button** on the selected text (or click **Format**), click **Font...**, then make the following changes: **18 pt**, **All Caps**.

❸ Click **OK** or press **[Enter]**.

❹ Click the **right mouse button** on the selected text (or click **Format**), click **Paragraph...**, then make the following changes: **Spacing Before 24 pt** and **Spacing After 6 pt**.

❺ Click **OK** or press **[Enter]**.

Jessica wants to add a rule to the Heading 2 style definition.

❻ Click the **¾ pt single rule** in the Line Style list box on the Borders toolbar, if necessary, then click the **Top Border button** 🔲.

TROUBLE? If the Borders toolbar is not displayed, click the Borders button ⊞ on the Formatting toolbar, then complete Step 6.

Now that Jessica has an example of the way she wants the Heading 2 style to appear, she is ready to redefine the style.

❼ Click the **Style list box** on the Formatting toolbar to select Heading 2, then press **[Enter]**. The Reapply Style dialog box appears for Heading 2. See Figure 5-21.

click to redefine style ─┐

Figure 5-21
Reapply Style
dialog box

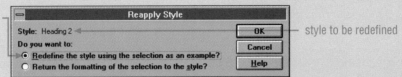

── style to be redefined

❽ Make sure the radio button for the option "Redefine the style using the selection as an example?" is selected, then click **OK** or press **[Enter]**.

❾ Scroll through the document to see that the new formatting characteristics for the Heading 2 style were also applied automatically to the headings Summary of Major Findings and Conclusion.

Next Jessica wants to change the formatting characteristics for the Heading 3 style and for the Body Text Indent style.

To redefine the Heading 3 and Body Text Indent styles by example:

❶ Select the heading **The Sample**. The entire heading must be highlighted. Use the Formatting toolbar to make the following font formatting changes: **Arial, 14 pt**.

❷ Click the right mouse button on the selected text (or click **Format**), click **Paragraph...**, then make the following changes: **Spacing After 12 pt**. (Spacing Before is already set to 12 pt.)

❸ Click **OK** or press **[Enter]**.

❹ Click the **Style list box** on the Formatting toolbar to select Heading 3, then press **[Enter]**. The Reapply Style dialog box appears.

❺ Make sure the radio button for the option "Redefine the style using the selection as an example?" is selected, then click **OK** or press **[Enter]**. Scroll through the document to see that all headings formatted with the Heading 3 style were automatically updated.

Now Jessica modifies the Body Text Indent style.

❻ Place the insertion point anywhere within a main text paragraph, then drag the indent markers on the ruler to the 1-inch mark.

❼ Click the **Justify button** ▤ on the Formatting toolbar.

❽ Repeat Steps 4 and 5 to complete modifying the Body Text Indent style by example. See Figure 5-22.

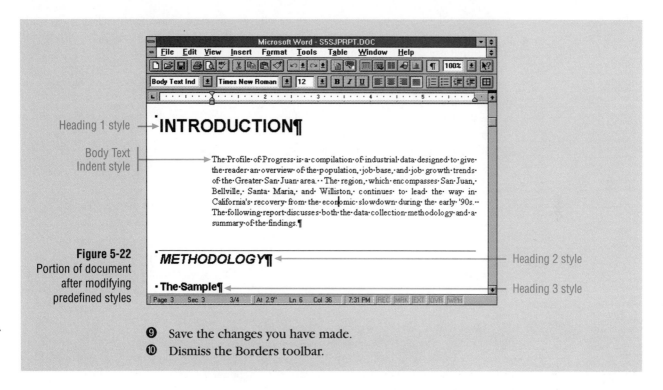

Heading 1 style

Body Text Indent style

Figure 5-22
Portion of document after modifying predefined styles

Heading 2 style

Heading 3 style

⑨ Save the changes you have made.
⑩ Dismiss the Borders toolbar.

Now that she has finished editing and formatting the text of her report, Jessica is ready to transfer the charts she created previously in another document.

Transferring Data Between Documents

One of the hallmarks of the Windows environment is the ease with which you can move or copy information. In previous tutorials, you learned ways to move or copy text *within* a document either by using the Clipboard or by using the drag-and-drop feature. The options for moving or copying information from one Word document to *another* Word document are basically the same as moving and copying text within a document. You can use either the Clipboard or the drag-and-drop feature.

Using the Clipboard to Transfer Data Between Documents

One way to transfer data between documents is by using the Clipboard. You can cut or copy selected text from one document, then paste the contents of the Clipboard in another document. Because the text is on the Clipboard, you can paste the cut or copied text as many times as you need to as many different documents as you need, including documents in other Windows applications.

Jessica thinks that the use of charts will enable the readers of the report to understand more easily the numeric data that she has gathered in her research. A **chart** is a visual display of numerical data in graph form. Jessica used Microsoft Graph to create the charts she needs to insert into the preliminary report and saved them in the file C5SJCHRT.DOC. Microsoft Graph is an **applet**, a small application designed to work with Windows programs such as Microsoft Word or Excel. To learn more about the use of Microsoft Graph, consult the *Microsoft Word User's Guide*.

Now Jessica needs to transfer the three charts she created in C5SJCHRT.DOC to their appropriate locations in S5SJPRPT.DOC. She marked the locations previously with bookmarks. She'll use the Go To command to move to the bookmarks.

To transfer the first chart using the Clipboard:

❶ Press **[F5]** to display the Go To dialog box, then click **Bookmark** in the Go to What list box.

❷ Click **figure1** in the Enter Bookmark Name list box, if necessary, then click **Go To** or press **[Enter]**. The insertion point moves to the selected bookmark. Close the Go To dialog box.

Now Jessica must open the document that contains the three charts she created.

❸ Open the file C5SJCHRT.DOC from your Student Disk. S5SJPRPT.DOC remains open, but it is not visible. Scroll through the chart document to view the three charts Jessica created: a 3-D column chart of population growth data for the area, a 3-D pie chart showing the different types of businesses in the area, and a 2-D stacked column chart showing projected job openings in the area. Each chart is on a separate page.

Jessica will follow the "select, then do" principle to copy the first chart to the Clipboard. To select a chart, you move the mouse pointer over the chart, then click. *Selection handles*, resembling small boxes, appear around the chart to indicate that it is selected. A selected chart is just as susceptible to change as selected text, *so be careful*.

❹ Move the mouse pointer over the 3-D Population column chart.

❺ Click the chart. Selection handles appear around the chart to indicate that it is selected. See Figure 5-23.

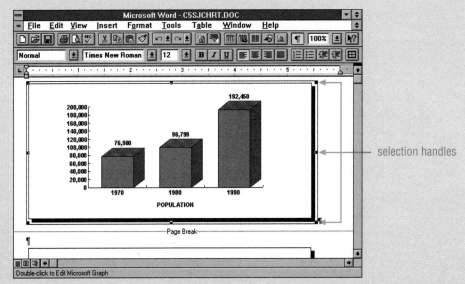

Figure 5-23
Selected
Population chart

TROUBLE? If you accidentally delete a chart, click the Undo button 🔄 on the Standard toolbar (or click Edit then click Undo Delete).

Now that the chart is selected, Jessica can copy it to the Clipboard.

❻ Click the **Copy button** 📋 on the Standard toolbar (or click **Edit** then click **Copy**).

Next Jessica will paste the copied chart from the Clipboard to its appropriate location in S5SJPRPT.DOC, but first she must make it the active document.

❼ Click **Window** then click **S5SJPRPT.DOC** to make it the active document. Notice that the insertion point is in the same location (figure1 bookmark) as it was before you switched. C5SJCHRT.DOC is still open, just not visible.

❽ Click the **Paste button** 📋 on the Standard toolbar (or click **Edit** then click **Paste**). The Population chart is pasted from the Clipboard to the report document. Notice that the bookmark has increased in size to match the size of the chart. See Figure 5-24. Press [↓] to see the entire chart.

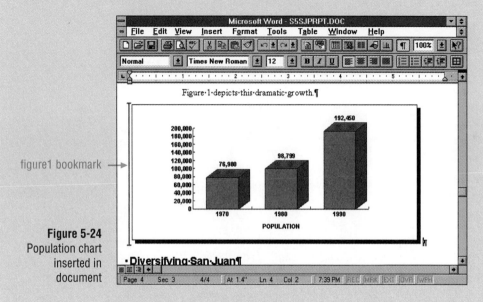

figure1 bookmark →

Figure 5-24
Population chart
inserted in
document

❾ Save the changes you have made.

Jessica next wants to transfer the pie chart from the chart document to the report document, but she decides to view both documents at once rather than switching between the two.

To arrange open documents on the screen:

❶ Go to the location of the figure2 bookmark in the report document, then close the Go To dialog box.

Rather than switch to the chart document, Jessica now arranges the screen so that both the chart document and the report document are visible at the same time.

❷ Click **Window**. Notice that C5SJCHRT.DOC and S5SJPRPT.DOC are the only two documents open.

TROUBLE? If other documents are listed, select them, then close them.

❸ Click **Arrange All**. Each document appears in its own document window, and S5SJPRPT.DOC is the active document. Notice also that the active document has its own document Control menu box and sizing buttons. See Figure 5-25.

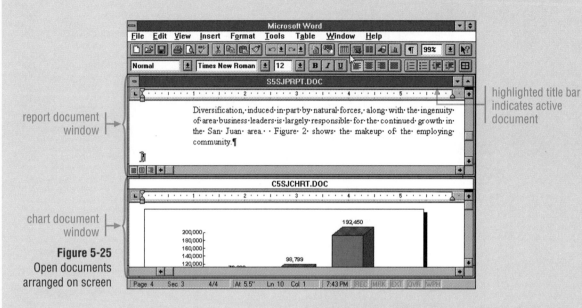

report document window

chart document window

Figure 5-25
Open documents arranged on screen

highlighted title bar indicates active document

❹ Click in the C5SJCHRT.DOC window (or press **[Ctrl][F6]**) to make it the active window, then move to page 2, the location of the pie chart.

❺ Click the pie chart to select it.

❻ Click the **Copy button** 📋 on the Standard toolbar (or click **Edit** then click **Copy**). The selected chart is copied to the Clipboard.

Next Jessica must paste the copied chart from the Clipboard to the report document.

❼ Click in the S5SJPRPT.DOC window (or press **[Ctrl][F6]**) to make it the active document. The insertion point is located at the figure2 bookmark.

❽ Click the **Paste button** 📋 on the Standard toolbar (or click **Edit** then click **Paste**). The pie chart is copied to its new location in the report document.

❾ Save the changes you have made.

Jessica has one more chart to copy to the report document. She decides to use the drag-and-drop feature to transfer the stacked column chart.

Using Drag-and-Drop Between Documents

In Tutorial 2 you learned to use drag-and-drop to move text within a document. With Word, you can also use drag-and-drop to *copy* text within a document simply by holding down the Control key as you drag the selected text. If you have the screen arranged so that two documents are visible at once, you can even use drag-and-drop to transfer data *between* documents.

To copy the third chart between the two documents using drag-and-drop:

❶ Go to the location of the figure3 bookmark in the report document, then close the Go To dialog box. The insertion point moves to the location of the figure3 bookmark.

❷ Click in the C5SJCHRT.DOC window (or press **[Ctrl][F6]**) to make it the active window, then move to page 3.

❸ Scroll until part of the stacked column chart is visible, then select the chart.

❹ Move the mouse pointer over the selected chart. Notice that the pointer changes to ☖ just as it does when it is over selected text.

❺ Press and hold **[Ctrl]** and hold down the **left mouse button**. The pointer changes to ☖⁺ to indicate that you are *copying* rather than *moving* the chart. See Figure 5-26. Do not release [Ctrl] until the copy is complete.

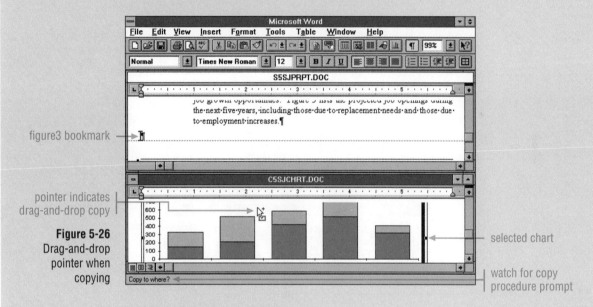

figure3 bookmark

pointer indicates drag-and-drop copy

Figure 5-26
Drag-and-drop
pointer when
copying

selected chart

watch for copy procedure prompt

❻ Drag the selected chart from the chart document over the title bar of C5SJCHRT.DOC until the dashed insertion point of the pointer is after the figure3 bookmark, then release [Ctrl] and the mouse button. The stacked column chart is copied from the chart document to the report and is still selected.

❼ Deselect the chart. Remember that when using the drag-and-drop procedure, the selected data is *not* placed on the Clipboard.

> **TROUBLE?** If you notice that the selected chart was moved instead of copied, you released [Ctrl] too soon. Click the Undo button ☑ on the Standard toolbar (or click Edit then click Undo Move), then repeat Steps 3 through 7.

Jessica no longer needs to see both documents at the same time.

❽ Click anywhere in the C5SJCHRT.DOC (or press **[Ctrl][F6]**), then close it without saving changes.

S5SJPRPT.DOC is still open but needs to be maximized.

❾ Click the **Maximize button** for the S5SJPRPT.DOC window.

❿ Save the changes you have made.

Now that Jessica has transferred the charts to the report document, she needs to format them by centering them and adding captions.

Adding Captions to Charts

Jessica formatted the charts when she created them in Microsoft Graph, but she thinks she can improve their appearance by centering them horizontally and adding an identifying caption.

To center the first chart and add a caption:

❶ Go to the figure1 bookmark, then click the chart to select it. If you use the Go To dialog box to move to the bookmarks in the steps, make sure you close the dialog box before continuing.

❷ Click the **Center button** 🔳 on the Formatting toolbar. The chart is centered across the page.

❸ With the chart still selected, click **Insert** then click **Caption....** The Caption dialog box appears with Figure 1 inserted in the Caption text box.

❹ After Figure 1, type : (a colon), press **[Spacebar]** twice, then type **Population Growth in the Greater San Juan Area**.

The Position list box indicates that the caption is to be inserted below the selected chart.

❺ Click **OK** or press **[Enter]**. The caption is centered below the chart. See Figure 5-27.

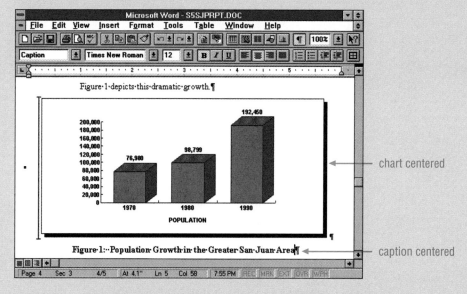

Figure 5-27
Formatted
Population chart

❻ Go to the figure2 bookmark, then select the pie chart. Repeat Steps 2 through 5, except insert the caption **Figure 2: Industrial Mix in the Greater San Juan Area**.

❼ Go to the figure3 bookmark, then select the stacked column chart. Repeat Steps 2 through 5, except insert the caption **Figure 3: Projected Job Openings**.

❽ Save the changes you have made.

Jessica wants to see how the pages split now that she has finished formatting her charts.

❾ Click the **Print Preview button** 🔍 on the Standard toolbar (or click **File** then click **Print Preview**). Notice the location of the charts on pages 4 and 5. See Figure 5-28.

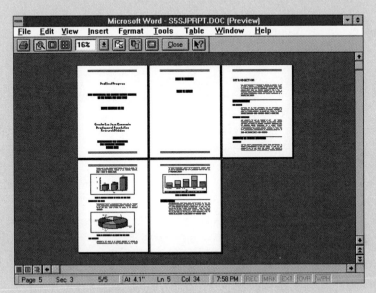

Figure 5-28
Formatted text and charts in print preview

TROUBLE? If you do not see all five pages, click the Multiple Pages button ▦ on the Print Preview toolbar, then select five pages.

❿ Click the **Close button** on the Print Preview toolbar.

Jessica no longer needs to see the bookmarks for the charts because she has inserted all three charts in her document. She can now deactivate the bookmarks.

To deactivate the bookmarks:
❶ Click **Tools**, click **Options...**, then click the **Bookmarks check box** on the View tab to deselect this option.
❷ Click **OK** or press **[Enter]**.

Jessica has finished formatting her report, and now she is ready to insert the table of contents.

Creating the Preface Page

In business reports, particularly long business reports, it's customary to include one or more preface pages immediately following the title page. The **preface pages** typically provide a list of the main topics so that a reader can go quickly to that topic without having to read the whole report. This list of main topics is called a **table of contents**. Word allows you to create a table of contents quickly, as well as a table of figures or a table of tables, if you have consistently applied styles to the various levels of topic headings or captions within a document.

Creating a Table of Contents

Jessica wants to insert a table of contents on the preface page between the title page and the text of the report.

To insert the table of contents for the report:

❶ Move to page 2, then place the insertion point immediately before the blank paragraph below the title Table of Contents.

❷ Click **Insert** then click **Index and Tables...**. The Index and Tables dialog box appears with the Index tab displayed.

❸ Click the **Table of Contents tab**.

Word provides a variety of formats for the Table of Contents page, but Jessica prefers the Formal style.

❹ Click **Formal** in the Formats box. Notice that the sample text in the Preview section changes to reflect the new formats. See Figure 5-29.

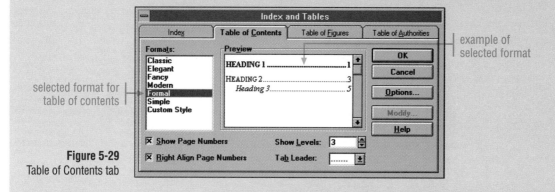

Figure 5-29
Table of Contents tab

Word will look for any text labeled with Heading 1, Heading 2, or Heading 3 styles, then display the text along with its corresponding page number in the Table of Contents.

❺ Click **OK** or press **[Enter]**. The Table of Contents based on text labeled with Heading 1, 2, or 3 styles appears at the insertion point. Recall that the title page used the styles Title 1 and Title 2, therefore, the text labeled with those styles was not included in the Table of Contents.

❻ Save the changes you have made.

Creating a Table of Figures

Next Jessica wants to insert a table of figures, which will list the names of the charts and their locations within the report. She will put the table of figures on the same page as the table of contents.

To insert a table of figures:

❶ Place the insertion point before the blank paragraph below the title Table of Figures on page 2.

❷ Click **Insert** then click **Index and Tables...**.

❸ Click the **Table of Figures tab**.

Jessica wants the table of figures to appear in a format similar to the table of contents.

❹ Click **Formal** in the Formats list box. See Figure 5-30.

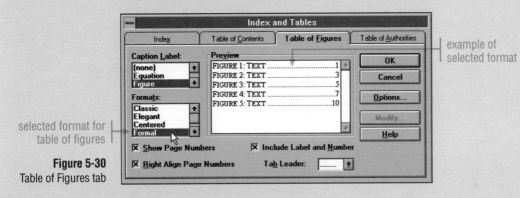

Figure 5-30
Table of Figures tab

❺ Click **OK** or press **[Enter]**. Word builds a table of figures based on the captions inserted below each chart.

❻ Save the changes you have made.

❼ Dismiss the Borders toolbar, if necessary.

Printing the Report

With her report complete, Jessica is anxious to print the document, but she decides to spell check it one more time because she has inserted text since she conducted the grammar check. After spell checking, she'll preview then print her document.

To spell check, preview, then print the document:

❶ Click the **Spelling button** on the Standard toolbar (or click **Tools** then click **Spelling...**) to spell check the document. If additional spelling errors are found, correct them, then save the changes.

❷ Click the **Print Preview button** on the Standard toolbar (or click **File** then click **Print Preview**). Jessica is satisfied with the appearance of her report.

❸ Click the **Print button** on the Print Preview toolbar. The printed document should be similar to Figure 5-31 on the following pages.

❹ Click the **Close button** on the Print Preview toolbar.

Profile of Progress

1995 Demographic and Industry Staffing Patterns for the Greater San Juan Area

Report Prepared for the

Greater San Juan Economic Development Foundation Research Division

Connolly/Bayle and Associates
San Francisco, California
August 1995

Figure 5-31
Jessica's completed
report (page 1 of 5)

Table of Contents

INTRODUCTION 3
METHODOLOGY 3
   The Sample 3
   Collection Procedures 3
SUMMARY OF MAJOR FINDINGS...3
   Population..3
   Diversifying San Juan...4
   Job Openings...4
CONCLUSION 5

Table of Figures

FIGURE 1: POPULATION GROWTH IN THE GREATER SAN JUAN AREA 4
FIGURE 2: INDUSTRIAL MIX IN THE GREATER SAN JUAN AREA 4
FIGURE 3: PROJECTED JOB OPENINGS..5

Figure 5-31
Jessica's completed report (page 2 of 5)

Profile of Progress

INTRODUCTION

The Profile of Progress is a compilation of industrial data designed to give the reader an overview of the population, job base, and job growth trends of the Greater San Juan area. The region, which encompasses San Juan, Bellville, Santa Maria, and Williston, continues to lead the way in California's recovery from the economic slowdown during the early '90s. The following report discusses both the data collection methodology and a summary of the findings.

METHODOLOGY

The Sample

The sample for this study was selected from the first quarter 1995 Employment and Wages report submitted to the California Department of Labor by the region's employers. The universe was stratified by standard industrial classification codes. Procedures involved all certainty cases.

Collection Procedures

The majority of the data was collected by mail. Each selected establishment received a structured schedule for their specific industry. The survey form included the following: instructions, occupational titles and definitions, business identification, and a standard industrial classification code. Survey procedures included three follow-up mailings to non-respondents. The telephone was used extensively to clarify data and to canvass critical non-respondents. The demographic statistics for the region were extracted from the 1990 census data.

SUMMARY OF MAJOR FINDINGS

Population

The 1995 Profile of Progress presents a growth statistic that continues to display the dynamic growth of the San Juan region. In 1990, the total population of the San Juan region was 192,457. This represents an increase of 48 percent over the 1980 figures and an increase of 150 percent

Figure 5-31
Jessica's completed
report (page 3 of 5)

increase over the 1970 figures. Greater numbers of jobs in the defense and computer industries accounted primarily for the population increases. Figure 1 depicts this dramatic growth.

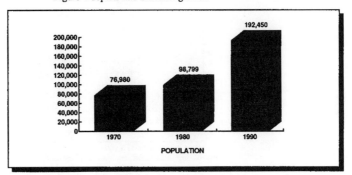

Figure 1: Population Growth in the Greater San Juan Area

Diversifying San Juan

Diversification, induced in part by natural forces, along with the ingenuity of area business leaders is largely responsible for the continued growth in the San Juan area. Figure 2 shows the makeup of the employing community.

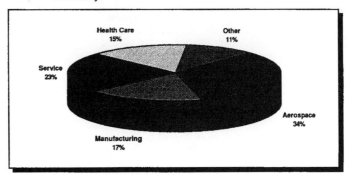

Figure 2: Industrial Mix in the Greater San Juan Area

Job Openings

According to our survey of the region's employers, on average, the occupational groups requiring the most education will also see the fastest

Figure 5-31
Jessica's completed
report (page 4 of 5)

Profile of Progress **Page 5**

job growth opportunities. Figure 3 lists the projected job openings during the next five years, including those due to replacement needs and those due to employment increases.

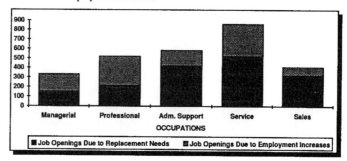

Figure 3: Projected Job Openings

CONCLUSION

Current population growth trends indicate that the Greater San Juan area will provide a steady job force for the next five to ten years. The diversity of the area's industries will continue to provide 4,000 to 5,000 new jobs over the next five years if current trends continue. These jobs will be largely in the professions, administrative support, and service industries. The San Juan region is a vital area that has grown rapidly over the past two decades and will continue to grow well into the twenty-first century.

Figure 5-31
Jessica's completed report (page 5 of 5)

Jessica has printed her document, but before she quits Word she wants to create a customized document template that will contain all the formatting and styles she has worked so hard to define in this report.

Creating a Customized Document Template

While Word's predefined document templates are indeed powerful, they might not exactly fit your needs, so you can create your own customized document templates. Once created, you use the user-defined document templates in the same way you use the predefined templates. Word provides you with several ways to create a customized document template, but the easiest way is to create a template from an existing document.

Jessica divided the original report document into three sections, each with its own specific formats such as headers and footers, margins, and vertical alignment. Although the formats and the styles she defined will be the same for future reports she might create, the text is likely to be different. Thus, her customized report template needs only to contain the styles and the section breaks. She must first prepare her document to be saved as a document template.

To prepare the document as a template:

❶   Make sure you have saved your most recent changes to S5SJPRPT.DOC.

Jessica wants to preserve the formatting in each of the three sections that she has created so she cannot delete any of the section breaks. She does not need any of the text in the document, however.

❷   Move to page 1, then select all the text on page 1 up to, but not including, the section break between pages 1 and 2. By not deleting the section break, the page-level changes made specifically for this section will be preserved.

❸   Press **[Del]**. Word deletes the text, but the styles applied to the text are still available.

Next Jessica moves to the page containing the table of contents. She does not want to delete the section break between pages 2 and 3.

❹   Move to page 2. Select the table of contents that you inserted, but *do not include* the title "Table of Contents" or the blank paragraph below the inserted table of contents.

❺   Press **[Del]**.

❻   Select the table of figures that you inserted, but *do not include* the title "Table of Figures" or the blank paragraph below the inserted table of figures.

❼   Press **[Del]**. The section break between pages 2 and 3 should not be deleted.

Finally, Jessica needs to delete all of the text in the report itself.

❽   Place the insertion point at the top of page 3, then press **[Ctrl][Shift][End]** to select all text and charts from the insertion point to the end of the document.

❾   Press **[Del]**.

Now Jessica is ready to save her prepared document as a customized document template.

To save the document as a template.

❶   Click **File** then click **Save As...**. The Save As dialog box appears.

❷   Click the **Save File as Type list box down arrow**, then click **Document Template**.

Ordinarily you would save your document templates to the Template subdirectory of the Winword directory along with Word's predefined document templates, but you will need to save this template to your Student Disk.

❸   Type **a:\s5report** in the File Name text box. Word will automatically add the template extension "DOT" to the filename. See Figure 5-32.

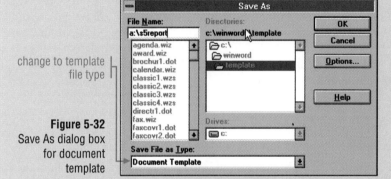

change to template file type

Figure 5-32
Save As dialog box for document template

❹   Click **OK** or press **[Enter]**. Notice the change in the title bar.

For future reference, Jessica wants to print the style sheet, which is a list of the formats defined for each style, for her customized document template.

❺   Click **File** then click **Print....**
❻   Click the **Print What list box down arrow**, then click **Styles**.
❼   Click **OK** or press **[Enter]**. The style sheet is printed.
❽   Close the document and exit Word. A message box appears asking if you want to save the changes you made to NORMAL.DOT. Recall that, at the beginning of this tutorial, you selected the option that displays this dialog box as a precaution. See Figure 5-33.

Figure 5-33
Microsoft Word message box

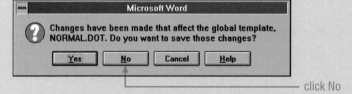

click No

Jessica does *not* want these changes to affect the NORMAL template.

❾   Click **No**. The following message appears: "You placed a large amount of text in the Clipboard. Do you want this text to be available to other applications after Word quits?"
❿   Click **No**.

Jessica submits the preliminary report to Henry. He is pleased with the report and is anxious to incorporate it into the final report.

Questions

1. What is the purpose of the Thesaurus feature?
2. What is the purpose of the Grammar feature?
3. What is the purpose of the Bookmark feature?
4. Under what circumstances would you want to insert a section break into a document?
5. What are two methods for inserting section breaks in a document?
6. What is the command sequence to go to section 3 in a document?
7. Describe the procedure for justifying a page vertically.
8. What is the significance of the Same as Previous indication in a header or footer?
9. How do you change page number formats within sections of a document?
10. Describe two procedures for defining a new style.
11. Describe three procedures for applying a new style.
12. Describe two procedures for redefining a style.
13. Describe the procedure for transferring information from one Word document to another Word document using the Clipboard.
14. Describe the procedure for transferring information from one Word document to another Word document using drag-and-drop.
15. Describe the procedure for arranging open documents on the screen so that they are all visible at the same time.
16. How do you know if a chart within a Word document is selected?
17. Describe the procedure for creating a document template from an existing document.
18. What is the procedure for inserting a table of contents in a document?
E 19. In the Print dialog box, how would you specify that you want to print only pages 3 through 5 in section 2 of a document?

Tutorial Assignments

Start Word, if necessary, and conduct a screen check. Open T5PROFIL.DOC from your Student Disk, then complete the following:
1. Save the document as S5PROFIL.DOC.
2. Use the Thesaurus to substitute an appropriate synonym for the word "variety" in the first paragraph on page 2.
3. Proofread the document for grammar and spelling errors, then save your changes.
4. Insert three bookmarks in the document to mark the appropriate locations of the three referenced charts. Make sure you place the bookmarks on the blank line following the figure references. Use the Tools Options command to display the bookmark symbol in your document, if necessary. Name the bookmarks Chart1, Chart2, and Chart3.
5. Substitute a Next Page section break for the page break between pages 1 and 2.
6. Insert a header into section 2 only. The header is to display on all pages except the first page of section 2. Section 1 should not contain a header at all.
7. Center the title page vertically.
8. Click Tools, click Options..., then click the Save tab, and make sure the Prompt to Save Normal.dot option is selected.
9. On the title page, apply the Heading 1 style to the following paragraphs: Profile of Progress and Greater San Juan Economic Development Foundation. Apply the Heading 2 style to the remaining headings on the title page. Save the changes.
10. Define a new style named "Main Text" for the main text paragraphs in section 2 of the document with the following paragraph formatting options: First Line Indentation set to 0.5" and Line Spacing set to double. Apply the style to the four text paragraphs in the Executive Summary.

11. In the Executive Summary, apply the Title style to the title Executive Summary; apply the Heading 3 style to the headings Population, Diversifying San Juan, and Job Openings.
12. Modify the Heading 3 style so that the Spacing After option is increased to 12 pt. Save the changes.
13. As header text for page 2, and all subsequent pages of section 2, insert the header "Executive Summary" at the left margin and the word "Page" plus the page number code at the right margin. Bold the entire header. Increase the Spacing After option for the header to 12 pt. Save the changes.
14. Open T5ESCHRT.DOC from your Student Disk, then copy the chart on page 1 to the Chart1 bookmark in S5PROFIL.DOC.
15. Copy the chart on page 2 of T5ESCHRT.DOC to the Chart2 bookmark in S5PROFIL.DOC.
16. Copy the chart on page 3 of T5ESCHRT.DOC to the Chart3 bookmark in S5PROFIL.DOC.
17. Close T5ESCHRT.DOC without saving any changes, center Figure 1 across the page, then insert the following caption above it: Figure 1: Population Growth in the Greater San Juan Area.
18. Center Figure 2 across the page, then insert the following caption above it: Figure 2: Industrial Mix in the Greater San Juan Area.
19. Center Figure 3 across the page, then insert the following caption above it: Figure 3: Job Openings. Save the changes.
20. Check the spelling in the document. Preview the document, making adjustments if necessary. (If the heading "Diversifying San Juan" appears as the last line on page 2, insert a hard page break before the heading to force it to the top of page 3.) Print the document.
E 21. Use Word Help to determine how to specify in the Header text area that page numbers are to start at page 1 of section 2. Make the change in your document, then save the changes as S5EXSUM.DOC. Preview the document then print just section 2.
22. Close the document. Do *not* save any changes to NORMAL.DOT.

Case Problems

1. Reporting on Printers at Buffington Engineering

Clinton Williams works as a hardware specialist in the Internal Information Technology Consulting Group of Buffington Engineering, a large consulting firm specializing in traffic engineering, urban planning, and engineering design of roadways, drainage, and structures. Buffington needs to upgrade the printers used by its staff, and Clinton's supervisor, Lyn Follmar, has assigned him to investigate the alternatives. After his initial investigation, Clinton wrote a memo to Lyn explaining his findings. He is now ready to insert a chart illustrating the data he gathered on printer sales.

Open P5PSALES.DOC from your Student Disk, then complete the following:
1. Save the document as S5BUFENG.DOC.
2. Check grammar usage and spelling in the document.
3. Attach the MEMO2 template to the document.
4. Apply the Title style to the heading Memorandum; apply the Message Header style to the paragraphs beginning "TO:..." through "...1995"; apply the Body Text Indent style to the memo text.
5. Open P5PSCHRT.DOC from your Student Disk, then copy the chart and place it a double space below the memo text in S5BUFENG.DOC.
6. Center the chart across the page.
7. Insert the following caption below the chart: Figure 1: Printer Sales.
8. Save the changes to the document.

   9. Preview the document, then print it.

E   10. Use Word Help to find out how to select vertical blocks of text. Select just the memo headings TO:, FROM:, RE:, and DATE:, then bold the vertical block of selected text. Save the document as S5VERT.DOC.

   11. Print then close the document.

2. Informational Handout on Inter-Tran Translation Services

Minh Vuong owns a language translation business, Inter-Tran, in Washington, D.C. She has prepared the basic text of a two-page informational handout about the services her company provides. She brings the document to you and asks you to help her improve the appearance of the handout.

   Open P5INTRAN.DOC from your Student Disk, then complete the following:

1. Review the document then save it as S5INTRAN.DOC.
2. Insert a Next Page section break between pages 1 and 2.
3. Center page 1 vertically.
4. Change the top margin of section 2 to 2" and the left and right margins to 1.75".
5. Insert appropriate headers and footers in sections 1 and 2.
6. Save the changes.
7. Click Tools, click Options..., then click the Save tab, and make sure the Prompt to Save Normal.dot option is selected.
8. Define attractive styles for the various elements of the handout, including at least two different styles for page 1 and two additional styles for page 2, one for the headings and one for the main text.
9. Apply the styles to the document. Save the changes.
10. Preview the document then print it.
11. Create a document template from S5INTRAN.DOC. Save it to your Student Disk as S5STYLES.DOT.
12. Print a style sheet for the styles used in your document.
13. Close the document. Do *not* save any changes to NORMAL.DOT.

3. Report on Career Opportunities

Write a double-spaced, two- to three-page report on the career opportunities in your major. Base your report on at least two sources, one of which should be the *Occupational Outlook Quarterly*. Consult your school's career counselor or reference librarian for other possible sources. Include in your report a discussion of potential job titles, salary expectations, academic preparation, and job mobility.

   Complete the following:

1. Type your report, including a title page. Use different levels of headings to break your report into subtopics. Save the document as S5CAREER.DOC.
2. Edit the report. Check for correct grammar and spelling, but also proofread the report very carefully on your own.
3. Format the report. Center the title page vertically. Insert appropriate headers and footers. Use the standard heading styles in Word or redefine them to fit your preferences. Save the changes.
4. Insert a Table of Contents.
5. Preview the report then print it. Also print the style sheet for the report.
6. Close the document. Do *not* save any changes to NORMAL.DOT.

OBJECTIVES

In this tutorial you will:

- Identify desktop publishing design elements
- Import text and clipart
- Use WordArt
- Use Organizer to copy styles
- Use outline view to reorganize a document
- Apply a newspaper-style column format
- Insert, size, and position frames
- Create a banner and drop caps
- Insert a masthead and a pull quote
- Layer text and graphics

Desktop Publishing with Word

Creating a Newsletter for Enviro-Disk

CASE

Enviro-Disk Al Wakefield, president of Wakefield Enterprises, is a new breed of entrepreneur: committed to saving the environment but also grounded in the realities of the free enterprise system. He has started a variety of companies, all with one common theme—to capitalize on the business opportunities becoming available with the nation's shift to a sound environmental policy. For instance, several years ago he realized that he was becoming inundated with old computer disks. He also knew that the cost of new disks was prohibitive for some people. He saw a business opportunity in recycling old disks by reformatting them, checking for and cleaning viruses, removing the old labels, then reselling the reclaimed disks at a greatly reduced price. To seize this business opportunity, Al founded the Enviro-Disk Company, just one of his many environmentally based companies.

Several months ago Al began publishing a local newsletter, called *Enviro-Newsletter*, to inform his customers of other companies in the burgeoning environmental business sector. His own efforts at desktop publishing were rather amateurish, so he decided to turn over the task of creating the newsletter to Keisha Beyah, currently in charge of marketing for Enviro-Disk, because of her past experience working on her college newspaper.

In this tutorial you will complete Keisha's task of creating the March issue of *Enviro-Newsletter*.

The finished newsletter will be a large file, requiring a significant amount of disk space. To ensure that your Student Disk will have enough space for the newsletter file, you'll first delete all the files you saved in Tutorial 1. (*Note*: If you do not want to delete these files, copy the files to another disk or directory. Once the files are copied to another location, delete the old files from your Student Disk.) Keep in mind that you might encounter storage problems if you choose not to delete some files from your Student Disk. Ask your instructor or technical support person for assistance, if necessary.

To delete the necessary files from your Student Disk:

❶ Turn on your computer, then insert your Student Disk in the disk drive.

❷ Using the Windows File Manager, delete all files beginning with "s1" from your Student Disk.

❸ Start Word then complete the screen check as described in Tutorial 1.

Introduction to Desktop Publishing

Publishing a professional-looking brochure, newsletter, program, advertisement, annual report, or any other marketing material previously took a great deal of effort by several people and could easily become quite expensive. With advances in computer technology and more sophisticated software, you can now typeset text, create graphics, layout a professional-looking publication, and get it ready for the printer right at your desktop computer—hence **desktop publishing** (DTP) was born.

DTP Design Elements

The trick to successful desktop publishing is to make your publications look as though they were done professionally. Before you can create your own desktop published documents, you must first know what design elements professionals use to make their documents look "professional." Figure 6-1 shows Keisha's final copy of the March issue of *Enviro-Newsletter* and illustrates some of the design elements that professionals typically include in their documents, which you can also accomplish using Word.

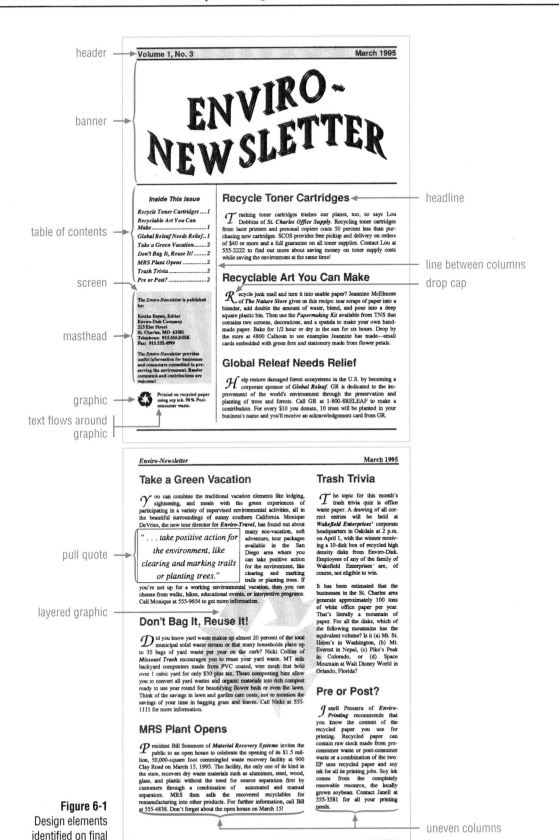

header → **Volume 1, No. 3**   **March 1995**

banner → # ENVIRO-NEWSLETTER

Recycle Toner Cartridges ← headline

*T*rashing toner cartridges trashes our planet, too, so says Lou Dobbins of *St. Charles Office Supply*. Recycling toner cartridges from laser printers and personal copiers costs 50 percent less than purchasing new cartridges. SCOS provides free pickup and delivery on orders of $40 or more and a full guarantee on all toner supplies. Contact Lou at 555-2222 to find out more about saving money on toner supply costs while saving the environment at the same time!

Recyclable Art You Can Make

*R*ecycle junk mail and turn it into usable paper? Jeannine McElmore of *The Nature Store* gives us this recipe: tear scraps of paper into a blender, add double the amount of water, blend, and pour into a deep square plastic bin. Then use the *Papermaking Kit* available from TNS that contains two screens, decorations, and a spatula to make your own handmade paper. Bake for 1/2 hour or dry in the sun for six hours. Drop by the store at 4800 Calhoun to see examples Jeannine has made—small cards embedded with green fern and stationery made from flower petals.

Global Releaf Needs Relief

*H*elp restore damaged forest ecosystems in the U.S. by becoming a corporate sponsor of *Global Releaf*. GR is dedicated to the improvement of the world's environment through the preservation and planting of trees and forests. Call GR at 1-800-8RELEAF to make a contribution. For every $10 you donate, 10 trees will be planted in your business's name and you'll receive an acknowledgement card from GR.

line between columns, drop cap →

Inside This Issue ← table of contents
Recycle Toner Cartridges 1
Recyclable Art You Can Make 1
Global Releaf Needs Relief.. 1
Take a Green Vacation......... 2
Don't Bag It, Reuse It! 2
MRS Plant Opens 2
Trash Trivia 2
Pre or Post? 2

screen →

masthead →

The *Enviro-Newsletter* is published by:

Keisha Beyah, Editor
Enviro-Disk Company
213 Elm Street
St. Charles, MO 63301
Telephone: 915.555.DISK
Fax: 915.555.4999

The *Enviro-Newsletter* provides useful information for businesses and consumers committed to preserving the environment. Reader comments and contributions are welcome!

graphic →
text flows around graphic → Printed on recycled paper using soy ink. 90% Post-consumer waste.

Enviro-Newsletter   **March 1995**

Take a Green Vacation

*Y*ou can combine the traditional vacation elements like lodging, sightseeing, and meals with the green experiences of participating in a variety of supervised environmental activities, all in the beautiful surroundings of sunny southern California. Monique DeVries, the new tour director for *Enviro-Travel*, has found out about many eco-vacation, soft adventure, tour packages available in the San Diego area where you can take positive action for the environment, like clearing and marking trails or planting trees. If you're not up for a working environmental vacation, then you can choose from walks, hikes, educational events, or interpretive programs. Call Monique at 555-9654 to get more information.

pull quote → *" . . . take positive action for the environment, like clearing and marking trails or planting trees."*

Don't Bag It, Reuse It!

*D*id you know yard waste makes up almost 20 percent of the total municipal solid waste stream or that many households place up to 35 bags of yard waste per year on the curb? Nicki Collins of *Missouri Trash* encourages you to reuse your yard waste. MT sells backyard composters made from PVC coated, wire mesh that hold over 1 cubic yard for only $30 plus tax. These composting bins allow you to convert all yard wastes and organic materials into rich compost ready to use year round for beautifying flower beds or even the lawn. Think of the savings in lawn and garden care costs, not to mention the savings of your time in bagging grass and leaves. Call Nicki at 555-1111 for more information.

layered graphic →

MRS Plant Opens

*P*resident Bill Sommers of *Material Recovery Systems* invites the public to an open house to celebrate the opening of its $1.5 million, 50,000-square foot commingled waste recovery facility at 900 Clay Road on March 15, 1995. The facility, the only one of its kind in the state, recovers dry waste materials such as aluminum, steel, wood, glass, and plastic without the need for source separation first by customers through a combination of automated and manual separators. MRS then sells the recovered recyclables into rich materials for remanufacturing into other products. For further information, call Bill at 555-4838. Don't forget about the open house on March 15!

Trash Trivia

*T*he topic for this month's trash trivia quiz is office waste paper. A drawing of all correct entries will be held at *Wakefield Enterprises'* corporate headquarters in Oakdale at 2 p.m. on April 1, with the winner receiving a 10-disk box of recycled high density disks from Enviro-Disk. Employees of any of the family of Wakefield Enterprises are, of course, not eligible to win.

It has been estimated that the businesses in the St. Charles area generate approximately 100 tons of white office paper per year. That's literally a mountain of paper. For all the disks, which of the following mountains has the equivalent volume? Is it (a) Mt. St. Helen's in Washington, (b) Mt. Everest in Nepal, (c) Pike's Peak in Colorado, or (d) Space Mountain at Walt Disney World in Orlando, Florida?

Pre or Post?

*J*anell Pessarra of *Enviro-Printing* recommends that you know the content of the recycled paper you use for printing. Recycled paper can contain raw stock made from pre-consumer waste or post-consumer waste or a combination of the two. EP uses recycled paper and soy ink for all its printing jobs. Soy ink comes from the completely renewable resource, the locally grown soybean. Contact Janell at 555-3581 for all your printing needs.

uneven columns →

← footer

Figure 6-1
Design elements identified on final version of newsletter

Figure 6-2 defines the design elements that you have not used so far in this book.

Element:	Definition:
Banner	The title of the newsletter, usually placed on the front page
Masthead	A list of the newsletter's address, phone number, subscription information, publication staff members, and other appropriate information
Screen	A shaded box appearing behind text to set it off and attract the reader's attention
Graphic	A photograph, drawing, chart, diagram, clipart, etc., used to enhance associated text and add visual interest
Headline	An article title, usually as brief as possible, that identifies the contents of the article and encourages the reader to continue reading the article
Drop Cap	A large uppercase letter, usually set in a different font, applied to the first character of a paragraph to add visual interest
Columns	Text formatted in two or more vertical columns of even or uneven width, creating shorter lines of text, which facilitate reading
Pull Quote	A phrase or quotation extracted from text in the document and formatted in a larger point size to attract the reader's attention
Layered Graphic	A graphic that appears dimmed behind text, so that it does not obscure the text, to add visual interest

Figure 6-2
Description of
design elements

Keisha has been given disks containing all eight articles for the newsletter. Although the articles take up the bulk of the newsletter, Keisha still has to create the banner, the table of contents, and the masthead. She is not ready to create the banner yet, and she can't create the table of contents until she is sure how the articles are best organized. She starts with the masthead information.

Inserting a Masthead

A **masthead** provides information about the publisher and a short mission statement. Typically, this information appears in a smaller font size than the text in the body of a newsletter. As shown in Figure 6-1, the masthead Keisha will create contains text on a screened background.

Keisha has not designed the banner for the name of the newsletter yet, but she does want to leave blank paragraphs as placeholders for the banner and for the table of contents. Therefore, before she types the text of the masthead, she'll insert some blank paragraphs.

To insert the masthead information:

❶ Press **[Enter]** three times to leave placeholders for the eventual placement of the banner and the table of contents and to allow for one blank line after the table of contents.

❷ Type the masthead information as it appears in Figure 6-3.

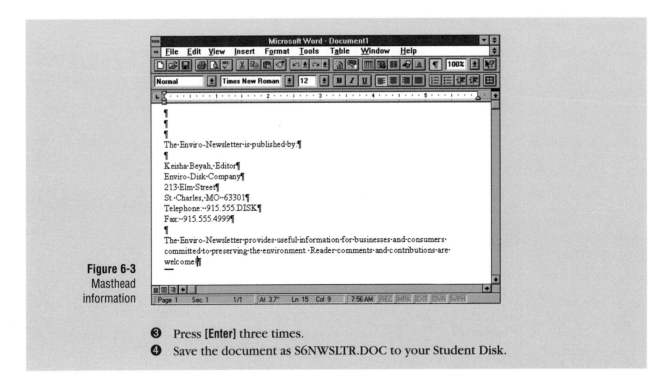

Figure 6-3
Masthead
information

❸ Press **[Enter]** three times.
❹ Save the document as S6NWSLTR.DOC to your Student Disk.

Now Keisha is ready to import the text for the articles in the newsletter.

Importing Text

You have learned several ways to transfer data within and between Word documents. You can also transfer data from a non-Word document into a Word document. To **import** a document means to insert either a non-Word document or a Word document file into another Word document. If you have installed the necessary conversion filters, you will notice no difference between importing a Word document and importing a **foreign-file** (non-Word) document. (See the *Microsoft Word User's Guide* for a list of conversion filters.) To insert a document into a Word document, you choose File from the Insert menu.

The newsletter readers have contributed eight articles to Keisha on disk: five in Word format, the rest in other formats. Rather than copying and pasting the text from the other documents into her newsletter document, she decides to import them using the File command on the Insert menu. She begins with the five Word articles. Let's import those now.

To import the five Word documents into the newsletter document:
❶ Make sure the insertion point is in the last blank paragraph at the end of the document (Ln 18).
❷ Click **Insert** then click **File....** The File dialog box appears.
❸ Switch to the drive containing your Student Disk, if necessary, then click **c6lou.doc** in the File Name list box. See Figure 6-4.

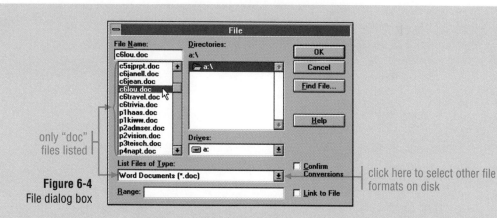

only "doc"
files listed

Figure 6-4
File dialog box

click here to select other file
formats on disk

④ Click **OK** or press **[Enter]**. The C6LOU.DOC document appears in the newsletter at the location of the insertion point. Notice that the formatting of the original document stays with the document.

⑤ Repeat Steps 2 through 4 to import the files C6JEAN.DOC, C6TRAVEL.DOC, C6JANELL.DOC, and C6TRIVIA.DOC (in that order) into your document immediately following C6LOU.DOC. *Do not press [Enter] between articles.*

⑥ Save your changes.

Next Keisha needs to insert those documents created using other word processing applications: C6NICKI.WP (a WordPerfect 5.1 document), C6RELEAE.M5 (a Word 5.0 for Macintosh document), and C6BILL.WRI (a Microsoft Write document).

To insert the foreign-format documents into the newsletter document:

❶ Click **Insert** then click **File....** The File dialog box appears. The File Name list box currently displays only those documents in Word format.

❷ Click the **List Files of Type list box down arrow**, then click **All Files (*.*)**. All files on your Student Disk are now listed in the File Name list box.

❸ Click **C6NICKI.WP**, then click **OK** or press **[Enter]**. A message appears briefly in the status bar indicating that Word is converting the file. The text of the WordPerfect file is inserted seamlessly into the newsletter document, as though it were a Word document. Notice that the formatting from the original document is transferred to the Word document. The WordPerfect code {PRIVATE} appears next to the article title as a result of the conversion, but it will not appear in the printed document.

TROUBLE? If the Convert File dialog box appears, click Cancel. Then click Insert, click File..., and click the Confirm Conversions check box to deselect it. Then repeat Step 3.

Next Keisha needs to insert the remaining documents that were created using other word processing applications.

❹ Repeat Steps 1 and 3 above to insert the files C6RELEAE.M5 and C6BILL.WRI into your document. Make sure that you have inserted all eight articles in the order specified. *Do not press [Enter] between articles.*

Even though the code after the heading of the WordPerfect document will not print, Keisha decides to delete it because it's distracting.

❺ Scroll up to the Don't Bag It, Reuse It article, select {PRIVATE} (make sure to include the braces), then press [Del]. The code is deleted from the document.

❻ Save your changes.

Now that all the text for the newsletter is in place, Keisha can begin to format the document.

Setting Mirror Margins

Attractive formatting is particularly important for desktop-published documents. Formatting should proceed in the same order for desktop-published documents as for other documents—page-level changes, paragraph-level changes, then font-level changes.

Page setup for a publication-style document is not necessarily as straightforward as with typical business communications. Consideration must be given early on as to how the document will be printed, whether the document will be duplexed (printed on both sides of the paper), whether the document will be printed in landscape or portrait orientation, whether the printed document will be bound, and whether it will be printed in color.

Word's Page Setup dialog box provides options for making these document-level decisions. The Mirror Margins option must be selected when you want to print duplexed pages. With **mirror margins**, the margins on facing pages "mirror" each other—that is, the inside margins are the same width and the outside margins are the same width. If a document is to be bound, you must also adjust the **gutter margin**, the additional space allowed on the inside margin of duplexed pages, to accommodate a binding.

Keisha wants the final newsletter to be printed with duplexed pages in portrait orientation. In addition, she wants the top, bottom, and right margins of the newsletter to be .75" and the left margin to be 1". Let's make these changes now.

To set the margins for the newsletter:
❶ Click **File** then click **Page Setup....** The Page Setup dialog box appears. Click the **Margins tab**, if necessary.

Keisha wants the final newsletter to be duplexed, or printed on both sides of the paper.

❷ Click the **Mirror Margins check box**. Notice that the Left option changes to Inside and the Right option changes to Outside, and that two facing pages appear in the Preview section.

❸ Change the Top, Bottom, and Outside margins to **.75"** and change the Inside margin to **1"**. See Figure 6-5.

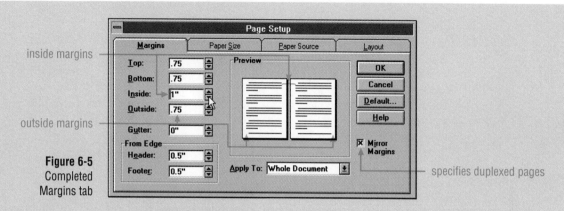

inside margins

outside margins

Figure 6-5
Completed
Margins tab

specifies duplexed pages

❹ Click **OK** or press **[Enter]**.
❺ Save your changes.

With the change in the margins, the entire width of the document is no longer visible on the screen. In order to see the entire width on the screen, Keisha decides to change the Zoom Control option to Page Width.

❻ Click the **Zoom Control list box down arrow** on the Standard toolbar, then click **Page Width** (or click **View**, click **Zoom...**, click the **Page Width button**, then click **OK** or press **[Enter]**).

The magnification percentage is reduced to 89% so that now the entire page width is visible on the screen.

TROUBLE? If the magnification percentage does not change to 89%, check the margins you just set in the Page Setup dialog box. Make sure you set them correctly, then repeat Step 6.

Now Keisha is ready to insert the banner, which is the name of the newsletter, at the top of the document.

Creating a Banner Using WordArt

Keisha wants the name of the newsletter in the banner to be impressive, so she decides to use **WordArt**, another applet like Microsoft Graph, provided with Word. WordArt allows you to create special effects with text—that is, create curved text or text that is turned on its side, angled, or even turned upside down.

When you choose Microsoft WordArt, you are no longer working in Word. Word is still running in the background, however. The process of running more than one application program at the same time is known as **multitasking**. Keisha will start Microsoft WordArt and use it to create the banner for her newsletter. When she is finished, she will exit WordArt and return to her Word document. The WordArt image she created will be inserted automatically into her document.

To start WordArt:
❶ Press **[Ctrl][Home]** to move the insertion point quickly to the top of the document. The insertion point should be in the first blank paragraph at the top of the document.

❷ Click **Insert** then click **Object....** The Object dialog box appears.

❸ In the Object Type list box, click **Microsoft WordArt 2.0**, then click **OK** or press **[Enter]**. WordArt starts and the Enter Your Text Here dialog box opens on top of your Word document. In your Word document the WordArt image, Your Text Here, appears surrounded by a crosshatched border. The WordArt menu bar and WordArt toolbar, used to choose the special effects to add to the text, also appear. See Figure 6-6.

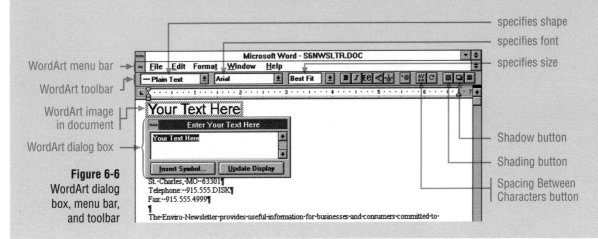

Figure 6-6
WordArt dialog
box, menu bar,
and toolbar

Keisha knows that she wants the banner to include the newsletter name, *Enviro-Newsletter*, but she's not sure of the special effects to add.

To create the WordArt image for the newsletter name:

❶ Type **ENVIRO-NEWSLETTER** (in all capital letters).

Keisha decides to use WordArt Help to look up a description of the special effects available in WordArt.

❷ Press **[F1]**. The Microsoft WordArt 2.0 Help window opens.

❸ Click the hot topic, **A Description of WordArt Special Text Effects**, then read the contents of the topic. Close the WordArt Help window.

Keisha decides to use the shape Wave2, the font Footlight MT Light, and the font size 50 pt for the banner.

❹ Click the **down arrow** next to Plain Text on the WordArt toolbar, then click the **Wave2 style** (row 4, last option). Click the **Font list box down arrow**, then click **Footlight MT Light**. Click the **Size list box down arrow**, then click **50**. The selected WordArt special effects are applied to the text.

Next Keisha decides to experiment with adding color, shading, and a shadow to the text.

❺ Click the **Shading button** ▨ on the WordArt toolbar. The Shading dialog box appears. Keisha wants the lettering to remain a solid pattern, but she wants to change the foreground color.

❻ Click the **Foreground list box down arrow** in the Color section, scroll through the list of colors, then click **Teal**. See Figure 6-7.

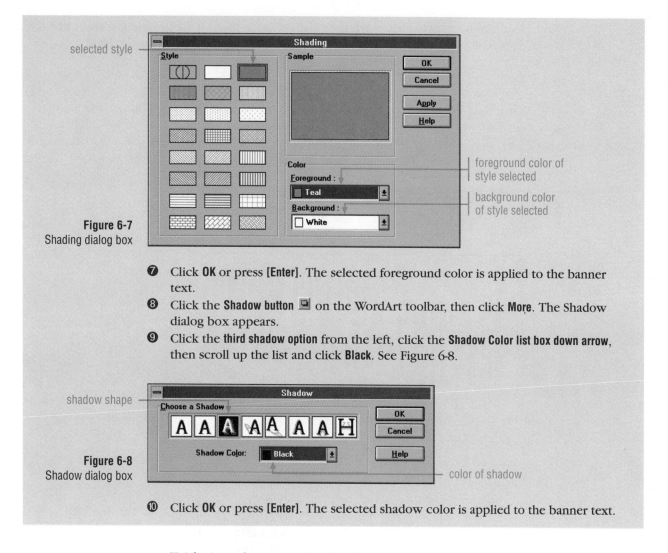

Figure 6-7
Shading dialog box

Figure 6-8
Shadow dialog box

❼ Click **OK** or press **[Enter]**. The selected foreground color is applied to the banner text.

❽ Click the **Shadow button** on the WordArt toolbar, then click **More**. The Shadow dialog box appears.

❾ Click the **third shadow option** from the left, click the **Shadow Color list box down arrow**, then scroll up the list and click **Black**. See Figure 6-8.

❿ Click **OK** or press **[Enter]**. The selected shadow color is applied to the banner text.

Keisha is ready to insert the WordArt image into her document.

Embedding an Object into a Word Document

After creating an image with WordArt, you can insert it into your document. The inserted image is considered an embedded object. An **embedded object** is an image, graphic, chart, or spreadsheet created and edited in another application, such as WordArt, but stored in a Word document. Keisha needs to embed the banner into her document.

To embed the WordArt image in the newsletter document:

❶ Click anywhere within the visible part of the document but outside the WordArt image and the dialog box. The WordArt image is updated in the document and appears surrounded by a border with selection handles, indicating it is selected.

Notice that the first paragraph mark now appears on the right side of the document, below the last letter of the banner.

Keisha notices that the image doesn't quite reach the right margin and, therefore, would not be balanced across the page. She decides to resize it using the handles.

To resize the WordArt image:

❶ Place the pointer on the middle handle on the right side of the image. The pointer changes to ↔.

❷ Click and drag the handle until it is even with the right margin, using the ruler as a guide. As you drag, the mouse pointer changes to +. See Figure 6-9.

Figure 6-9
Resizing the
WordArt image

resize image to right margin

pointer during resizing

❸ Release the mouse button. Note that the first paragraph mark moves back to the left side of the screen.

TROUBLE? If the first paragraph mark still appears on the right side of your screen, you did not resize the image far enough to the right. Repeat Step 2, making sure you drag the handle to the right margin. The first paragraph mark will move back to the left margin if you have resized the image correctly.

Keisha wants to switch to print preview to see how the banner looks in relation to the rest of the page.

❹ Click the **Print Preview button** 🔍 on the Standard toolbar (or click **File** then click **Print Preview**).

❺ Click the **Close button** on the Print Preview toolbar.

❻ Save your changes.

After viewing the document in print preview, Keisha decides to make some changes to the banner.

Editing an Embedded Object

Keisha decides that the text "ENVIRO" needs to be emphasized, so she decides to split the title after the hyphen in ENVIRO-NEWSLETTER, dropping "NEWSLETTER" to the next line. Then, she must edit the embedded image. To edit an embedded WordArt object, you double-click the object to start the application, or select the object then choose WordArt Object from the Edit menu.

To edit the WordArt image:

❶ Double-click the **WordArt image** (or select the WordArt image, click **Edit**, click **WordArt Object**, then click **Edit**) to start WordArt.

❷ Place the insertion point after the hyphen (-) in the Enter Your Text Here dialog box, then press **[Enter]**. "NEWSLETTER" moves to the next line.

Now that the banner text is on two lines, Keisha decides that rather than force the size of the font to 50 pt, she will let Word choose the best font size to fit the current image area.

❸ Click the **Font Size list box down arrow**, scroll up the list then click **Best Fit**.

Because of the black shadow behind the letters of the banner, some letters appear to be touching one another. Keisha thinks the letters in the name would look better if they weren't so close together. She decides to add more space between the letters.

❹ Click the **Spacing Between Characters button** 🔲 on the WordArt toolbar. The Spacing Between Characters dialog box appears.

❺ Click the **Loose radio button**. This setting will increase the spacing to be 120% of the original image size, as indicated in the Custom box.

❻ Click **OK** or press **[Enter]**. Extra space is inserted between each character.

❼ Click anywhere within the visible part of the document to embed the edited WordArt image in the Word document. The image appears selected in the document.

Keisha wants to separate the banner from the rest of the newsletter with a rule across the page.

To place a rule below the banner:

❶ Place the insertion point in the blank paragraph immediately below the banner (Ln 2).

❷ Activate the Borders toolbar, insert a 2¼ pt single rule at the bottom of the line space, then dismiss the Borders toolbar. See Figure 6-10.

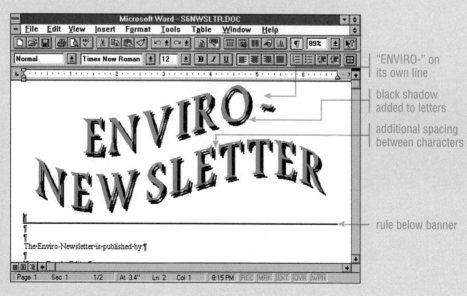

Figure 6-10
Newsletter banner
completed

❸ Save your changes.

To save time formatting the *Enviro-Newsletter*, Keisha decides to use the styles she saved in a template for another newsletter. She wants to copy only the paragraph and character styles, not the other text and formatting features of the template. Keisha can use the Organizer to copy the necessary styles.

Copying Styles Using the Organizer

Once you have defined styles for a document or template, you can share those style definitions with any other Word document or template without having to recreate them, thus saving production time. You can use Word's **Organizer** dialog box to copy styles between other documents or templates. You can also use the Organizer to delete or rename styles.

The styles Keisha wants to use are stored in a template named C6OLDNEW.DOT. She'll use the Organizer to copy the styles from this template. Before she does, however, she needs to prevent Word from automatically saving any style changes to the NORMAL template. As you learned in Tutorial 5 when defining styles, style changes can alter the NORMAL template.

To prevent changes to the NORMAL template:
❶ Click **Tools** then click **Options...**. The Options dialog box appears.
❷ Click the **Save tab**.
❸ Make sure the Prompt to Save Normal.dot check box is selected. If it is not, click it to select it. With this setting activated, Word will display a message box asking you to confirm any changes to the NORMAL template.
❹ Click **OK** or press [Enter].

Now Keisha is ready to copy the styles she needs.

To copy styles using the Organizer:
❶ Click **Format** then click **Style...**. The Style dialog box appears. The Styles list box displays only those styles currently in use in the document.

   TROUBLE? If the List box indicates All Styles, you are seeing a complete list of predefined styles. Click the List box down arrow, then click Styles in Use.

❷ Click **Organizer...**. The Organizer dialog box appears with the Styles tab displayed. The styles in use currently for S6NWSLTR.DOC appear on the left side of the Organizer dialog box, and the styles for the NORMAL template appear on the right. See Figure 6-11.

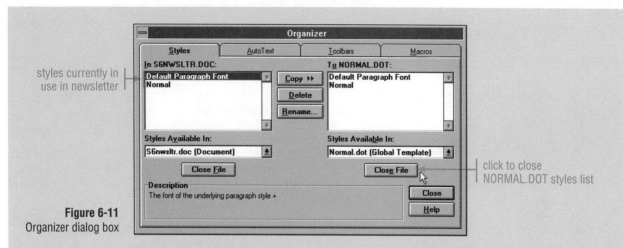

styles currently in use in newsletter

click to close NORMAL.DOT styles list

Figure 6-11
Organizer dialog box

Keisha needs to display the styles for the C6OLDNEW template instead of those for the NORMAL template.

❸ Click **Close File** below the NORMAL template list of styles. (See Figure 6-11.) The Close File button changes to the Open File… button.

❹ Click **Open File…**. The Open dialog box appears with all file types displayed.

   TROUBLE? If all files are not listed, select All Files (*.*) from the List Files of Type list box in the Open dialog box.

❺ Select the drive containing your Student Disk, click **C6OLDNEW.DOT**, then click **OK** or press **[Enter]**.

   The right side of the Organizer dialog box now lists the styles for C6OLDNEW.DOT. You can select multiple styles at one time, rather than selecting and copying each style individually. To select consecutive styles in a range, click the first name in the range to be selected, hold down [Shift], then click the last style name in the range. To select non-adjacent styles, click the first style to be selected, then press [Ctrl] while clicking the remaining style names to be selected. To deselect individual styles, press and hold [Ctrl] then click the style name to be deselected.

❻ Click **Article Text**, hold down **[Shift]**, scroll to the bottom of the list, click the last name in the list, **Recycle**, then release [Shift]. All the names in the list are selected. Notice that the arrows on the Copy button now point to the left, indicating that the styles will be copied *from* the C6OLDNEW.DOT template to the current document.

   TROUBLE? All style names for C6OLDNEW.DOT should be highlighted. If not, repeat Step 6.

Keisha decides that she doesn't want to overwrite the Normal style or the Default Paragraph Font style with those same style names from the C6OLDNEW template. She must deselect those two styles from the list.

❼ Press and hold **[Ctrl]** while you click **Normal**, then click **Default Paragraph Font** in the C6OLDNEW.DOT styles list. The two styles are deselected while the remaining styles are still selected.

❽ Click **Copy**. The selected style names now appear in the style list for S6NWSLTR.DOC. See Figure 6-12.

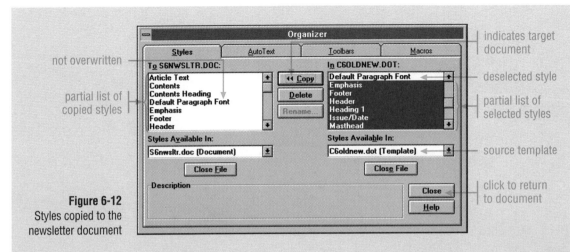

Figure 6-12
Styles copied to the
newsletter document

⑨ Click **Close** in the lower-right corner of the dialog box (*do not click either of the Close File buttons*).

Keisha wants to make sure that the styles from the C6OLDNEW.DOT template have been transferred to her current document.

⑩ Click the **Style list box down arrow** on the Formatting toolbar. The new styles are listed. Press **[Esc]** to close the Style list without making a selection, then save your changes.

Now that she has copied the styles, Keisha is ready to apply them to the appropriate elements of her newsletter.

Displaying the Style Area

To make sure that you apply the correct style to different parts of your documents, you can display the style area along the left margin. The **style area** displays the name of the style applied to the adjacent paragraph. The style area is usually hidden, but you can display it by specifying a style area width on the View tab of the Options dialog box. The style area can be seen only in normal or in outline view.

Keisha decides to display the style area to help ensure that she applies the appropriate styles to her document. Let's do that now.

To display the style area:
❶ Click **Tools** then click **Options....** The Options dialog box appears.
❷ In the Window section of the View tab, increase the Style Area Width option to **0.5"**.
❸ Click **OK** or press **[Enter]**.
Keisha still wants to be able to see the full width of the document on the screen.
❹ Click the **Zoom Control list box down arrow**, then click **Page Width**. Notice that the style area is now visible and that only the Normal style has been used so far in the document. See Figure 6-13.

style area

Figure 6-13
Style area displayed

Now that the style area is displayed, Keisha can apply appropriate styles to the various design elements of the newsletter.

Applying Styles Using Shortcut Keys

Keisha had assigned shortcut keys to the paragraph and character styles that she copied into the current document from the old newsletter template. Figure 6-14 lists the style names and their assigned shortcut keys.

Style Name:	Shortcut Key:	Style Name:	Shortcut Key:
Article Text	[Alt][t]	Heading 1	[Alt][Shift][1]
Contents	[Alt][n]	Issue/Date	[Alt][i]
Contents Heading	[Alt][c]	Masthead	[Alt][m]
Emphasis	[Ctrl][Shift][e]	Recycle	[Alt][r]

Figure 6-14
Shortcut keys for
copied styles

Let's apply these styles now.

To apply the paragraph styles using shortcut keys:

❶ Select the masthead information, beginning with the blank paragraph (Ln 4) above the words "The Enviro-Newsletter is published..." through "...welcome!", then press **[Alt][m]**. The formats defined for the Masthead style are applied to the selected text. Notice the change in the Style list box and in the style area in the left margin. See Figure 6-15.

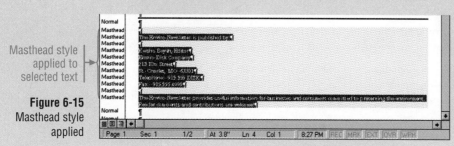

Masthead style
applied to
selected text

Figure 6-15
Masthead style
applied

TROUBLE? If the shortcut keys do not work as described in these steps, apply the styles to the appropriate text by selecting the styles from the Style list box on the Formatting toolbar.

Keisha wants to check the attributes of the Masthead style using Reveal Formats.

❷ Click the **Help button** 🔍 on the Standard toolbar, move the mouse pointer over the masthead text, then click. The attributes assigned to the Masthead style are displayed in the Reveal Formats box. Press **[Esc]** to dismiss the Reveal Formats box.

❸ Place the insertion point in the headline for the first article, Recycle Toner Cartridges, then press **[Alt][Shift][1]**. The Heading 1 style is applied to the headline. Notice the change in the Style list box and in the style area. Use the Reveal Formats feature to view the attributes for the newly applied style.

❹ Place the insertion point in the text of the first article, then press **[Alt][t]**. The Article Text style is applied to the text. Notice the change in the Style list box and in the style area. Use the Reveal Formats feature to view the attributes for the applied style.

❺ Apply the Heading 1 style to the headlines and apply the Article Text style to the text paragraphs for the remaining articles. Notice that the document now extends to three pages.

❻ Save your changes.

Keisha also created a character style, called Emphasis, for words that need to be emphasized in the newsletter. The character attributes for the style are italics and bold. Keisha decides to apply the Emphasis style to the first occurrence of the specific company's name in each article using the shortcut key combination, [Ctrl][Shift][e].

To apply the character style to selected text in the newsletter:

❶ In the Recycle Toner Cartridges article, select **St. Charles Office Supply** then press **[Ctrl][Shift][e]** to apply the Emphasis character style.

❷ In the next article, select **The Nature Store** then press **[F4]** (Repeat) to apply the Emphasis style again.

❸ In the remaining articles, select the first instance of each company's name— Enviro-Travel, Enviro-Printing, Wakefield Enterprises', Missouri Trash, Global Releaf, and Material Recovery Systems—then press **[F4]** to apply the Emphasis character style. Then save your changes.

Keisha notices that the name of the newsletter, Enviro-Newsletter, should appear in italics as well as bold in the masthead. The text is already bold, as specified by the Masthead style. Therefore, she cannot apply the Emphasis style to this text because doing so would remove the bolding from it. Keisha simply needs to italicize the text.

❹ Italicize both occurrences of **Enviro-Newsletter** in the masthead.

Keisha has applied all the styles and can now close the style area.

❺ Click **Tools** then click **Options....** On the View tab, decrease the Style Area Width option to **0"**.

❻ Click **OK** or press **[Enter]**.

Keisha wants to be able to see as much of the document as possible.

❼ Click the **Zoom Control list box down arrow**, then click **Page Width**.

Next, Keisha needs to format the newsletter in columns. To do so, she'll work in page layout view.

Activating Paste-Up Tools

The traditional means of arranging the text of a publication is called creating a **dummy**, or a **paste-up**, of the page layout of the document. It is essential to be able to see how a document will fit best within the allotted pages. You can approximate this step electronically with some of Word's view options. Page layout view, which you used previously in Tutorials 3 and 5, gives you the most accurate What-You-See-Is-What-You-Get (WYSIWYG) display of text as it will print, a capability essential for "pasting up" dummy documents. Unlike normal view, page layout view displays headers and footers and, more importantly for desktop publishing projects, newspaper-style columns and how text will wrap around graphics. Another essential tool available in page layout view is the vertical ruler, which enables you to judge the placement of objects more accurately. Also, you can see two pages side by side when you use page layout view in combination with the Zoom Control command.

During the paste-up process, you also need to differentiate the various text areas within your document. Word considers the main text of a document, graphics, headers, footers, frames, and footnote reference marks each to be different text areas. By activating the **Text Boundaries** option, you can display dotted boxes around the different text areas and crop marks at the corners. In traditional typesetting, **crop marks**—the notations at the top, bottom, and side margins—were used to indicate the limits of the print area.

Before Keisha formats the newsletter for newspaper-style columns and adds the graphics, she needs to change to page layout view so she can see the effect of these changes as she is working. Text boundaries are visible only in page layout view. She also wants to be able to distinguish the different text areas in the document.

To activate Word's paste-up tools:

❶ Press **[Ctrl][Home]**.

❷ Click the **Page Layout View button** 🔲 in the horizontal scroll bar (or click **View** then click **Page Layout**).

❸ Click the **Zoom Control list box down arrow**, then click **Two Pages**. You should see the first two pages of the newsletter.

Now Keisha wants to display text boundaries so that she can see the different text areas.

❹ Click **Tools** then click **Options…**. The Options dialog box appears.

❺ Click the **View tab**, if necessary, then click the **Text Boundaries check box** (if it is not already selected) in the Show section.

❻ Click **OK** or press **[Enter]**. The document is now displayed with crop marks at the margins on the four corners of the page, and the document text area is outlined with a dashed border. See Figure 6-16.

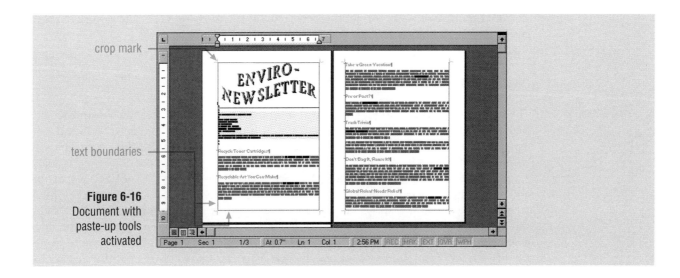

crop mark

text boundaries

Figure 6-16
Document with
paste-up tools
activated

    Next Keisha will insert the headers and footers for the newsletter document.

Inserting Alternating Headers and Footers

Headers and footers are essential design elements for desktop-published documents. They not only provide the reader with valuable information, but can also be used to add visual interest to the appearance of the page. One way to add interest to the headers and/or footers is to alternate the information on the odd and even pages of a document, putting one piece of information on the inside margins and another on the outside margins.

    Keisha wants to insert alternating headers to contain the volume number and month issued, and the newsletter name and month issued. She also wants to insert a footer containing the page number on every page but the first.

To insert alternating headers into the newsletter document:

❶ Click **View** then click **Header and Footer**. The Header and Footer toolbar appears.

❷ Click the **Page Setup button** 🔲 on the Header and Footer toolbar. The Page Setup dialog box appears. If necessary, click the **Layout tab**.

Keisha wants different headers and footers on the first page, on all even pages, and on all odd pages.

❸ Click the **Different Odd and Even check box**, then click the **Different First Page check box** in the Headers and Footers section.

❹ Click **OK** or press **[Enter]**. The insertion point moves into the First Page Header text area. See Figure 6-17.

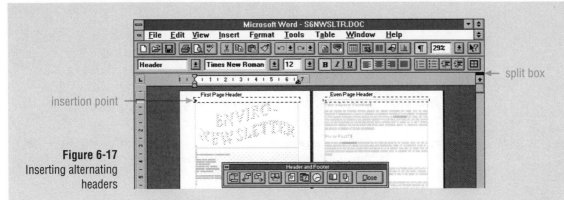

Figure 6-17
Inserting alternating
headers

Keisha wants to insert the volume number and month issued on all odd pages, and the newsletter title and month issued on all even pages, but first she needs to split the window so that she can see what she is typing. Word allows you to split the document window into two *panes* by double-clicking the split box (see Figure 6-17).

❺ Double-click the **split box** above the vertical scroll bar. The window splits into two panes, showing two views of the same document.

❻ Click in the lower pane, then switch to **75%** Zoom view. The top pane remains in Two Pages view, but the magnification of the lower pane is increased so that you can see the text more clearly. See Figure 6-18.

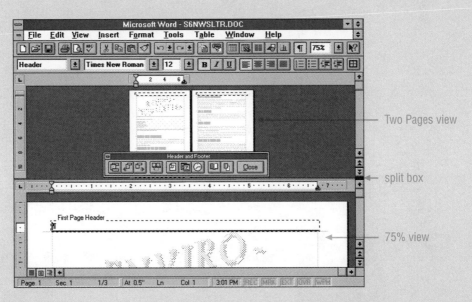

Figure 6-18
Document split in
page layout view

❼ Make sure the First Page Header text area is visible, type **Volume 1, No. 3** and press **[Tab]**, then type **March 1995**. The Header style specifies bold text and provides only one tab in the ruler, located at the right margin.

Keisha wants to use the additional attributes of the Issue/Date style for this text.

❽ With the insertion point anywhere in the First Page Header text area, press **[Alt][i]**, the shortcut key to apply the Issue/Date style. The attributes of the style are applied to the text.

On even-numbered pages, Keisha wants the newsletter name on the outside (left) margin and the date on the inside (right) margin.

⑨ Click the **Show Next button** 🔲 on the Header and Footer toolbar to move to the Even Page Header text area at the top of page 2. Type **Enviro-Newsletter** and press **[Tab]**, then type **March 1995**. Italicize Enviro-Newsletter.

On odd-numbered pages (except the first page), Keisha wants the date on the inside (left) margin and the newsletter name on the outside (right) margin.

⑩ Click 🔲 to move the insertion point to the Odd Page Header text area. Type **March 1995** and press **[Tab]**, then type **Enviro-Newsletter**. Italicize Enviro-Newsletter.

Now Keisha is ready to insert the footers into her document. For the footer on all pages, except page 1, Keisha wants a 2¼ pt rule at the top of the line space and the page number centered. The style for the footer in the OLDNEW template overwrote the predefined footer style, so a rule has already been added to all footers. Keisha just needs to insert a page number code in both the even and odd page footers.

To insert the footers into the newsletter document:

① Click the **Switch Between Header and Footer button** 🔳 on the Header and Footer toolbar. The insertion point moves to the Odd Page Footer text area.

② Press **[Tab]** then click the **Page Numbers button** 🔲 on the Header and Footer toolbar.

③ Click the **Show Previous button** 🔲 on the Header and Footer toolbar to move the insertion point to the Even Page Footer text area.

④ Press **[Tab]** then click 🔲 .

⑤ Close the Header and Footer toolbar.

⑥ Double-click the split box between the two panes to remove the split screen.

Keisha wants to see all three pages at one time.

⑦ Click the **Print Preview button** 🔲 on the Standard toolbar. The document appears in print preview. See Figure 6-19.

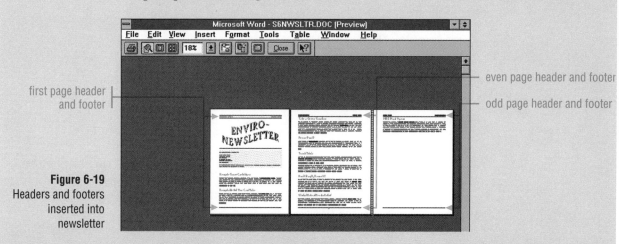

Figure 6-19
Headers and footers inserted into newsletter

first page header and footer

even page header and footer

odd page header and footer

TROUBLE? If you do not see all three pages of the newsletter, click the Multiple Pages button 🔲 on the Print Preview toolbar, then drag across two pages. Because the Mirror Margins option is activated, each page in print preview is actually two facing pages.

TROUBLE? If you cannot see the rule in the footer on page 1, close print preview, display the First Page Footer text area, place the insertion point in the First Page Footer text area, then press [Tab]. This will fix the problem and display the rule in the footer. Then repeat Step 7.

❽ Click the **Close button** on the Print Preview toolbar.

❾ Save your changes.

Applying a Newspaper-Style Column Format

Another design element of desktop-published documents is the use of **newspaper-style columns**, where the text flows down one column to the bottom of the page, then begins at the top of the next column and continues down that column, until all columns are filled on a page. Newspaper-style columns are popular because text set in narrow columns is easier to read and understand than text set in longer line lengths.

There are two ways to create columns. You can click the Columns button on the Standard toolbar and highlight the number of columns that you want, or for more layout choices you can select the Columns command on the Format menu. Because formatting in columns is a document-level formatting decision, if you want only a part of the document formatted in columns, you must insert a section break between the different parts of the document.

Now Keisha wants to format the copy text into multiple columns. She wants the banner and the rule below it to extend across the entire width of the page (in one column), however, so she must insert a section break between the rule and the copy text. She's not sure how many columns will look good, so she decides to begin with three even-width columns with a vertical line between each column.

To apply a newspaper-style column format to the newsletter document:

❶ Place the insertion point in the first blank paragraph below the rule between the banner and the masthead (Ln 3).

TROUBLE? If it is difficult to move the insertion point to the correct location in Two Pages Zoom view, then return to Page Width Zoom view. If you do switch to Page Width Zoom view, return to Two Pages Zoom view after completing Step 8.

❷ Click **Format** then click **Columns...**. The Columns dialog box appears.

❸ In the Presets section, click the **Three icon**, then click the **Line Between check box**. Notice the changes in the Preview section.

Keisha wants these changes to affect only the text from the insertion point to the end of the document, so she needs to insert a section break.

❹ Click the **Apply To list box down arrow**, then click **This Point Forward**. This option inserts a section break at the insertion point. See Figure 6-20.

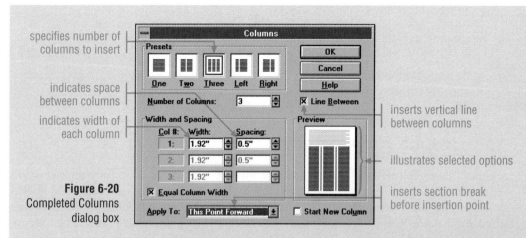

specifies number of
columns to insert

indicates space
between columns

indicates width of
each column

Figure 6-20
Completed Columns
dialog box

inserts vertical line
between columns

illustrates selected options

inserts section break
before insertion point

❺   Click **OK** or press **[Enter]**. Notice that the text below the banner flows into three columns, the length of the document is reduced to two pages, and the insertion point is now in section 2. A section break is indicated below the banner.

Keisha thinks the page layout would look better with just two columns in section 2, and the first column narrower than the second column.

❻   With the insertion point in section 2, click **Format** then click **Columns...**.

❼   In the Presets section, click the **Left icon**, then decrease the Spacing option for column 1 to **0.3"**. Notice the change in the Preview section. These changes will affect only the current section—section 2.

❽   Click **OK** or press **[Enter]**. See Figure 6-21.

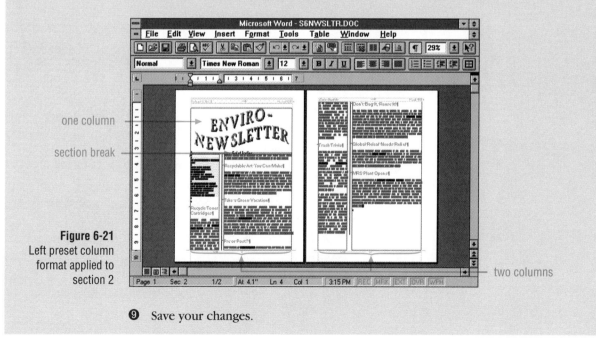

one column

section break

Figure 6-21
Left preset column
format applied to
section 2

two columns

❾   Save your changes.

Next Keisha decides to rearrange the order of the articles in the newsletter.

Using Outline

Word's **outline** feature allows you to create a topic outline with up to nine heading levels for a document, with a level 1 heading being the broadest topic and level 2 through 9 headings being increasingly subordinate topics. To help you easily distinguish the various levels within your document, Word applies a different predefined heading style to each heading level. For instance, all level 1 headings in a Word outline are assigned the predefined Heading 1 style. Although this capability to create an outline is valuable, of more benefit during the desktop publishing process is the ability in outline view to reorganize a Word document quickly.

To switch to outline view, you click the Outline View button on the horizontal scroll bar or choose Outline from the View menu. In outline view the ruler is replaced with the Outline toolbar. Among other things, you can use the Outline toolbar to move a heading and the text below it to a different point in the document.

Keisha decides to rearrange the order of the articles in the newsletter so that she can fit the copy better on the two pages. Because she has applied the predefined Heading 1 style to all the headlines in the newsletter, she decides to use outline view to help her reorganize the document.

To reorganize the newsletter document using outline view:

❶ Click the **Outline View button** 📑 on the horizontal scroll bar (or click **View** then click **Outline**). The ruler disappears and is replaced by the Outline toolbar. Scroll through the document in outline view.

Keisha wants to view just the headlines so it will be easier to tell where she is moving the articles.

❷ Click the **Show Heading 1 button** 1️⃣ on the Outline toolbar to display just the headlines that have been assigned the Heading 1 style. The line below each headline indicates that text is associated with that heading, but the text is hidden from view.

TROUBLE? If the Show Formatting button 🄰 on the Outline toolbar is activated, the headings will appear formatted. Click 🄰 to deactivate it.

Keisha wants to move the Pre or Post article to the end of the newsletter.

❸ Place the insertion point anywhere in the Pre or Post heading, then click the **Move Down button** ⬇️ on the Outline toolbar. The article title moves down one line. This means that the title and the text associated with it now come after the article Trash Trivia.

❹ Click ⬇️ three more times to move the Pre or Post article to the end of the newsletter.

Keisha wants to move the Global Releaf Needs Relief article up to be the third article.

❺ Place the insertion point anywhere in the Global Releaf Needs Relief title, then click the **Move Up button** ⬆️ on the Outline toolbar three times to move the selected article after the article, Recyclable Art You Can Make.

❻ Continue using the Move Up and Move Down buttons to rearrange the article titles so that the final order of the titles matches Figure 6-22.

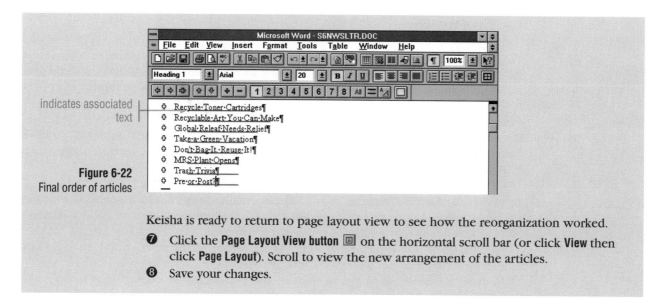

indicates associated
text

Figure 6-22
Final order of articles

Keisha is ready to return to page layout view to see how the reorganization worked.

❼ Click the **Page Layout View button** 🔲 on the horizontal scroll bar (or click **View** then click **Page Layout**). Scroll to view the new arrangement of the articles.

❽ Save your changes.

If you want to take a break and resume the tutorial at a later time, you can do so now. However, if you do exit Word at this point, the shortcut keys for applying styles will no longer be available. To take a break, turn off Text Boundaries, close the document, then exit Word. Click No if a message displays asking if you want to save changes to the NORMAL template. When you want to resume the tutorial, start Word, place your Student Disk in the disk drive, then complete the screen check procedure described in Tutorial 1. Open S6NWSLTR.DOC, change to page layout view, make sure the Text Boundaries option is activated, select Two Pages Zoom view, then continue with the tutorial.

◼   ◼   ◼

Keisha sees now that she needs to force the text for the first article on page 1 to the top of the second column.

Inserting a Column Break

Sometimes you might want to end a column of text in newspaper-style columns before the text reaches the end of the column, thus forcing the remaining text to the top of the next column. You can accomplish this in Word by choosing the Column Break option in the Break dialog box.

Keisha wants to force the headline for the first article, Recycle Toner Cartridges, to the top of the second column on the first page of the newsletter.

To insert the column break:

❶ Place the insertion point in front of the "R" in Recycle Toner Cartridges.

❷ Click **Insert** then click **Break...**. The Break dialog box appears.

❸ Click the **Column Break radio button** in the Insert section, then click **OK** or press **[Enter]**. A row of dots appears across the bottom of column 1 to indicate a column break.

The article is forced to the top of the second column and the text of all subsequent articles reflows through the columns. See Figure 6-23.

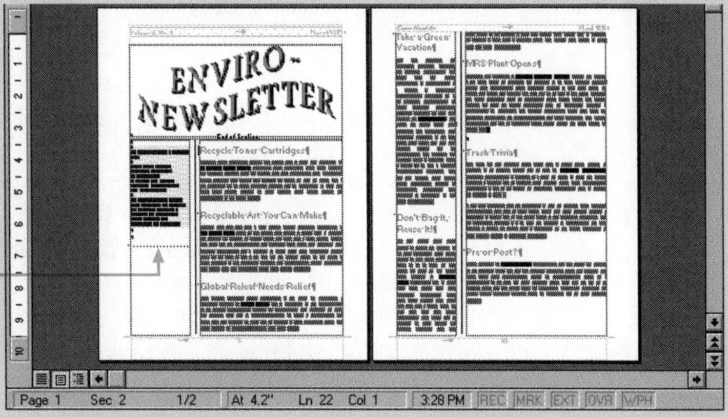

column break —

Figure 6-23
Column break
inserted

❹ Save your changes.

Keisha wants to add some variety to her newsletter layout, so she decides to change the column formatting for page 2.

Changing Column Formatting

You might want to change the layout of the columns from page to page. Because the columns feature is a document-level formatting decision, you must first remember to insert a section break at the point where you want to change the column arrangement.

Keisha wants to vary the column arrangement on the second page of the newsletter by making the right column narrower than the left column, and by removing the line between columns. She doesn't want this change to affect the column arrangement on page 1, however.

To modify the column formatting:
❶ Place the insertion point in front of the "T" in Take a Green Vacation, at the top of page 2.
❷ Click **Format** then click **Columns...**. The Columns dialog box appears.

Keisha wants this change to affect the document only from the insertion point to the end of the document. She must insert a section break as well as make the necessary column formatting changes.

❸ In the Presets section, click the **Right icon**, click the **Line Between check box** to deselect it, decrease the Spacing option for column 1 to **0.3"**, click the **Apply To list box down arrow**, then click **This Point Forward**.
❹ Click **OK** or press **[Enter]**. Notice that the text on page 2 is reformatted to fit the new arrangement of columns. Also notice that the insertion point is in section 3, indicating that a section break has been inserted at the bottom of page 1.

Keisha wants the Trash Trivia article always to start at the top of the second column (page 2) even if she makes changes to the preceding text.

❺   Place the insertion point in front of the "T" in Trash, click **Insert**, click **Break...**, then click **Column Break**.

❻   Click **OK** or press **[Enter]**.

When Keisha inserted the section break at the top of page 2, the header for the page changed. When she originally inserted the headers and footers for her newsletter, she decided to have different headers and footers on the first page. Now that the document contains multiple sections, this option applies to *all* sections. Page 2 is the first page for the new section, and the header changed to match the previous first page header, showing the volume number and issue date for the newsletter. Keisha needs to change the Page Setup options for the new section.

❼   Double-click the Header text area, which is visible in page layout view, at the top of page 2 to display the Header and Footer toolbar.

❽   Click the **Page Setup button** 🔲 on the Header and Footer toolbar, then click to deselect the **Different First Page check box** in the Headers and Footers section on the Layout tab. This change will apply to only the current section—section 3. Click **OK** or press **[Enter]**.

❾   Close the Header and Footer toolbar. See Figure 6-24.

Figure 6-24
Newsletter after
modifying column
format

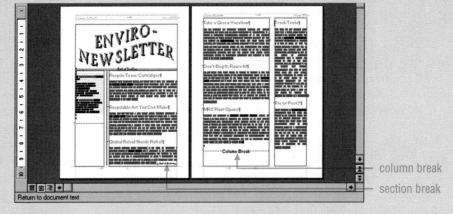

column break

section break

Keisha is satisfied with the arrangement of the columns and the text in the columns. She no longer needs to view both pages at one time in page layout view.

❿   Click the **Zoom Control list box down arrow**, then click **Page Width**.

Now that Keisha has finalized the text and the arrangement of the articles, she is ready to insert the table of contents at the top of column 1 in section 2 on page 1. Besides providing information about the articles and their locations in the newsletter, a table of contents can be designed to provide another point of visual appeal to the reader.

To insert a table of contents into the newsletter document:

❶   Place the insertion point in the first blank paragraph on page 1 (Ln 4) below the section break and the rule, then type **Inside This Issue** as the contents heading.

❷ With the insertion point in the contents heading, click the **Style list box down arrow**, then click **Contents Heading**.

❸ Place the insertion point after the "e" in Issue, then press **[Enter]**. You need a blank paragraph before you generate the table of contents.

Because Keisha assigned the Heading 1 style to all the headlines of the articles, the headlines can be used to create the table of contents.

❹ Click **Insert** then click **Index and Tables...**. The Index and Tables dialog box appears.

❺ Click the **Table of Contents tab**.

Keisha has several choices of formats for the table of contents, but she decides that the Elegant format is most appropriate for the newsletter.

❻ In the Formats section click **Elegant**, click the **Tab Leader list box down arrow**, then select the dot leader style.

❼ Click **OK**.

The table of contents is inserted, but it is formatted incorrectly for the column; the page numbers do not fit in the first column.

TROUBLE? If the text for the first article is forced to page 2, then the table of contents will reflect the wrong page numbers. Delete the table of contents. Then check to make sure you have only two blank paragraphs above the masthead and only two blank paragraphs below the masthead in column 1 of page 1. Delete any extra blank paragraphs then repeat Steps 4 through 7.

Keisha needs to apply the table of contents style that she used in the previous newsletter.

❽ Select the table of contents from the title for the first article, Recycle Toner Cartridges, through Pre or Post, click the **Style list box down arrow**, then click **Contents**. Notice the addition of a right-aligned tab stop in the ruler as a result of applying the style. Deselect the table of contents. See Figure 6-25.

table of contents →

Figure 6-25
Table of contents
inserted in
newsletter

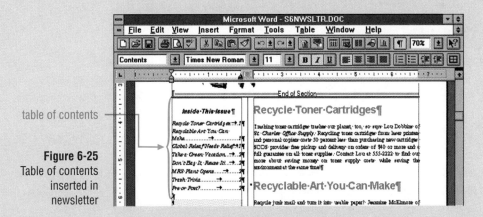

TROUBLE? If the format of the entire table of contents did not change, you did not select the entire table of contents. The table of contents automatically turns a dark gray shade when the insertion point is within it, but it is not selected unless it is highlighted.

❾ Save your changes.

Now Keisha is ready to add another design element, a graphic, that will add visual interest to her newsletter.

Inserting Word ClipArt

Graphics add variety to documents, and Word supports a variety of graphic file formats. You can insert a graphic from another Windows application by copying it to the Clipboard, then pasting the image in your document; or you can import a graphic directly by using the Picture command on the Insert menu. Word has its own clipart library, located in a subdirectory named CLIPART, which contains several graphic images in Windows Metafile format (WMF).

Keisha wants to insert a recycle graphic between the masthead and the headline for the first article.

To import the recycle graphic:

❶ Place the insertion point in the second blank paragraph (Ln 30) below the masthead, before the Column Break.

❷ Click **Insert** then click **Picture….** The Insert Picture dialog box appears.

❸ Scroll through the File Name list box, then click **recycle.wmf.**

❹ Click the **Preview Picture check box**, if necessary. The selected graphic file displays in the Preview section. See Figure 6-26.

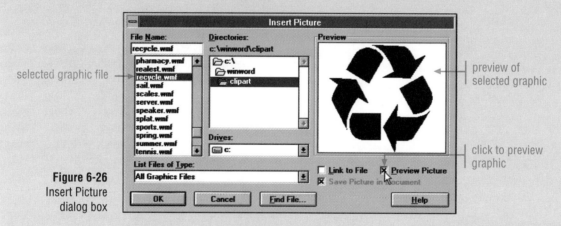

selected graphic file

preview of selected graphic

click to preview graphic

Figure 6-26
Insert Picture
dialog box

❺ Click **OK** or press **[Enter]**. The recycle graphic appears in the document at the insertion point, but because of its size, it forces the text after it to flow to the next page.

❻ Save your changes.

Keisha must make the graphic smaller so that it will fit in column 1 and the articles will be correctly placed in column 2.

Sizing Graphics

After inserting a picture into a document, you might need to resize it to fit the surrounding text. Word allows you to **scale** a picture, that is, change the picture's proportions, or to **crop** a picture, that is, to cut off any part of the picture. You can scale or crop a picture using either the mouse or the Picture command on the Format menu.

REFERENCE WINDOW

Sizing a Graphic

To use the mouse to scale or crop a graphic:

- Select the graphic to be resized.
- Drag the corner handles to size the graphic proportionally.
- Press and hold [Shift] then drag the center handle on any side of the graphic to crop it.

To use the Picture dialog box to scale or crop a graphic:

- Click Format then click Picture.... The Picture dialog box appears.
- To scale a selected picture, indicate the percentage to increase or decrease the width or height in the Scaling section of the Picture dialog box.
- To crop a selected picture, choose the side or sides to crop, then indicate the exact measurement to cut from the picture.
- Click OK or press [Enter].

Keisha wants to resize the recycle graphic to be .4 x .4-inch square so that it will fit in the first column.

To resize the recycle graphic using exact measurements:

❶ Click the **recycle graphic** to select it, if necessary. Selection handles appear around the graphic.

Keisha could use the selection handles to size the graphic, but she wants a more precise measurement.

❷ Click **Format** then click **Picture...**. The Picture dialog box appears.

❸ Decrease the Width option in the Size section to **0.4"**. Notice that the options in the Scaling section change as well.

❹ Decrease the Height option in the Size section to **0.4"** also. See Figure 6-27.

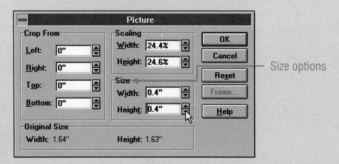

Figure 6-27
Completed Picture dialog box

❺ Click **OK** or press **[Enter]** then deselect the graphic. The graphic now fits in the first column. See Figure 6-28.

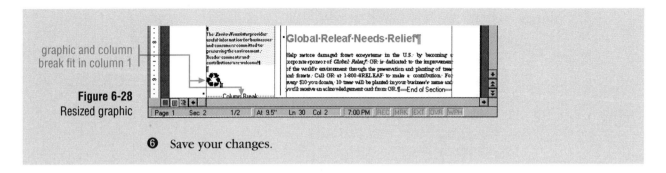

graphic and column
break fit in column 1

Figure 6-28
Resized graphic

❻   Save your changes.

Keisha is pleased with the size of the graphic; now she can insert the appropriate text next to it.

Wrapping Text Around a Picture

Another design element that adds interest to a document is to have text wrap around an object on a page. You can create this effect with Word by inserting a frame around the selected text, graphic, or table. A **frame** is a container or enclosure for an object. When working with frames, it is recommended that the document be in page layout view so that you can see the exact location of the frame.

You use frames to position text, graphics, tables, or other objects in your documents. You can either insert a blank frame then insert text or graphics in the frame at a later time, or you can insert a frame around existing text or graphics so that they can be repositioned.

Keisha wants to insert informational text beside the recycle graphic explaining to the reader that the newsletter was printed on recycled paper and describing the specific content of the recycled paper.

To wrap text around the recycle graphic:
❶   With the insertion point in front of the paragraph mark to the right of the recycle graphic (Ln 30), type **Printed on recycled paper using soy ink. 90% Post-consumer waste.** As you type, the recycle graphic and the text move to the top of the second column. Notice also that the typed text does not appear directly next to the recycle graphic.

Keisha must insert a frame around the graphic so that the text will flow beside the picture.
❷   Click the **recycle graphic** to select it.
❸   Click **Insert** then click **Frame**. A frame is inserted around the graphic. A framed object appears to have a crosshatched border. Notice that the text now flows next to the framed graphic, and the text and graphic now appear at the bottom of the first column.

TROUBLE?   If a message appears asking whether you want to switch to page layout view, click Yes.

Now Keisha needs to apply the Recycle style to the text.
❹   Place the insertion point anywhere within the paragraph text next to the graphic, click the **Style list box down arrow**, then click **Recycle**. The Recycle style is applied to the selected text. See Figure 6-29.

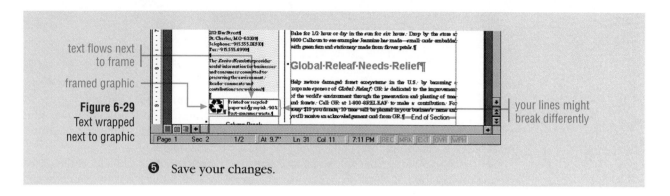

text flows next to frame

framed graphic

Figure 6-29
Text wrapped next to graphic

your lines might break differently

❺ Save your changes.

Next Keisha adds several design elements to page 2 of the newsletter.

Inserting a Pull Quote

Keisha wants to insert a pull quote into the newsletter to draw attention to the text in one of the articles. A **pull quote** is a phrase or quotation formatted in a larger point size and/or with a border or extra space between lines. Keisha wants to emphasize part of the text in the article, Take a Green Vacation. To achieve this effect she must insert an empty frame first, then copy the text for the quotation from the article into the frame.

To insert an empty frame for the pull quote:
❶ Place the insertion point in the Take a Green Vacation article text on page 2.
❷ Click **Insert** then click **Frame**. The pointer changes to +.
❸ Place the pointer in the center of the article, below the third line of the article, then press and drag the mouse to insert an empty frame approximately 1" square. You will size the frame more precisely later.
❹ Release the mouse button. See Figure 6-30. Notice that the text of the article wraps around the blank frame and that the frame is outlined with a crosshatched border. Word automatically inserts a thin border around an empty frame. An anchor symbol also appears to the left of the first line of the paragraph to which the frame is "anchored." Both the horizontal and vertical rulers indicate the size of the frame. The adjacent text is underlined but will not appear so when printed.

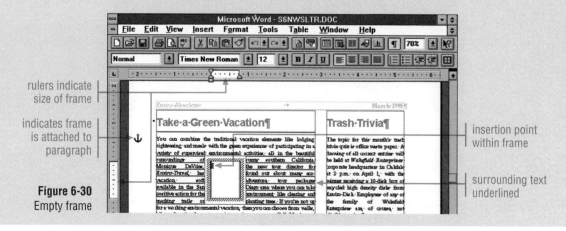

rulers indicate size of frame

indicates frame is attached to paragraph

Figure 6-30
Empty frame

insertion point within frame

surrounding text underlined

Now Keisha needs to size the frame more precisely.

Sizing a Frame

You can size a frame using the mouse by dragging the sizing handles—just as you do to size a graphic. When the pointer is over one of the sizing handles, it changes to ↔ indicating that you can size the frame by dragging the pointer to a new location. If you require a more precisely sized frame, you can specify the exact width and height measurements of the frame using the Frame command on the Format menu.

Keisha approximates that she wants the frame to be about 2.5" wide and 1.5" high to hold the text for the pull quote in this article. She can adjust the frame size later, if necessary.

To size the frame for the pull quote:
- ❶ Point to the crosshatched border of the empty frame. The pointer changes to ⊕.
- ❷ Click the crosshatched border of the frame to select it. The selection handles appear.
- ❸ Click **Format** then click **Frame…**. The Frame dialog box appears. Notice that Around is the default Text Wrapping option.
- ❹ In the Size section, increase the Width option to **Exactly** At **2.6"** and the Height option to **Exactly** At **1.4"**. See Figure 6-31.

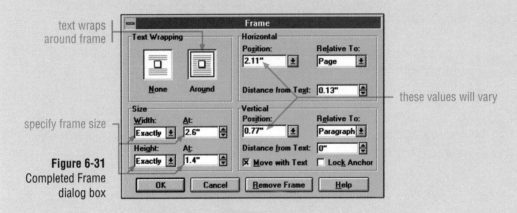

Figure 6-31
Completed Frame dialog box

text wraps around frame

specify frame size

these values will vary

TROUBLE? Your values in the Horizontal and Vertical Position list boxes will most likely be different; continue with the tutorial.

- ❺ Click **OK** or press **[Enter]**. The frame becomes the size specified in the Frame dialog box. The text in the second column temporarily moves to page 3.

TROUBLE? If the text in the second column does not move to page 3, just continue with the tutorial.

Now Keisha can insert text into the empty frame. She could type the text, but she decides to copy it instead to prevent typing errors.

To insert the text for the pull quote in the frame:
- ❶ Select the following text in the Take a Green Vacation article: **take positive action for the environment, like clearing and marking trails or planting trees.** (include the period).

❷ Click the **Copy button** 🖹 on the Standard toolbar (or click **Edit** then click **Copy**).

❸ Place the insertion point in the empty frame, then click the **Paste button** 🖹 on the Standard toolbar (or click **Edit** then click **Paste**). The copied text appears in the frame.

Keisha decides to add an ellipsis (. . .) to indicate that the copied text is a partial quotation.

❹ Place the insertion point in the frame in front of the "t" in "take."

❺ Type " . . . press [**Spacebar**], move the insertion point to the end of the quotation after the period, then type ". Make sure you press [Spacebar] to separate the points of the ellipsis.

❻ Save your changes.

Now Keisha needs to format the pull quote so that it will stand out.

Formatting Text in a Frame

Text in a frame is formatted in the same manner as regular text. If you want the formats to apply to all the contents of the frame, click the outside of the frame to select it; otherwise, select just that portion of the text within the frame to be formatted.

Keisha wants to format all the text in the frame.

To format the text in the frame:

❶ Click the crosshatched border of the frame to select it.

❷ Click **Format** then click **Font...**. The Font dialog box appears.

❸ In the Font Style list box, click **Italic**, then in the Size list box click **16**.

❹ Click **OK** or press [**Enter**]. The text in the frame is formatted with the selected font attributes.

Keisha wants the line spacing to be set at exactly 1.5 times the applied font size (16 pt).

❺ Click **Format** then click **Paragraph...**. The Paragraph dialog box appears. If necessary, click the Indents and Spacing tab.

❻ Click the **Line Spacing list box down arrow**, then click **Exactly**.

❼ Click the **At up arrow** to **24 pt** (16 x 1.5).

❽ Click the **Alignment list box down arrow**, then click **Centered**.

❾ Click **OK** or press [**Enter**]. See Figure 6-32.

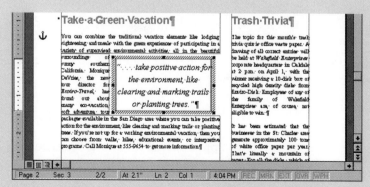

Figure 6-32
Formatted pull quote

❿ Save your changes.

Keisha doesn't like the position of the pull quote; she decides to position it more precisely.

Positioning a Frame

You can use the mouse to drag a frame to any location on the page. To position a frame with the mouse, you must first select it. The pointer changes to ✛ when it is over the edge of the frame, indicating that the frame can be moved. Then you simply drag the frame to a new location.

To position a frame more precisely, you can use the Frame command on the Format menu, which allows you to specify the frame's horizontal and vertical position, as well as a reference point—page, column, margin, paragraph—for each position. Keisha wants to position the framed pull quote at the left edge of the first column, approximately halfway down the article.

To position the framed pull quote using the Frame command:

❶ Click the framed pull quote to select it, if necessary, click **Format**, then click **Frame….** The Frame dialog box appears.

❷ In the Horizontal section, click the **Position list box down arrow**, then click **Left**.

❸ In the Horizontal section, click the **Relative To list box down arrow**, then click **Column**.

❹ In the Position box of the Vertical section, type **1"**.

❺ In the Vertical section, click the **Relative To list box down arrow**, then click **Paragraph**, if necessary. See Figure 6-33.

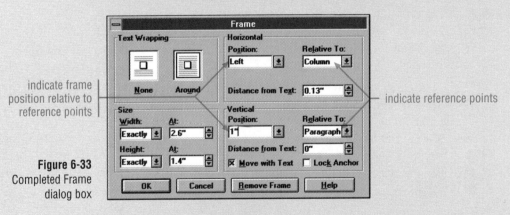

indicate frame position relative to reference points

indicate reference points

Figure 6-33
Completed Frame
dialog box

❻ Click **OK** or press [Enter]. The pull quote moves to the left side of the column and is also adjusted vertically.

TROUBLE? If the Trash Trivia article still appears on page 3, reduce the size of the frame around the pull quote until the article moves back to page 2.

❼ Save your changes.

Next Keisha wants to apply one of the more traditional design elements to her newsletter—a stylized first letter for each article.

Creating Drop Caps

Another special text effect you can create with frames is a drop cap. A **drop cap** is a large, uppercase character applied usually to the first character of a paragraph with the top part of the drop cap even with the top of the line and the rest of the drop character extending downward into the paragraph below. The surrounding text wraps around the drop cap. With Word, you can also specify that the selected text be displayed as a drop cap in the left margin.

Keisha wants the first character of the first paragraph of each article to begin with a drop cap. She wants the character to extend down into the next line.

To insert drop caps in the articles:

❶ Place the insertion point anywhere in the text paragraph of the article, Recycle Toner Cartridges.

❷ Click **Format** then click **Drop Cap…**. The Drop Cap dialog box appears.

Keisha wants the character to be dropped within the paragraph rather than in the margin, and she wants to use a more stylish font for the drop cap.

❸ Click the **Dropped icon** in the Position section.

❹ Click **Monotype Corsiva** in the Font list box.

> **TROUBLE?** If Monotype Corsiva is not available in your Font list, choose Brush Script MT.

Keisha wants the drop cap to extend downward through two lines of text, and to be set off .05" from the surrounding text.

❺ Decrease the Lines to Drop option to **2**.

❻ Increase the Distance from Text option to **.05"**. Make sure you type .05 and not .5. See Figure 6-34.

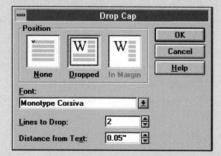

Figure 6-34
Completed Drop Cap
dialog box

❼ Click **OK** or press **[Enter]**. Word automatically formats the first character of the paragraph containing the insertion point as a drop cap with the specified attributes. Notice that a frame has been inserted around the character. See Figure 6-35.

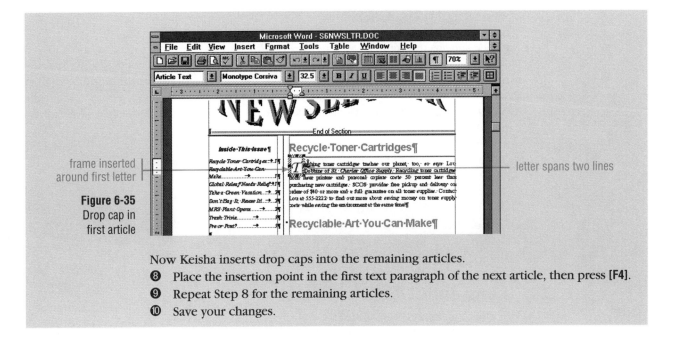

frame inserted around first letter

Figure 6-35
Drop cap in first article

letter spans two lines

Now Keisha inserts drop caps into the remaining articles.

❽ Place the insertion point in the first text paragraph of the next article, then press **[F4]**.

❾ Repeat Step 8 for the remaining articles.

❿ Save your changes.

Keisha notices that her document has several areas with large gaps of space between words; this is caused by the justified text. She decides to correct this problem by hyphenating the document.

Hyphenating a Document

One of the hazards of formatting text in narrow columns and then justifying the text is that Word often inserts noticeable white space in order to accommodate the justified paragraphs. By hyphenating a document, you can eliminate some of the large gaps of space between words. Word's **Hyphenation** command allows you to hyphenate a document automatically with Word making all the decisions for you or manually where Word allows you to accept, reject, or change the suggested word division.

Keisha decides to hyphenate her document to eliminate as many of the large gaps of space between words as possible.

To hyphenate the document:

❶ Make sure you have saved your most recent changes.

❷ Place the insertion point in the blank paragraph directly before the beginning of the masthead.

❸ Click **Tools** then click **Hyphenation...**. The Hyphenation dialog box appears.

Keisha wants as much of a word as possible to fit on a line, so she needs to make the hyphenation zone narrower. She also wants to limit the number of consecutive hyphenated words to 3.

❹ Decrease the Hyphenation Zone option to **0.1"**.

❺ Change the Limit Consecutive Hyphens To option to **3**. See Figure 6-36.

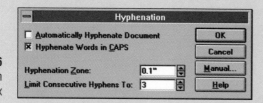

Figure 6-36
Hyphenation
dialog box

Keisha could have Word automatically hyphenate the newsletter but she wants to make each decision.

❻ Click **Manual...**. Word stops at the first instance of the need for a hyphenated word, and displays the Manual Hyphenation dialog box. See Figure 6-37.

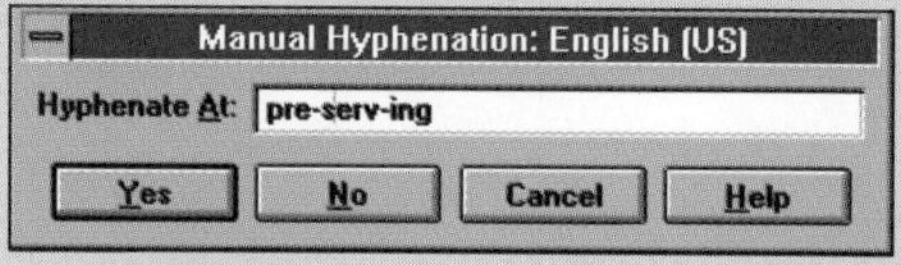

Figure 6-37
Manual Hyphenation
dialog box

TROUBLE? Depending on the type of printer you're using, the word identified in your Manual Hyphenation dialog box might be different. Continue with the steps.

Keisha can decide to either accept Word's suggestion for hyphenation, move the hyphenation point to another syllable in the word, or not hyphenate the word at all. She decides to accept Word's suggestion.

❼ Click **Yes** or press **[Enter]**. Word hyphenates the word and moves to the next instance of a word that needs hyphenating.

❽ Continue accepting all suggestions by Word for hyphenation *except* for proper nouns and words in headlines.

TROUBLE? If the hyphenation process stalls at the end of first page, press [Esc] to cancel the option. Move the insertion point to the top of page 2, then repeat Steps 2, 3, and 6. If the process stalls at any other point, press [Esc], then repeat Steps 2, 3, and 6 beginning at the last stalled location.

❾ Click **OK** or press **[Enter]** in the Word message box that indicates the hyphenation process is complete. Then save your changes.

For a final design element, Keisha wants to insert the same recycle graphic she used below the masthead. This time, however, she wants to layer the graphic so that it appears behind the text on page 2.

Layering Text and Graphics

Another design element that provides a great deal of visual interest in a document is the layering of a graphic behind text, such that a drawing or text on a lower layer shows through to the upper layers. In the past only the most sophisticated desktop publishing packages could accomplish this effect, but now you can do so with Word.

As illustrated in Figure 6-38, every Word document is made up of four layers. The header/footer layer is on the bottom and can include header/footer text, as well as drawings, that appears on every page. You access the header/footer layer through the View menu, whereas you access the background and foreground drawing layers through the Drawing toolbar. The text layer contains the text of the document.

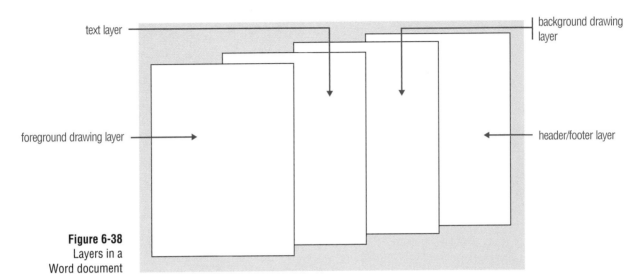

text layer

background drawing layer

foreground drawing layer

header/footer layer

Figure 6-38
Layers in a
Word document

In Word, a drawing object is different from a picture. A **drawing object** is a graphic that you create using the Drawing toolbar; a **picture** is an existing graphic that you import from a graphics program. Another distinction concerns the placement of the graphic itself. You can add *drawings* to *any* layer of a document, but you can add *pictures* only to the *text* layer. Drawings are visible only in page layout view or print preview.

Keisha wants to add the recycle symbol to the center of the last page, but she doesn't want it to obscure any text nor does she want to use a frame to flow text around the symbol; she wants it to show through the text. A graphic, such as the recycle symbol, can be placed on one of the drawing layers only if it is first changed to a drawing object. You can change a graphic to a drawing object by surrounding it with a text box. Keisha must convert the recycle picture to a drawing object in order to accomplish the layered effect.

To layer the recycle symbol behind the text on page 2:
❶ Place the insertion point on page 2, if necessary.
❷ Click the **Drawing button** 🖉 on the Standard toolbar. The Drawing toolbar appears at the bottom of the screen. See Figure 6-39.
❸ Click the **Text Box button** 🔲 on the Drawing toolbar. The pointer changes to + when you move it into the document.

As in Windows Paintbrush, to create a perfect shape with a drawing tool, hold down the Shift key while dragging the mouse.

❹ In the approximate center of page 2, press and hold [**Shift**], then drag to insert a text box about 3.5" by 3.5". You will adjust the size of the text box more precisely later. Release [Shift] and the mouse button. An empty text box appears. See Figure 6-39.

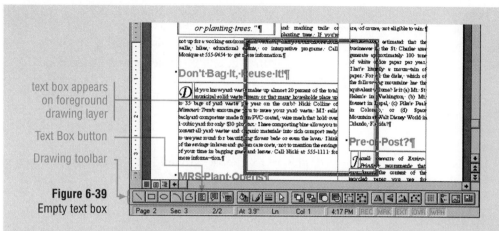

text box appears
on foreground
drawing layer

Text Box button

Drawing toolbar

Figure 6-39
Empty text box

Because the empty text box is inserted on the foreground drawing layer, it does not interfere with the text on the layer below, which is the text layer. Even though the text box is inserted as a framed object, the document text does not wrap around it because the text and the text box are on different layers.

As with an empty frame, Word automatically adds a border to a text box. Keisha doesn't want a border around the text box, however.

❺ Move the mouse pointer over the border of the text box. The pointer changes to ⬚. Click to select the object.

❻ Click **Format** then click **Drawing Object...**. The Drawing Object dialog box appears.

❼ Click the **Line tab**, then click the **None button** in the Line section to select the option (if it is not already selected).

Next Keisha must size and position the text box to a more precise location on the page.

❽ Click the **Size and Position tab** in the Drawing Object dialog box, then make the changes shown in Figure 6-40.

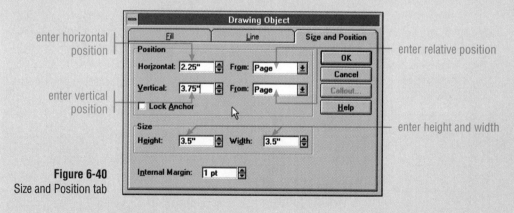

enter horizontal
position

enter vertical
position

enter relative position

enter height and width

Figure 6-40
Size and Position tab

❾ Click **OK** or press **[Enter]**. The text box is repositioned according to your specifications.

Now Keisha is ready to insert the recycle symbol into the empty text box.

To insert the recycle symbol into the text box:

❶ Click **Insert** then click **Picture....** The Insert Picture dialog box appears.

❷ Scroll through the File Name list box, then double-click **recycle.wmf** to insert the graphic into the text box. Notice that the recycle symbol blocks out the text on the layer behind it.

❸ Save your changes.

Keisha will move the recycle picture to the background layer, but first she needs to change the color of the picture.

Adding Color to a Graphic

Keisha must edit the color of the picture because the black of the image will obscure the text even when she moves the picture to the background layer. To edit a picture, you use the Picture toolbar.

To change the color of the recycle graphic:

❶ Double-click the **recycle graphic** (or click the graphic with the *right* mouse button, then click **Edit Picture**). The Picture toolbar and the recycle graphic are now the only objects on the screen. Word changes the magnification of the screen to 100%.

Keisha reduces the screen magnification so she can bring more of the graphic into view.

❷ Click the **Zoom Control list box down arrow**, then click **Page Width**.

❸ Scroll down the screen until the entire graphic is in view.

You cannot change the color of a WMF file, but you can change the color of a Word drawing object. Keisha must convert the picture to a Word drawing object in order to change its color.

❹ Click the **Select Drawing Objects button** 🔲 on the Drawing toolbar, then click and drag to insert a selection box around the recycle graphic. See Figure 6-41.

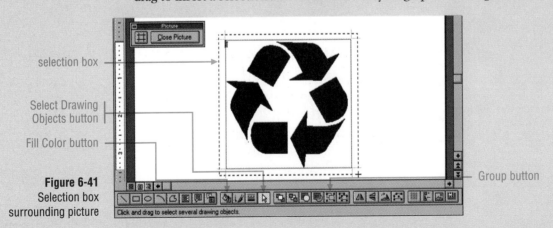

Figure 6-41
Selection box
surrounding picture

selection box

Select Drawing
Objects button

Fill Color button

Group button

❺ Release the mouse button. Selection handles appear around every individual piece of the WMF object.

⑥ Click the **Group button** 🔲 on the Drawing toolbar to transform the WMF object into a Word drawing object.

Now Keisha is ready to change the fill color from black to light gray so that text on the text layer will show through.

⑦ Click the **Fill Color button** 🌢 on the Drawing Toolbar. The Fill Color palette appears. See Figure 6-42.

click to select this
color for picture

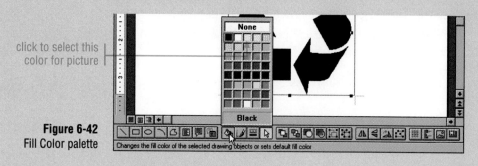

Figure 6-42
Fill Color palette

⑧ Click the **light gray color** (first row, third option). The color of the recycle graphic changes to light gray.

⑨ Click the **Close Picture button** on the Picture toolbar.

Now Keisha is ready to send the drawing object to the background drawing layer; that is, the layer behind the text.

Moving an Object to the Background Drawing Layer

Even though the color of the picture is lighter, it still blocks the text of the newsletter. Keisha must move the object to the background drawing layer.

To move the recycle graphic to the background drawing layer:

❶ Select the **recycle graphic**, if necessary. Make sure selection handles appear around the outside of the graphic.

❷ Click the **Send Behind Text button** 🔲 on the Drawing toolbar. The recycle graphic moves behind the text layer.

❸ Click outside the graphic to deselect it.

❹ Click the **Drawing button** 🔲 to dismiss the Drawing toolbar.

❺ Turn off the Text Boundaries option on the View tab of the Options dialog box.

❻ Save your changes.

Keisha will electronically transmit her completed newsletter file to Janell at Enviro-Printing, but she needs to print a hard copy for her records. She will spell check then preview the document one more time before she prints it.

To spell check, preview, then print the newsletter document:

❶ Click the **Spelling button** 🔤 on the Standard toolbar (or click **Tools** then click **Spelling...**) to spell check the document.

❷ Click the **Print Preview button** 🔍 on the Standard toolbar (or click **File** then click **Print Preview.**)

❸ Click the **Print button** 🖨 on the Print Preview toolbar. The document might take a while to print. Your printed document should look like Figure 6-1.

❹ Click the **Normal View button** 📄 on the horizontal scroll bar to return to normal view. Scroll through the document to see how the newsletter looks in normal view.

❺ Close any supplementary toolbars.

❻ After the newsletter prints, close the document, then exit Word.

❼ Click **No** in the message box asking if you want to save changes to NORMAL.DOT.

Keisha reviews her printed newsletter then electronically distributes it to Janell for printing.

Questions

1. Define the term desktop publishing.
2. Define the following design elements:
   a. banner
   b. masthead
   c. newspaper-style columns
   d. drop cap
   e. pull quote
3. Describe the procedure for importing an entire Word document into the current Word document.
4. Describe the procedure for importing an entire foreign-format file into the current Word document.
5. When do you activate the Mirror Margins option?
6. Explain the purpose of WordArt.
7. Describe the procedure for copying styles from one document or template to another document or template using the Organizer.
8. Describe the procedure for displaying the style area of the Word screen.
9. What features can be displayed while in page layout view?
10. What is the purpose of the Text Boundaries option?
11. Describe the procedure for inserting columns into a document.
12. What are two uses of outline view?
13. Describe the procedure for inserting a column break.
14. Describe the procedure for importing a graphic from Word's CLIPART subdirectory.
15. Describe the procedure for sizing a selected graphic.
16. Define the term "frame."
17. Describe the procedure for making text wrap around a selected picture.
18. Describe the procedure for sizing a selected frame.
19. Describe the procedure for precisely positioning a selected frame.

20. Describe the procedure for creating drop caps.
21. Describe the procedure for hyphenating a document.
22. Explain each of Word's four layers.
23. Explain the difference between a drawing object and a picture.

E   24. Using a newsletter you've received, identify the design elements of the newsletter. List the procedures for recreating the newsletter using Word. Submit your annotated newsletter and your list of procedures.

Tutorial Assignments

Start Word, if necessary, and conduct a screen check. Open a new document window in preparation for creating the newsletter shown in Figure 6-43.

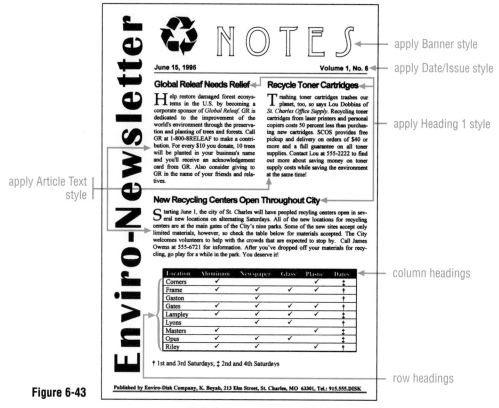

Figure 6-43

Complete the following:

1. Switch to page layout view, start WordArt, then create the following image:
   a. Type "Enviro-Newsletter" as the text for the banner.
   b. Format the banner with the Bottom to Top pattern (first row, last option) in the Style list box, and with the Brittanic Bold font in 72 points.
   c. Click the Spacing Between Characters button, then click the Loose radio button.
   d. Embed the WordArt image in the document.
2. Save the document as S6NOTES.DOC.
3. Insert a frame around the WordArt image, then format the position of the frame using the following options. (Note that you need to type the setting 1" for both position options.)
   a. Horizontal section: Position 1"; Relative To Page; Distance from Text .25"
   b. Vertical section: Position 1"; Relative To Page
4. Save the document.

5. Insert the following text into the document:
   a. Type "Notes" then press [Enter].
   b. Type "June 15, 1995" then press [Tab]; type "Volume 1, No. 6" then press [Enter].
   c. Import the following article files (in order): T6RELEAF.M5, T6LOU.DOC, T6SITES.DOC.
6. Make the following document-level formatting changes:
   a. Left Margin: 2"; Right Margin: 1"
   b. Footer, type: Published by Enviro-Disk Company, K. Beyah, 213 Elm Street, St. Charles, MO 63301, Tel.: 915.555.DISK (*Note:* The footer text will be formatted automatically when you copy styles in the next step.)
7. Copy the styles from T6NOTES.DOT to S6NOTES.DOC without overwriting the Default Paragraph Font style or the Normal style. Click Yes to All to overwrite all other existing style entries.
8. Apply the styles as indicated in Figure 6-43.
9. Insert section breaks so that articles 1 and 2 appear in two-column format with the Spacing option set at .3" and the last article appears in one column.
10. Place the insertion point at the top of the document in front of the "N" in Notes, then insert the recycle graphic. Resize the graphic so that it is exactly 1" square.
11. Insert a space between the graphic and the "N" in Notes.
12. Save the document.
13. Place the insertion point at the end of the document, then press [Enter] once.
14. Insert a 10 x 6 table with the following specifications:
    a. Type the text for the column headings—Location, Aluminum, Newspaper, Glass, Plastic, Dates. See Figure 6-43.
    b. Type the text for the row headings in the table as shown in Figure 6-43.
    c. Insert the checkmark symbol (✓) from the Wingdings character set, and the symbols (†) and (‡) from the (normal text) character set to indicate acceptable materials and open dates.
    d. Select the completed table, then format it using the List 4 table format.
    e. Center align the cells containing symbols.
    f. Select the table then center the entire table horizontally.
    g. Place the insertion point below the table, press [Enter], then type the note indicating the meaning of the symbols used in the Dates column of the table.
    h. Save the document.
15. Insert appropriate drop caps in the three articles. Specify that the drop caps extend to 2 lines, and use a distance from text of .05".
16. Hyphenate the newsletter using a hyphenation zone of .1" and a limit of 3 consecutive hyphenations. Perform a manual hyphenation.
17 Save the document.
18. Preview then print the newsletter.
E 19. Create a new template for the Notes newsletter saving it to your Student Disk as S6NOTES2.DOT.
E 20. Delete appropriate text so that just the skeleton document template is displayed. Save the changes to the template.
21. Print the remaining document template and its style sheet.

Case Problems

1. Cerfing The Internet Newsletter

James Dougherty, the director of Technological Services for the Commonwealth of Massachusetts board of higher education, began an electronic bulletin board service for the state's faculty and students concerning the uses of technology in the classroom. It became so popular that he decided to publish a monthly newsletter with worldwide distribution focused on the applications of the information superhighway, the Internet, in the educational environment. You'll create the monthly newsletter, called *Cerfing The Internet*, shown in Figure 6-44.

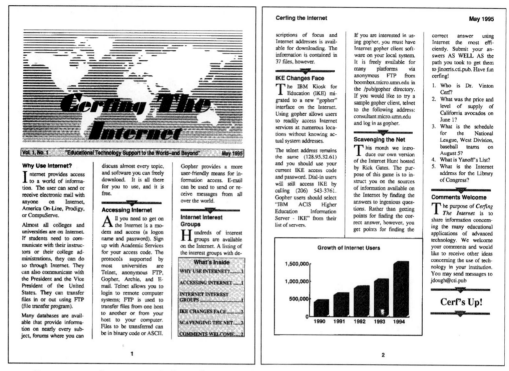

Figure 6-44

Open a new document window, then complete the following:

1. Save the document as S6NETNEW.DOC.
2. Change the left and right margins to 1".
3. At the top of the document, insert CONTINEN.WMF, a Word clipart picture.
4. Resize the graphic so that it is even with the right margin.
5. Place the insertion point in the blank paragraph below and to the right of the graphic, then press [Enter] to insert a blank paragraph mark.
6. Type "Vol. 1, No. 1" then press [Tab]; type the following text *including* the quotation marks: "Educational Technology Support to the World—and Beyond" then press [Tab]; type "May 1995" then press [Enter].
7. Insert the article P6WHY.DOC. Delete the WordPerfect code, {PRIVATE}, after the article title.
8. Place the insertion point in the blank paragraph at the end of the document, insert DIVIDER2.WMF, a Word clipart picture, then press [Enter].
9. Insert the following files (in order): P6ACCESS.MCW, P6GROUPS.WRI, P6IKE.DOC, P6HUNT.DOC, P6COMMEN.DOC, and P6CERFUP.DOC. Make sure your file list shows all types of files. After inserting each file, insert the DIVIDER2.WMF clipart picture, pressing [Enter] after inserting each divider except the last.
10. Save your changes.
11. Insert the following header and footer:
    a. Header: No header on the first page; for subsequent pages, type "Cerfing The Internet" press [Tab]; then type "May 1995." (The text will align properly after you copy styles in Step 12.)
    b. Footer: To appear on all pages, insert a page number code at the center tab.
    c. Save your changes.

12. Copy the styles from P6INET.DOT to S6NETNEW.DOC, without overwriting the Default Paragraph Font style or the Normal style. Click Yes to All to overwrite all other existing style entries.

13. Apply the Issue/Date style to the issue/date information; apply the Heading 1 style to all article titles; apply the Article Text style to all paragraphs; apply the Hunt Questions style to the numbered list. (Note that after you apply the Hunt Questions style to the paragraphs formatted as a numbered list, you must reformat the text as a numbered list.)

14. Switch to page layout view, then format the articles below the issue/date information in three columns with the Line Between option selected.

15. Switch to Two Pages view, then insert frames as placeholders as indicated below.
    a. Bottom of column 3 on page 1—Size section: Width set Exactly At 1.9"; Height set Exactly At 2.3". Horizontal section: Position 5.65"; Relative To Page. Vertical section: Position 7.6"; Relative To Page.
    b. Bottom of column 1 (and extending to the bottom of column 2) on page 2—Size section: Width set Exactly At 4.4"; Height set Exactly At 3". Horizontal section: Position .99"; Relative To Page. Vertical section: Position 7"; Relative To Page. Remove the border from the frame.
    c. Save the document.

16. Insert a table of contents using the following steps:
    a. Place the insertion point in the empty frame at the bottom of the third column on the first page, then type "What's Inside." Press [Enter] twice. Apply the Contents Title style to the text you typed.
    b. Place the insertion point at the last blank paragraph mark under the contents title. Insert a table of contents. Select the Formal style. If necessary, delete the blank paragraph mark below the table of contents after it is generated.
    c. Save your changes.

17. Select the empty frame at the bottom of page 2. Insert the file P6NETCHT.DOC into the selected frame. Save the document.

18. Insert a 1 1/2 pt single line border around the chart.

19. With the chart selected, click Format then click Picture.... Select the following options in the Size section: Width 4.4"; Height: 2.8"

20. Save your changes.

21. Insert drop caps in the first paragraph of all articles. Drop the cap to 2 lines, and increase the distance from text to .05". Save the document.

22. Hyphenate the newsletter using a hyphenation zone of .1" and a limit of 3 consecutive hyphens. Save the document.

23. Insert text on top of the banner graphic using the following steps.
    a. Place the insertion point at the top of the document, then display the Drawing toolbar.
    b. Draw a text box at the center bottom of the graphic, then format the drawing object so that it is positioned as follows: Position section: Horizontal 1" From Page; Vertical 2.7" From Page. Size section: Height 1.6"; Width 6.5".
    c. Type "Cerfing The Internet" then apply the Banner style.
    d. Change the font size of the letters "C," "T," and "I" to 48 pt.
    e. Save the changes.

24. Print the newsletter and its style sheet.

E 25. Use the microcomputer symbol in the Wingdings character set to indicate the following locations on the banner graphic:
    a. Cambridge, Massachusetts
    b. Houston, Texas
    c. Buenos Aires, Argentina
    d. London, England
    e. Toronto, Ontario
    f. Cairo, Egypt

g. Moscow, Russia

h. Sydney, Australia

26. Save the document as S6NET2.DOC, then print page 1 of the document.

2. Butterfly World Parents Newsletter

Elaine Kozinski is the director of the Butterfly World Educational Center in Evanston, Indiana. Butterfly World is a nationally syndicated childcare day school. She has asked the leaders of the pre-kindergarten (Caterpillars) and the kindergarten (Butterflies) to submit articles for inclusion in the September parents' newsletter. You'll create the parents' newsletter, shown in Figure 6-45.

Figure 6-45

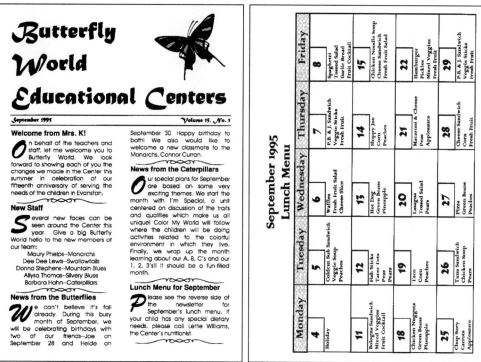

Open a new document window and complete the following:

1. Save the document as S6BWNEWS.DOC.

2. At the top of the document, insert BUTTRFLY.WMF, a Word clipart picture, then insert it in a frame. Format the frame's position with the following attributes:
   a. Size section: Width set Exactly At 1.88"; Height set Exactly At 1.82"
   b. Horizontal section: Position 5.1"; Relative To Page. Vertical section: Position 0.1"; Relative To Paragraph

3. Place the insertion point at the top of the document, type the banner text "Butterfly World Educational Centers," then press [Enter].

4. Type the date/issue text "September 1995" then press [Tab]; type "Volume 15, No. 1" then press [Enter]. Save the document.

5. Insert the article P6MRSK.DOC.

6. Insert DIVIDER3.WMF, a Word clipart picture, then press [Enter].

7. Insert the following articles (in order): P6STAFF.DOC, P6BUTTER.MCW, P6PIL-LAR.DOC, and P6LUNCH.WRI, each followed by the DIVIDER3.WMF picture. Press [Enter] after each DIVIDER3.WMF picture, except the one after the last article. Save your changes.

8. Copy the styles from P6BWNEWS.DOT to S6BWNEWS.DOC without overwriting the Default Paragraph Font style or the Normal style. Overwrite any other existing style entries.

9. Apply the Banner style to the newsletter title; apply the Date/Issue style to the date/issue information; apply the Heading 1 style to all article titles; apply the Article Text style to all paragraphs. If necessary, adjust the position of the framed banner graphic so that it appears even with the right margin, and so that the words "Educational Centers" in the banner wrap to the line below the graphic. Save your changes.

10. Insert a section break so that the articles appear in two-column format.

11. Place the insertion point at the end of the document, then insert another section break to begin on the next page. Make the following adjustments to the new section:
   a. Change the page orientation to landscape.
   b. Change the top and bottom margins to 1".
   c. Format in one-column format.
   d. Change the vertical alignment to centered.
   e. Save your changes.

12. Insert the file P6MENU.DOC.

13. Insert a drop cap in the first paragraph of all articles with the following attributes:
   a. Change the font to Brush Script MT.
   b. Drop the cap 3 lines.
   c. Save your document.

14. Center the teachers' names in the New Staff article, as well as each of the DIVIDER3.WMF pictures. Save the document.

15. Print the newsletter and its style sheet.

E 16. Use the Rectangle drawing tool to draw a border around the entire first page with the following formatting specifications for the drawing object:
   a. A 2 pt line with rounded corners.
   b. Position section: Horizontal -.5" From Margin; Vertical -.4" From Margin.
   c. Size section: Height 10"; Width 7".
   d. Send the drawing object behind the text.
   e. Save the document.

17. Change the issue number to 2, save the document as S6BORDER.DOC, then print the first page of the newsletter.

18. Dismiss the Drawing toolbar.

3. Word Help Desk Newsletter

Create a newsletter that could be used by co-workers and/or clients as a source of up-to-date information about Word. Include in the newsletter articles covering four to six features of Word that you feel are the most useful, along with the purpose and procedures to use each feature correctly. Also consider including a "tips and techniques" section, as well as your most often used shortcut keys.

Complete the following:

1. Create the articles to include in the newsletter, saving each one in a separate file.

2. Decide on a general layout for your newsletter.

3. Create a banner for the newsletter, using WordArt. Save the document as S6HELPDK.DOC.

4. Import the articles into S6HELPDK.DOC.

5. Insert a masthead, using your name as editor.

6. Insert appropriate headers and/or footers.

7. Create or copy styles for the newsletter, then apply them where appropriate. Save the document.

8. Insert attractive design elements to enhance the appearance of your newsletter, including graphics, drop caps, pull quotes, multiple columns, text wrapped around graphics, a table of contents, shading, and, if you have access to a color printer, color. Save the document.

9. Print the newsletter and its style sheet.

Index

Special Characters

_ (end mark), W 10, W 11
↲ (new line mark), W 78-79
¶ (paragraph mark), W 67
→ (tab character), W 71

A

activating
    document views, W 13
    paste-up tools, W 241-242
    ruler, W 15
    Show/Hide ¶ button, W 16
    toolbars, W 14
aligning
    paragraphs, W 82-85
    title page, vertically, W 189-190
alternating headers and footers, W 242-245
antonyms, finding, W 181-182
applet, W 231
applying styles, W 134-136, W 198-202
    shortcut keys, W 200-202, W 239-240
    Style command, W 200
applying type styles, W 42-44
    multiple type styles, W 43-44
ascending order sorts, W 123
AutoCorrect feature, W 107-109
automatic formatting, tables, W 138-139
automatic hyphenation, W 260
available text area, W 63

B

Backspace key, error correction, W 22
banners, W 231-236
bindings, gutter margins, W 232-233
blank lines, inserting in documents, W 21, W 23
blank rows, inserting in tables, W 121
blank table structure, creating with Insert Table
    button, W 106-107
bold type style, W 42
    applying, W 43

bookmarks, W 185-186
borders
    paragraphs, W 85-86
    tables, W 138-139
Borders and Shading command, W 67, W 85-86
bullets, W 45-46

C

calculations, tables, W 124-125
captions
    centering, W 140-141
    charts, W 210-211
    inserting in tables, W 125-126
cells, W 104
    centering text, W 140
    deleting contents, W 121-122
    selecting, W 119
centered alignment, paragraphs, W 82-84
centered tabs, W 73
    setting using ruler, W 74-75
centering
    captions, W 140-141
    charts, W 210-211
    column headings, W 139-141
    tables, W 139-141
    text in cells, W 140
changes, undoing, W 33-34, W 41, W 67
changing
    column formatting, W 249-250
    column width, W 136-138
    converting existing text to tables, W 110-112
    document views, W 12-13
    font and character spacing using Font command,
        W 89-90
    font and point size using Formatting toolbar,
        W 90-91
    indentations, W 67-71
    line spacing, W 81-82
    margins, W 63-64
    several character attributes at once, W 89-90
    styles, W 202-205
    table structure, W 120-122
character attributes, W 87. *See also* font formatting

character sets, W 91-92
Character Spacing tab, W 90
character style, W 131
    applying to selected text, W 240
characters, W 87
    deleting, W 22
    spacing between, W 90
charts, W 205
    bookmarks, W 185-186
    captions, W 210-211
    centering, W 210-211
    transferring between documents, W 206-207
clearing tab stops, W 75
click-and-drag technique, W 40
clipart, W 252-254
    importing graphics, W 252
    sizing graphics, W 252-254
CLIPART subdirectory, W 252
Clipboard, W 112-116
    copying and pasting text, W 113-114
    cutting and pasting text, W 114-116
    transferring data between documents, W 205-208
closing documents without saving changes, W 19-20
codes
    date field, W 160
    merge field, W 161-164, W 171-172
color, graphics, W 264-265
column breaks, W 248-249
column headings, centering, W 139-141
columns
    changing width, W 136-138
    deleting, W 121
    desktop publishing, W 227
    formatting, W 249-250
    inserting and deleting, W 121
    newspaper-style, W 245-246
    selecting, W 119
Columns command, W 245-246
context-sensitive Help, W 48-49
Control menu box
    document window, W 10, W 11
    Word window, W 10, W 11
Copy command, W 113-114
copying
    information using the Clipboard, W 112-114
    footers, W 130
    styles using Organizer, W 236-238
    tables, W 120
    text, W 113-114
    transferring data between documents, W 208-209
correcting errors. *See* error correction

Create Data Source command, W 155-156
crop marks, W 241
CTI WinApps icon group, W 6-7
custom tab stops, W 72-75
Customize dialog box, W 201
customized templates, W 219-220
cutting text, W 114-115

D

data fields, W 154, W 155-156
data forms, W 157-160
data records, W 154
data source. *See* merging documents
Date and Time command, W 161
date field code, inserting in main document, W 160
dates, entering in documents, W 22
deactivating
    ruler, W 15
    toolbars, W 14
decimal-aligned tabs, W 73
default settings, W 20
    line spacing, W 81
    margins, W 63
    tab stops, W 71-72
    tab style, W 73
    templates, W 131
defining styles. *See* styles
deleting. *See also* removing
    characters, W 22
    columns, W 121
    contents of cells, W 121-122
    files, W 225
    paragraph mark ¶, W 67
    rows, W 121, W 122
    spaces, W 22
    tab characters, W 71
    text, W 32-33
descending order sorts, W 123
deselecting text, W 41-42
design elements, desktop publishing, W 225-227
desktop publishing (DTP), W 224-266
    alternating headers and footers, W 242-245
    applying styles using shortcut keys, W 239-240
    clipart, W 252-254
    column breaks, W 248-249
    column formatting, W 245-246
    copying styles using Organizer, W 236-238
    creating banners using WordArt, W 231-236
    design elements, W 225-227

displaying style area, W 238-239
drop caps, W 259
hyphenating documents, W 260
importing text, W 228-230
inserting tables of contents, W 250-251
layering text and graphics, W 261-266
mastheads, W 227
mirror margins, W 230-231
newspaper-style column format, W 245-246
outline view, W 247-248
paste-up tools, W 241-242
pull quotes, W 255
wrapping text around pictures, W 254-255
displaying. *See* viewing
.DOC filename extension, W 25
document templates. *See* templates
document view buttons, W 10, W 11, W 12
document views, W 12-13
    activating, W 13
    changing, W 12-13
document windows, W 12
    Control menu box, W 10, W 11
    organizing, W 17-20
    Restore button, W 10, W 11
    sizing, W 13
    views, W 12-13
documents, W 4. *See also* reports
    arranging on screen, W 207-208
    attaching templates, W 132, W 133-134
    closing without saving changes, W 19-20
    creating, W 4, W 20-24
    data source. *See* merging documents
    desktop publishing. *See* desktop publishing (DTP)
    dummy, W 241
    duplexed, W 230
    editing. *See* editing documents
    embedding objects, W 233
    entering dates, W 22
    entering text, W 20-24
    formatting. *See* font formatting; formatting documents;
    page setup options; paragraph formatting hyphenating, W 260-261
    importing, W 228-230
    inserting blank lines, W 21, W 23
    main. *See* merging documents
    merging. *See* mailing labels; merging documents
    new, opening, W 17-18
    opening, W 17-18, W 27-28
    planning, W 20
    previewing, W 46-47
    printing. *See* printing
    saving as templates, W 219-220
    saving for first time, W 25-26
    selecting, W 40
    switching between, W 18-19
    transferring data between. *See* transferring data between documents
.DOT filename extension, W 131
drag-and-drop technique
    moving text within documents, W 60-61
    transferring data between documents, W 208-209
drawing objects, W 262. *See also* graphics
drives, selecting, W 8
drop caps, W 227, W 259
drop shadows, W 85
dummy, W 241
duplexed documents, W 230

E

Edit Data Source button, W 164
editing
    data source, W 164
    embedded objects, W 234-236
editing documents, W 4, W 27-39
    checking spelling, W 36-39
    deleting text, W 32-33
    inserting new text, W 21-32
    main documents, W 160-164
    moving insertion point, W 28-31
    opening existing documents, W 27-28
    Overtype mode, W 34-35
    undoing changes, W 33-34
    updating files, W 35-36
embedding objects, W 233
    editing objects, W 234-236
end mark _ , W 10, W 11
entering. *See also* inserting
    dates in documents, W 22
    text, W 20-24, W 21-32
envelopes, printing, W 51-52
Envelopes and Labels dialog box, W 52
error correction, W 22
grammatical errors, W 182-185
    spelling errors, W 36-39, W 107, W 184-185
    tables, W 107
example
    defining styles by, W 194-196
    modifying styles by, W 203-205
exiting Word 6.0 for Windows, W 26-27

F

filenames, W 25
 extensions, W 25, W 131
files. *See also* documents
 renaming, W 60
 updating, W 35-36
Find File command, W 228-229
Find in Field dialog box, W 168
finding and replacing text, W 116-118
finding files, W 228-229
first-line indent marker, W 68
Font command, W 89-90
font formatting, W 87-92
 changing font and point size using Formatting
  toolbar, W 90-91
 changing several character attributes at once,
  W 89-90
 character style, W 131, W 244
 inserting special symbols, W 91-92
Font tab, W 89
fonts, W 87
 changing using Formatting toolbar, W 90-91
 checking settings, W 17
 listing, W 88
 printer, W 88
 screen, W 88
 size. *See* point size
 TrueType, W 88
footers, W 126-127
 alternating, W 242-245
 copying and pasting, W 130
 formatting, W 129-130
 inserting, W 129-130
 in multi-section documents, W 190-194
 viewing footer information, W 130
foreign-format documents, importing, W 229-230
formatting
 columns, W 249-250
 documents. *See* font formatting; formatting
  documents; page setup options; paragraph
  formatting
 fonts. *See* font formatting
 footers, W 129-130
 main document, W 166
 moving text within documents, W 60-62
 options, W 62. *See also* font formatting; page
  setup options; paragraph formatting
 page numbers, W 192
 paragraphs. *See* paragraph formatting
 sections in documents, W 189-190
 tables. *See* formatting tables
 text in frames, W 257
formatting documents, W 4. *See also* font formatting;
 page setup options; paragraph formatting
 bullets, W 45-46
 sections, W 189-190
 "select, then do" principle, W 39-42
 type styles, W 42-45
formatting tables, W 136-144
 automatically, W 138-139
 centering tables, W 139-141
 changing column width, W 136-138
Formatting toolbar, W 10, W 11, W 14, W 67
 changing font and point size, W 90-91
 paragraph alignment, W 83
Frame command, positioning frames, W 258
frames, W 254-258
 drop caps, W 259-260
 formatting text in, W 257
 positioning, W 258
 pull quotes, W 255-258
 sizing, W 256
 wrapping text around pictures, W 254-255

G

Go To command, W 76
Grammar command, W 182-185
graphics, W 227
 color, W 264-265
 layering, W 261-266
 wrapping text around, W 254-255
Gridlines option, W 105
gutter margins, W 230

H

hard page breaks, W 65-66
header rows, W 154
 creating, W 155-156
headers, W 126-127
 alternating, W 242-245
 inserting, W 127-129
 in multi-section documents, W 190-194
headings, applying styles using Style command,
 W 200
headlines, W 227
Help buttons, W 48
Help Contents window, W 49-50

Help system, W 48-51
    context-sensitive Help, W 48-49
    Help Contents window, W 49-50
    Search feature, W 50-51
hot topics, W 49-50
hot words, W 49
hyphenating documents, W 260-261

I

importing text, W 228-230
indenting, W 67-71
    all lines of paragraph, W 70-71
    first line of paragraph, W 69-70
    numbered lists, W 81
Insert Caption command, W 125-126
Insert Picture command, W 252
Insert Table command, W 106-107, W 109-110
inserting. *See also* entering
    alternating footers, W 244-245
    alternating headers, W 242-243
    blank lines in documents, W 21, W 23
    captions in tables, W 125-126
    date field code, W 160
    drop caps, W 259-260
    footers, W 129-130
    hard page breaks, W 65-66
    headers, W 127-129
    leader characters, W 76-78
    mastheads, W 227-228
    merge field codes, W 161-162
    pull quotes, W 255-258
    rows and columns, W 121
    tables of contents, W 212, W 250-251
    tables of figures, W 213
    text for pull quotes, W 256-257
insertion point, W 10, W 11
    moving, W 28-31
    moving in tables, W 107
italic type style, W 42-43

J

justified alignment, paragraphs, W 83, W 84-85

K

keyboard. *See also* shortcut keys
    moving text, W 61-62
    moving within tables, W 107
Label Options dialog box, W 171
labels. *See* mailing labels
landscape orientation, W 63
layer graphics, W 227
layering text and graphics, W 261-266
    adding color, W 264-265
    moving objects to background drawing layer,
        W 265-266
leader characters, W 76-78
left-aligned tab, W 73
left alignment, paragraphs, W 82
left indent marker, W 68
    line spacing, W 81-82
default setting, W 81
lines (of text)
    new, starting, W 78-79
    selecting, W 40
lines (rules). *See* rules
lists, indenting, W 81

M

Mail Merge facility. *See* mailing labels; merging
    documents
Mail Merge Helper dialog box, W 153
Mail Merge toolbar, W 160
mailing labels, W 169-173
    creating, W 169-172
    creating main document, W 170-171
    formatting, W 172-173
    inserting merge field codes into document,
        W 171-172
    printing, W 173
main document. *See* mailing labels; merging
documents Make Word Student Disk window, W 7-8
Manual Hyphenation dialog box, W 261
manual page breaks, W 65-66
margins
    changing, W 63-64
    default settings, W 63
    gutter, W 230
    mirror, setting, W 230-231
mastheads, W 227
mathematical calculations, tables, W 124-125
menu bar, W 10, W 11

merge field codes, W 161-164
  inserting, W 161-162, W 171-172
merging documents, W 150-173
  adding records to data source, W 168
  attaching data source, W 155
  creating data source, W 154-160
  creating main document, W 153-154
  data form, W 157-160
  editing data source, W 164
  editing main document, W 160-164
  formatting main document, W 166
  mailing labels. *See* mailing labels
  moving to records within data source, W 159
  printing data source records, W 168-169
  printing documents, W 166-167, W 169
  process, W 152-153
  saving data source, W 159
  selecting data source records, W 167-169
  sorting data source records, W 164-165
  switching to main document, W 165
  viewing data source, W 159-160
  viewing documents, W 166
  viewing merged document, W 166
Microsoft Graph, W 205
Microsoft Office group window, W 8-9
Microsoft Word message box, W 220
mirror margins, W 232-234
misspellings, correcting, W 36-39, W 107, W 184-185
mistakes, correcting. *See* error correction
Modify Numbered List dialog box, W 81
Modify Style command, W 200-201
modifying. *See* changing
mouse
  changing column width, W 136-137
  click-and-drag technique, W 40
  drag-and-drop technique, W 60-61
  positioning frames, W 258
  selecting text, W 40
  sizing frames, W 256
  sizing graphics, W 252-254
mouse pointer, W 10, W 11
Move command, W 61-62
moving
  information using the Clipboard, W 112
  data between documents, W 205-210
  within data source, W 159
  insertion point, W 28-31
  insertion point in tables, W 107
  between pages, W 76
  tab stops, W 75
  text within documents, W 60-62

within tables, W 107
multi-section documents
  formatting sections, W 189-190
  headers and footers, W 190-194
  inserting section breaks, W 187-189
multitasking, W 231

N

naming files, W 60. *See also* filenames
New dialog box, W 17-18
new documents, opening, W 17-18
New Line command, W 78-79
new line mark (↵), W 78-79
New Style dialog box, W 198
newsletters. *See* desktop publishing (DTP)
nonprinting characters, viewing, W 15-16
NORMAL template, W 131
  preventing changes, W 195, W 236
normal view, W 12
numbering paragraphs, W 80-81
numbers, pages. *See* page numbers

O

objects
  drawing, W 262. *See also* graphics
  embedding. *See* embedding objects
on-line Help system. *See* Help system
opening
  existing documents, W 27-28
  new documents, W 17-18
Organizer, copying styles, W 236-238
Outline toolbar, W 247
outline view, W 12, W 247-248
Overtype mode, W 34-35

P

page breaks
  hard (manual), W 65-66
  soft, W 65
page layout view, W 12-13
page numbers
  formatting, W 192
  headers, W 127-128
  right margin, W 128-129
page orientation, W 63

page setup options, W 63-67
    changing margins, W 63-64
    hard page breaks, W 65-66
    soft page breaks, W 65
pages. *See also* title pages
    moving between, W 76
    multiple, previewing and printing, W 92-95
    preface, W 211-213
Paragraph command, W 67, W 81-82
paragraph formatting, W 67-87
    aligning paragraphs, W 82-85
    borders and rules, W 85-87
    changing indentations, W 67-71
    custom tab stops, W 72-75
    default tab stops, W 71-72
    leader characters, W 76-78
    line spacing, W 81-82
    moving between pages, W 76
    moving tab stops, W 75
    New Line command, W 78-79
    numbering paragraphs, W 80-81
paragraph mark (¶), W 67
paragraph style, applying, W 134
    shortcut keys, W 239
paragraph styles, W 131
paragraphs
    aligning, W 82-85
    borders and rules, W 85-87
    selecting, W 40, W 67
paste-up tools, W 241-242
    activating, W 241-242
pasting
    footers, W 130
    tables, W 120
    text, W 113-114, W 115-116
Picture dialog box, sizing graphics, W 253
pictures, W 262. *See also* graphics
planning documents, W 20
point size, W 88
    changing using Formatting toolbar, W 90-91
    checking settings, W 17
portrait orientation, W 63
positioning frames, W 258
preface pages, W 211-213
previewing
    documents, W 46-48
    multiple pages, W 92-95
    templates, W 132-133
Print dialog box, W 47
print preview. *See* previewing
print settings, checking, W 47

printer fonts, W 88
printing
    on both sides of paper, W 230
    documents, W 4, W 46-48
    envelopes, W 51-52
    mailing labels, W 173
    merged documents, W 166, W 169
    multiple pages, W 92-95
    page orientation, W 63
    reports, W 213-218
productivity strategy, W 4-5
pull quotes, W 227, W 255

R

records, sorting, W 164-165
rectangle, indenting paragraphs, W 68
removing. *See also* deleting
    borders and rules, W 87
    type styles, W 45
renaming files, W 60
Replace command, W 116-118
replacing text, W 117-118
reports, W 178-220
    adding captions to charts, W 210-211
    bookmarks, W 185-186
    checking grammar, W 182-185
    customized templates, W 219-220
    formatting sections, W 187-190
    headers and footers in multi-section documents,
        W 190-194
    preface page, W 211-213
    printing, W 213-218
    styles. *See* styles
    Thesaurus command, W 181-182
    transferring data between documents. *See*
        transferring data between documents
Restore button, document window, W 10, W 11
Reveal Formats feature, W 135-136, W 240
right-aligned tabs, W 73
    setting using ruler, W 74-75
right alignment, paragraphs, W 83
right indent marker, W 68
Row tab, W 140
rows
    deleting, W 121, W 122
    header. *See* header rows
    inserting and deleting, W 121
    selecting, W 119
    sorting, W 122-124

ruler, W 10, W 11, W 14, W 63
    activating and deactivating, W 15
    changing indentations, W 68-71
    moving tab stops, W 75
    setting custom tabs, W 74-75
    viewing, W 15
rules
    desktop publishing, W 235
    paragraphs, W 86-87

S

Save As command, W 26, W 60, W 219-220
saving
    data source, W 159
    documents, for first time, W 25-26
    documents as templates, W 219-220
screen, arranging documents, W 207-208
screen check, W 12-17
    checking document view, W 12-13
    checking font and point size settings, W 17
    displaying nonprinting characters, W 15-16
    sizing document windows, W 13
    sizing Word window, W 14
    viewing toolbars and ruler, W 14-15
screen elements, W 9-11
screen fonts, W 88
screens (desktop publishing), W 227
scroll bars, W 10, W 11
Search feature, W 50-51
section breaks, inserting, W 187-189
"select, then do" principle, W 118
    formatting documents, W 39-46
    indenting paragraphs, W 68-71
selecting
    cells, W 119
    columns, W 119
    documents, W 40
    drives, W 8
    lines, W 40
    paragraphs, W 40, W 67
    rows, W 119
    sentences, W 40-41
    tables, W 119
    within tables, W 118-120
    text, W 39-42
    text blocks, W 40
    words, W 40
selection bar, W 40
sentences, selecting, W 40-41

setting
    custom tabs, W 72-75
    mirror margins, W 230-231
shading tables, W 138-139
shadow borders, W 85
shortcut keys
    applying styles, W 200-202, W 239-240
    line spacing, W 81
    paragraph alignment, W 83
shortcut Toolbar menu, W 14-15
Show/Hide ¶ option, W 15-16, W 71
sizing
    document windows, W 13
    frames, W 256
    graphics, W 252-254
    Word window, W 14
    WordArt images, W 234
sizing buttons, W 10, W 11
soft page breaks, W 65
Sort command, W 123
sorting
    data source records, W 164-165
    rows, W 122-124
spaces, deleting, W 22
spacing, between characters, W 90
special symbols, inserting, W 91-92
spelling, checking, W 36-39, W 107, W 184-185
Spelling command, W 36-39
    tables, W 107
splitting windows, W 243
Standard toolbar, W 10, W 11, W 14
starting
    Word 6.0 for Windows, W 8-9
    WordArt, W 231-232
status bar, W 10, W 11
    elements, W 20-21
structure, tables, W 105, W 106-107
Student Disk, W 6-8
style area, displaying, W 238-239
Style command
    applying heading styles, W 200
    defining styles, W 196-198
    modifying styles, W 202-203
Style Gallery feature, W 132-133
style sheets, W 131
styles, W 131-136, W 194-205
    applying, W 134-136, W 198-202
    checking attributes, W 240
    copying using Organizer, W 236-238
    defining by example, W 194-196
    defining using Style command, W 196-198

modifying, W 202-205
of outline headings, W 247
Reveal Formats features, W 135-136
templates, W 131-134
switching
to main document, W 165
between open documents, W 18-19
to outline view, W 247
symbols, inserting, W 91-92
synonyms, finding, W 181-182

T

tab characters (→), W 71
deleting, W 71
tab stops, W 71-75
clearing, W 75
custom, W 72-75
default settings, W 71-72
moving, W 75
tab style, default settings, W 73
Table AutoFormat command, W 138-139
Table button, W 105-107
Table Cell Height and Width command, W 136
Table Formula command, W 124-125
table structure, W 105, W 106-107
modifying, W 120-122
tables, W 104-112
AutoCorrect feature, W 107-109
centering, W 139-141
converting existing text to, W 110-112
copying, W 120
elements, W 105
entering text, W 107, W 108
formatting. *See* formatting tables
inserting captions, W 125-126
mathematical calculations, W 124-125
moving within, W 107
pasting, W 120
selecting, W 119
selecting within, W 118-120
Table button, W 105-107
Table Insert command, W 109-110
tables of contents, W 211-212
inserting into document, W 256-257
tables of figures, W 212-213
Tabs dialog box, W 77
templates, W 20
attaching to documents, W 132, W 133-134
customized, W 219-220

preparing documents as, W 219
preventing alteration, W 195
preventing changes, W 236
previewing, W 132-133
saving documents as, W 219-220
styles, W 131-134
text
centering in cells, W 140
converting to tables, W 110-112
copying, W 113-114
cutting, W 114-115
deleting, W 32-33
deselecting, W 41-42
entering, W 20-24
entering in tables, W 107, W 108
finding and replacing, W 116-118
formatting in frames, W 257
importing, W 228-230
inserting, W 21-32
layering, W 262-263
pasting, W 113-114, W 115-116
pull quotes, W 256-257
selected, applying character style, W 240
selecting, W 39-42
wrapping around pictures, W 254-255
text blocks, selecting, W 40
Thesaurus command, W 181-182
title bar, W 10, W 11
title pages, vertical alignment, W 189-190
toolbars. *See* Formatting toolbar; Standard toolbar
activating and deactivating, W 14
Mail Merge, W 160
Outline, W 247
viewing, W 14-15
ToolTip feature, W 12-13
topic outlines, W 247-248
topics, hot, W 49-50
transferring data between documents, W 205-209
TROUBLE? paragraphs, W 6
TrueType fonts, W 88
tutorials, using effectively, W 5-6
Two Pages view, W 241, W 243
type styles, W 42-45, W 89
applying, W 42-44
removing, W 45
typing. *See* entering
typing errors, correcting. *See* error correction

U

underlined type style, W 42
    applying, W 44
    removing, W 45
undoing changes, W 33-34, W 41, W 67
updating files, W 35-36

V

viewing
    data source, W 159-160
    footer information, W 130
    merged documents, W 166
    nonprinting characters, W 15-16
    normal view, W 12
    outline view, W 247-248
    page layout view, W 12-13, W 245
    ruler, W 15
    rules for flagged grammatical errors, W 183-184
    soft page breaks, W 65
    style area, W 238-239
    toolbars, W 14-15

W

Window menu, W 19
windows
document. *See* document windows
    Help Contents, W 49-50
    Make Word Student Disk, W 7-8
    Microsoft Office group, W 8-9
    splitting, W 243
    Word. *See* Word window
Windows Metafile format (WMF), W 252
Word 6.0 for Windows
    exiting, W 26-27
    starting, W 8-9
Word window, W 12
    Control menu box, W 10, W 11
    sizing, W 14
    sizing buttons, W 10, W 11
word wrap, W 23, W 107
WordArt, W 231-236
    editing embedded objects, W 234-236
    embedding objects into documents, W 233
    sizing images, W 234
    starting, W 231-232

words
    hot, W 49
    selecting, W 40
workspace, W 10, W 11

TASK REFERENCE
Microsoft Word 6.0 for Windows
Italicized page numbers indicate the first discussion of each task.

TASK	MOUSE	MENU	KEYBOARD
Apply or define a style, *W 134*	Click Style box arrow, click style	Click Format, click Style..., choose style options, click Apply	[Alt][O], [S], choose style options, [Alt][A] or [Enter]
Arrange open documents, *W 207*		Click Window, click Arrange All	[Alt][W], [A]
Attach a template, *W 131*		Click File, click Templates..., choose template, click OK	[Alt][F], [T], choose template, [Enter]
AutoCorrect entries, change, *W 107*		Click Tools, click AutoCorrect..., make changes, click OK	[Alt][T], [A], make changes, [Enter]
Between character spacing, change, *W 90*		Click Format, click Font..., click Character Spacing tab, change spacing options, click OK	[Alt][O], [F], [Alt][R], change spacing options, [Enter]
Bold selected text, *W 43*	**B**	Click Format, click Font..., click Font tab, click Bold, click OK	[Alt][O], [F], [Alt][N], click Bold, [Enter]
Bookmark, assign, *W 185*		Click Edit, click Bookmark..., enter bookmark information, click Add	[Alt][E], [B], enter book-mark information, [Alt][A] or [Enter]
Border or shading, add to selected paragraphs and tables, *W 85*	⊞, choose border and shading options in Borders toolbar	Click Format, click Borders and Shading..., click appropriate tab, choose border and shading options, click OK	[Alt][O], [B], [B] or [S], choose border and shading options, [Enter]
Bulleted list, create, *W 45*	☰	Click Format, click Bullets and Numbering..., click Bulleted tab, click list format, click OK	[Alt][O], [N], [Alt][B], choose list format, [Enter]
Calculations, perform in tables, *W 124*		Click Table, click Formula..., enter calculation, click OK	[Alt][A], [O], enter calculation, [Enter]
Caption, insert, *W 125*		Click Insert, click Caption..., specify caption and format, click OK	[Alt][I], [I], specify caption and format, [Enter]
Center a selected table, *W 139*		Click Table, click Cell Height and Width..., click Row tab, click Center, click OK	[Alt][A], [W], [Alt][R], [Alt][T], [Enter]
Center selected text, *W 82*	▤	Click Format, click Paragraph..., click Indents and Spacing tab, click Alignment arrow, click Centered, click OK	[Ctrl][E], or [Alt][O], [P], [Alt][I], [Alt][G], choose Centered, [Enter]
Close a document, *W 19*	Double-click document Control menu box	Click File, click Close	[Alt][F], [C]
Column break, insert, *W 248*		Click Insert, click Break..., click Column Break, click OK	[Alt][I], [B], [Alt][C], [Enter]
Column width, change, *W 136*	Drag boundary between columns using ◄╫►	Click Table, click Cell Height and Width..., click Column tab, change column width options, click OK	[Alt][A], [W], [Alt][C], change column width options, [Enter]

TASK REFERENCE
Microsoft Word 6.0 for Windows

Italicized page numbers indicate the first discussion of each task.

TASK	MOUSE	MENU	KEYBOARD
Columns, format into, *W 245*	▦	Click Format, click Columns..., choose column options, click OK	[Alt][O], [C], choose column options, [Enter]
Continuous section break, insert, *W 187*		Click Insert, click Break..., click Continuous, click OK	[Alt][I], [B], [Alt][T], [Enter]
Convert existing text to a table, *W 110*	▦	Click Table, click Convert Text to Table..., choose table options, click OK	[Alt][A], [V], choose table options, [Enter]
Copy selected text or graphics to Clipboard, *W 113*	📋	Click Edit, click Copy	[Ctrl][C], or [Alt][E], [C]
Copy selected text without using the Clipboard, *W 61*			[Shift][F2], place insertion point in location, [Enter]
Copy styles, *W 236*		Click Format, click Style..., click Organizer..., click Styles tab, choose styles to copy, click Close	[Alt][O], [S], [Alt][O], [Alt][S], choose styles to copy, [Enter]
Crop a selected graphic, *W 253*	Press and hold [Shift], drag any center handle	Click Format, click Picture..., specify cropping dimensions, click OK	[Alt][O], [R], specify cropping dimensions, [Enter]
Cut selected text or graphics to Clipboard, *W 114*	✂	Click Edit, click Cut	[Ctrl][X], or [Alt][E], [T]
Date and time, insert, *W 160*		Click Insert, click Date and Time..., click format, click OK	[Alt][I], [T], click format, [Enter]
Decimal tab, insert, *W 73*	⊥	Click Format, click Tabs..., click Decimal, click OK	[Alt][O], [T], [Alt][D], [Enter]
Double-space text, *W 81*		Click Format, click Paragraph..., click Indents and Spacing tab, click Line Spacing arrow, click Double, click OK	[Ctrl][2], or [Alt][O], [P], [Alt][I], [Alt][N], choose Double, [Enter]
Drawing object, add, *W 262*	▱		
Drop cap, insert into a selected paragraph, *W 259*		Click Format, click Drop Cap..., choose drop cap options, click OK	[Alt][O], [D], choose drop cap options, [Enter]
Exit Word, *W 26*	Double-click Word Control menu box	Click File, click Exit	[Alt][F4], or [Alt][F], [X]
Font, change, *W 88*	Click Font list box arrow, click font	Click Format, click Font..., click Font tab, click font, click OK	[Alt][O], [F], [Alt][N], choose font, [Enter]
Formats, display, *W 135*	Click ▯?, then click text		
Formatting toolbar, activate/deactivate, *W 14*		Click View, click Toolbars..., click Formatting, click OK	[Alt][V], [T], click Formatting, [Enter]
Frame, insert, *W 254*		Change to page layout view, click Insert, click Frame	Change to page layout view, [Alt][I], [F]
Frame, position selected, *W 258*		Click Format, click Frame..., specify horizontal and/or vertical reference points, click OK	[Alt][O], [M], specify horizontal and/or vertical reference points, [Enter]

TASK REFERENCE
Microsoft Word 6.0 for Windows

Italicized page numbers indicate the first discussion of each task.

TASK	MOUSE	MENU	KEYBOARD
Frame, size selected, *W 256*		Click Format, click Frame..., specify frame size, click OK	[Alt][O], [M], specify frame size, [Enter]
Go to a position in a document, *W 76*		Click Edit, click Go To...	[F5], or [Alt][E], [G], or [Ctrl][G]
Grammar, check, *W 183*		Click Tools, click Grammar...	[Alt][T], [G]
Graphic, insert, *W 252*		Click Insert, click Picture..., click graphic name, click OK	[Alt][I], [P], click graphic name, [Enter]
Graphic, size selected, *W 253*		Click Format, click Picture..., specify graphic size, click OK	[Alt][O], [R], specify graphic size, [Enter]
Hard page break, insert, *W 65*		Click Insert, click Break..., click Page Break, click OK	[Ctrl][Enter], or [Alt][I], [B], [Alt][P], [Enter]
Headers and footers, insert, *W 127*		Click View, click Header and Footer, enter headers and footers, click Close	[Alt][V], [H], enter headers and footers, click Close
Help, access, *W 48*	▶?	Click Help, click Contents	[F1], or [Alt][H], [C]
Hyphenate a document, *W 260*		Click Tools, click Hyphenation..., choose hyphenation options, click OK	[Alt][T], [H], choose hyphenation options, [Enter]
Import a document, *W 228*		Click Insert, click File..., click document name, click OK	[Alt][I], [L], click document name, [Enter]
Indent selected paragraph to next tab stop, *W 70*	🔲		[Ctrl][M]
Italicize text, *W 42*	*I*	Click Format, click Font..., click Font tab, click Italic, click OK	[Ctrl][I], or [Alt][O], [F], [Alt][N], click Italic, [Enter]
Justify text, *W 83*	▤	Click Format, click Paragraph..., click Indents and Spacing tab, click Alignment arrow, click Justified, click OK	[Ctrl][J], or [Alt][O], [P], [Alt][I], [Alt][G], choose Justified, [Enter]
Left-align text, *W 82*	▤	Click Format, click Paragraph..., click Indents and Spacing tab, click Alignment arrow, click Left, click OK	[Ctrl][L], or [Alt][O], [P], [Alt][I], [Alt][G], click Left, [Enter]
Left-aligned tab, insert, *W 73*	▣	Click Format, click Tabs..., click Left, click OK	[Alt][O], [T], [Alt][L], [Enter]
Mail merge process, start, *W 153*		Click Tools, click Mail Merge...	[Alt][T], [R]
Margins, change, *W 63*		Click File, click Page Setup..., click Margins tab, change margin settings, click OK	[Alt][F], [U], [Alt][M], change margin settings, [Enter]
Merged mailing labels, create, *W 170*		Click Tools, click Mail Merge..., click Create, click Mailing Labels...	[Alt][T], [R], [Alt][C], [M]
Move selected text without using the Clipboard, *W 61*			[F2], place insertion point in location, [Enter]

TASK REFERENCE
Microsoft Word 6.0 for Windows

Italicized page numbers indicate the first discussion of each task.

TASK	MOUSE	MENU	KEYBOARD
Move to previous location in a document, *W 87*			[Shift][F5]
New line mark, insert, *W 78*			[Shift][Enter]
Next Page section break, insert, *W 187*		Click Insert, click Break..., click Next Page, click OK	[Alt][I], [B], [Alt][N], [Enter]
Normal view, change to, *W 12*	▤	Click View, click Normal	[Alt][V], [N]
Numbered list, create, *W 80*	▤	Click Format, click Bullets and Numbering..., click Numbered tab, click list format, click OK	[Alt][O], [N], [Alt][N], choose list format, [Enter]
Open a new document, *W 17*	▢	Click File, click New..., click a template, click OK	[Ctrl][O], or [Alt][F], [N], click a template, [Enter]
Open an existing document, *W 27*	▣	Click File, click Open..., click document name, click OK	[Ctrl][F12], or [Alt][F], [O], click document name, [Enter]
Outline view, change to, *W 12*	▤	Click View, click Outline	[Alt][V], [O]
Overtype mode, activate/ deactivate, *W 34*	Double-click OVR in the status bar	Click Tools, click Options..., click the Edit tab, click Overtype Mode, click OK	[Insert] or [Alt][T], [O], click the Edit tab, click Overtype Mode, [Enter]
Page layout view, change to, *W 12*	▣	Click View, click Page Layout	[Alt][V], [P]
Paste text or graphics from the Clipboard, *W 113*	▣	Click Edit, click Paste	[Ctrl][V], or [Alt][E], [P]
Point size, change, *W 89*	Click Font Size box arrow, click size	Click Format, click Font..., click Font tab, click size, click OK	[Alt][O], [F], [Alt][N], choose size, [Enter]
Print a document, *W 46*	▣	Click File, click Print..., specify print options, click OK	[Ctrl][P], or [Alt][F], [P], specify print options, [Enter]
Print an envelope, *W 51*		Click Tools, click Envelopes and Labels..., click Envelopes tab, click Print	[Alt][T], [E], [Alt][E], [Alt][P]
Print Preview a document, *W 46*	▣	Click File, click Print Preview	[Alt][F], [V]
Redo a previous undone action, *W 33*	▣	Click Edit, click Redo	[Ctrl][Y], or [Alt][E], [R]
Rename a file, *W 60*		Click File, click Save As..., type filename, click OK	[Alt][F], [A], type filename, [Enter]
Repeat last action, *W 125*			[F4]
Replace text or formatting, *W 116*		Click Edit, click Replace..., specify replace options, click Replace or Replace All	[Ctrl][H] or [Alt][E], [E], specify replace options, [Alt][R] or [Alt][A]
Right-align text, *W 83*	▤	Click Format, click Paragraph..., click Indents and Spacing tab, click Alignment arrow, click Right, click OK	[Ctrl][R], or [Alt][O], [P], [Alt][I], [Alt][G], click Right, [Enter]

TASK	MOUSE	MENU	KEYBOARD
Right-aligned tab, insert, *W 73*	⬛	Click Format, click Tabs..., click Right, click OK	[Alt][O], [T], [Alt][R], [Enter]
Save a document for the first time, *W 25*	💾, enter filename, click OK	Click File, click Save or Save As..., enter filename, click OK	[Ctrl][S] or [Alt][F], [S] or [A], enter filename, [Enter]
Save a document, *W 35*	💾	Click File, click Save	[Ctrl][S], or [Shift][F12], or [Alt][F], [S]
Single space text, *W 81*		Click Format, click Paragraph..., click Indents and Spacing tab, click Line Spacing arrow, click Single, click OK	[Ctrl][1], or [Alt][O], [P], [Alt][I], [Alt][N], click Single, [Enter]
Sort rows in a table, *W 122*		Click Table, click Sort..., specify sort options, click OK	[Alt][A], [T], specify sort options, [Enter]
Spacing before or after a selected paragraph, change, *W 137*		Click Format, click Paragraph..., click Indents and Spacing tab, change Spacing Before or After options, click OK	[Alt][O], [P], [Alt][I], change Spacing Before or After options, [Enter]
Spelling, check, *W 36*	✔	Click Tools, click Spelling...	[Alt][T], [S], or [F7]
Standard toolbar, activate/deactivate, *W 14*		Click View, click Toolbars..., click Standard, click OK	[Alt][V], [T], click Standard, [Enter]
Style area, display, *W 238*		Change to normal view, click Tools, click Options..., click View tab, click Style Area Width option, click OK	Change to normal view, [Alt][T], [O], click View tab, choose Style Area Width option, [Enter]
Style Gallery, access, *W 132*		Click Format, click Style Gallery...	[Alt][O], [G]
Switch between open documents, *W 18*		Click Window, click document name	[Ctrl][F6], or [Alt][W], click document name
Switch between panes, *W 243*	Click in pane		[F6]
Symbol, insert, *W 91*		Click Insert, click Symbol..., click Symbols tab, click symbol, click Insert, click Close	[Alt][I], [S], [Alt][S], click symbol, [Alt][I], [Enter]
Table, create, *W 105*	▦	Click Table, click Insert Table..., choose table options, click OK	[Alt][A], [I], choose table options, [Enter]
Table, format, *W 138*		Click Table, click Table AutoFormat..., choose format options, click OK	[Alt][A], [F], choose format options, [Enter]
Table of contents, insert, *W 212*		Click Insert, click Index and Tables..., click Table of Contents tab, choose table of contents options, click OK	[Alt][I], [X], [Alt][C], choose table of contents options, [Enter]
Table of figures, insert, *W 213*		Click Insert, click Index and Tables..., click Table of Figures tab, choose table of figures options, click OK	[Ctrl][N], or [Alt][I], [X], [Alt][F], choose table of figures options, [Enter]

TASK REFERENCE
Microsoft Word 6.0 for Windows

Italicized page numbers indicate the first discussion of each task.

TASK	MOUSE	MENU	KEYBOARD
Text boundaries, display, *W 241*		Change to page layout view, click Tools, click Options..., click View tab, click Text Boundaries, click OK	Change to page layout view, [Alt][T], [O], click View tab, [Alt][X], [Enter]
Thesaurus, access, *W 181*		Click Tools, click Thesaurus...	[Shift][F7], or [Alt][T], [T]
ToolTips, activate/deactivate, *W 14*		Click View, click Toolbars..., click Show ToolTips, click OK	[Alt][V], [T], [Alt][S], [Enter]
Underline text, *W 44*	U	Click Format, click Font..., click Font tab, click Underline arrow, click underline option, click OK	[Ctrl][U], or [Alt][O], [F], [Alt][N], [Alt][U], click underline option, [Enter]
Undo last action, *W 33*	↺	Click Edit, click Undo	[Ctrl][Z], or [Alt][E], [U]
Unindent text to previous tab stop, *W 71*	⇤		[Ctrl][Shift][M]
Vertical alignment, change, *W 189*		Click File, click Page Setup..., click Layout tab, click Vertical Alignment option, click OK	[Alt][F], [U], [Alt][L], [Alt][V], choose alignment option, [Enter]
WordArt image, create, *W 232*		Click Insert, click Object..., click Create New tab, click Microsoft WordArt, click OK	[Alt][I], [O], [Alt][C], click Microsoft WordArt, [Enter]
WordArt image, edit selected, *W 235*	Double-click the image	Click Edit, click WordArt Object, click Edit	[Alt][E], [O], [E]
WordArt image, resize selected, *W 234*	Click and drag a handle using ↔	Click Format, click Picture..., specify sizing options, click OK	[Alt][O], [R], specify sizing options, [Enter]
Zoom Page Width view, change to, *W 159*	Click Zoom Control box arrow, click Page Width	Click View, click Zoom..., click Page Width, click OK	[Alt][V], [Z], [Alt][P], [Enter]
Zoom Two Pages view, change to, *W 241*	Change to page layout view, click Zoom Control box arrow, click Two Pages		